The Art of the Compromise
Second Edition, Revised and Expanded

The Art of the Compromise

Second Edition, Revised and Expanded

RETURNING AMERICAN DEMOCRACY TO
BETTER DAYS

David L. Page, Ph.D.

Warped Minds Press

Knoxville, Tennessee

The Art of the Compromise
Second Edition, Revised and Expanded

Copyright © 2025 by David L. Page, Ph.D.

All rights reserved. No part of this publication may be reproduced, distributed, or transmitted in any form or by any means—electronic, mechanical, photocopying, recording, or otherwise—without the prior written permission of the publisher, except in the case of brief quotations used in critical reviews and certain other noncommercial uses permitted by copyright law.

First edition published in hardcover 2024.
Second edition (revised and expanded) published in paperback 2025.

Library of Congress Control Number: 2025921911

ISBN (paperback, second edition): 979-8-9906504-0-4
ISBN (hardcover, first edition): 979-8-9906504-1-1
ISBN (eBook, second edition): 979-8-9906504-2-8

Warped Minds Press
Knoxville, Tennessee

For my wife Lisa and my daughter Grace.

> "I have always figured that a half a loaf is better than none, and I know that in the democratic process you're not going to always get everything you want."
>
> —Ronald Reagan

Preface

I AM NEVER HAPPY with the final copy of an academic article, a newspaper column, or a book chapter, and this revised and expanded edition of *The Art of the Compromise* is no exception. I am no more pleased with this version than I was with the first hardcopy edition. Yet at some point, one must declare it finished and move on.

The writing process, for me, is never truly complete. The process feels like sculpting a delicate three-dimensional bust from a bowl of strawberry Jell-O. I hold an impression in my mind's eye of the form that I want to achieve—though that impression is neither precise nor stable—and my hands struggle to coax the Jell-O blobs before slipping through my grasp. In the end, I look back. I read. I re-read. And still, I am not happy. I see flaws. Thoughts remain half-shaped, but we ultimately must move on.

As Leonardo da Vinci said, "Art is never finished, only abandoned." So, I must abandon this new version to the reader's hands and ask forgiveness, just as I once left the first hardback to stand on its own. I ask the reader to look past my flaws as a writer and to seek the more important ideas hidden inside these pages—ideas about what political compromise means in a large, fractious republic.

This Revised and Expanded Edition includes more than minor spelling and punctuation corrections—of which there were many—but also introduces new material in each chapter. This revised material derives from a small discussion group in

Knoxville during the Spring of 2025. We called the group *Donuts for Democracy,* and we did indeed consume a few delicious toroidal confections while we argued about the meaning of compromise in our raucous Republic. The insights and feedback from that group helped hone the original arguments and added new ones that sharpened this book's message. The chapters now include charts and graphs that paint a more data-rich context for the ideas expressed. These visuals evolved from the need to translate the words on the pages into shared, tangible points for discussion. I hope that readers will find them engaging and enlightening.

The most significant change comes in the final chapter. Where the hardcover edition concluded with a focus on Congress and the reforms necessary to restore deliberation, the paperback turns inward. The new chapter, *Beyond the Deal*, calls attention not only to the failures of transactional politics but also to the responsibility of each citizen to practice *The Art of the Compromise* in daily life. I continue to draw a sharp contrast with Donald Trump—whose conservative policies I often support but whose leadership style I do not embrace. The survival of our Republic does not rest on Congress alone. It also depends on whether we, as individuals, can resist the Tyranny of the Deal and recover the wisdom of genuine compromise.

I have not intended this book to be definitive, but rather to be useful. If the arguments give the reader pause, stir a conversation, or challenge an assumption, then the book has done its job. We are living through a moment when compromise feels like weakness and when social media—with its resounding gongs and clanging cymbals*—drowns out dialogue. I may be a fool, but I believe—perhaps stubbornly—that the American experiment in self-government still works if we are willing humbly to submit to compromise.

As I write this preface, tragedy weighs upon our nation. On September 10, 2025, an assassin's bullet cut short the life of Charlie Kirk, a young conservative who made his mark by engaging in political dialogue on college campuses. One need not agree with his message to recognize his courage to enter the arena. In a time when too many walk away from the table or drown out their opponents with noise, Kirk chose to speak, debate, and risk persuasion. His murder is a stark reminder that violence must never be the answer to our disagreements. If America has strength, it lies not in the unity of our thought but in the unity of our ideals, expressed and tested through words rather than weapons.

So let us begin, not with fear, but with curiosity—and perhaps, like Charlie, with a little courage, too.

---

*My clumsy allusion with this phrase is to 1 Corinthians 13:1, where the Apostle Paul is writing to the early Christian church in Corinth. "If I speak in the tongues of men or of angels, but do not have love, I am only a resounding gong or a clanging cymbal" (Yancey & Stafford, 2024a).

Contents

Introduction 1
Chapter 1. Out of Many 21
Chapter 2. Into One Soul 61
Chapter 3. Of Two Minds 107
Chapter 4. With Compromise 161
Chapter 5. Beyond the Deal 195
Acknowledgments 237
Further Reading 241
Work Cited 247
Index 273
About the Author 289

INTRODUCTION

Fear Not!

DON'T PANIC. NO NEED to secede from the Union. No need to move to Canada. No need to get rid of the Electoral College. America is not imploding—unless we want it to do so. Yes, our democracy is messy. Yes, Trump is a demagogue—an effective one. And yes, he is an SOB—his words, not mine.* Yes, January 6 was a riot, but it was not an insurrection. Insurrections do not end at dusk after only four hours. We may not be at our political best, but we

---

*Donald Trump has, in a moment of gallows humor, confessed to being a "son of a bitch." In January 2020, while hosting the Louisiana State University football team at the White House following their national championship win, President Trump remarked that while the country had "a great president," Congress wanted to "impeach the son of a bitch" (Bogage, 2020). The line landed as a joke, but like many Trumpian asides, his humor blurs the line between self-awareness and spectacle.

have been here before or in similar situations where the peril of American democracy seems imminent. We must step back from the perceived abyss and take a deep breath. The American political system is working despite the news headlines to the contrary.

Nothing to Fear

Consider the following brief scan of our history. When our nation was young, the Founders stumbled through Shays's Rebellion, a low point and near insurrection as well. Shays exposed the weakness of the Articles of Confederation, and we emerged stronger with the writing of the Constitution as our new form of government. Then, the Founders struggled for a few decades to navigate the tensions of partisanship, which led to the emergence of our first demagogue, President Andrew Jackson. Jackson, however, kept the lid on the festering problem of slavery that would eventually erupt into the Civil War. When the awful war did come, Abraham Lincoln took the federal reins of government and led us through that terrible struggle. Lincoln's stalwart leadership again strengthened the nation by fulfilling our Creed that "all men are created equal."

Yet the turbulent history continued to wax and wane. The ensuing Reconstruction years saw more turmoil with anarchist and populist movements. The ebb and flow of these dark valleys and sunny mountaintops have taken on a natural rhythm in American democracy, going into the 20th century with the Great World War, the Great Depression, the Second World War, the Nuclear Age, the violent Sixties, and most recently January 6. In the moment, each oscillation of our history has the feeling of the end being near. However, to panic would be to give in to the darkness. Give in to the fear, which

The Art of the Compromise

we cannot and should not do. Our forebears never gave in. We should not.

Franklin D. Roosevelt understood this need to resist giving in to fear. At his inauguration on March 4, 1933,* the Great Depression gripped the nation, and fear was widespread. The stock market crashed in 1929, and the American economy was in shambles. Massive unemployment, home foreclosures, drought-stricken farms, spiraling deflation, and banking failures paralyzed America. Americans stood in long lines for jobs, food, and shelter. Citizens lost confidence in the U.S. government to deliver on the American Dream. Businesses failed by the thousands, but the government could not be allowed to do the same. Unlike a business, a government cannot fold its doors when the ledger bleeds red.†

FDR offered hope. His expansive optimism echoed through his inaugural address as he confronted the nation's fear: "This great nation will endure as it has endured, will revive and will prosper. So, first of all, let me assert my firm

---

*Franklin Roosevelt's 1933 inauguration was the last to occur on March 4. The Twentieth Amendment—often called the "lame duck" amendment—had been ratified earlier that year and shifted future presidential inaugurations to January 20. Authored by progressive Nebraska Senator George Norris, the amendment aimed to shorten the long and often unproductive interval between a president's election in November and the transfer of power in January (Mann & Ornstein, 2006).

†One critical difference between a business and the United States government is that businesses can fail. They go bankrupt, dissolve, and disappear. Governments—at least the ones worth preserving—are meant to endure. During the Great Depression, many businesses collapsed. Homes were lost; fortunes vanished. Yet the federal government had no such luxury. "Going out of business" was never an option.

belief that the only thing we have to fear is fear itself" (Roosevelt, 1933), He understood that fear, left unchecked, paralyzes the effort to turn retreat into advance.

The panic and tension surrounding government and politics in America today—as in FDR's time—generate the same destructive force and induce self-fulfilling prophecies. Fear once again grips the nation. Gavin de Becker, a security specialist and best-selling author, has written about the danger of misplaced fear and how it fabricates unproductive, unhealthy behaviors. Fear and worry, he warns, "will not bring solutions" (De Becker & Stechschulte, 1997). "It will more likely distract you from finding solutions." Fear can become paralysis.

The writing of this book is my own attempt to escape this fear spiral and to rediscover a path of progress—a path paved with compromise. Today, compromise has become a four-letter word in our Republic, discarded from our political lexicon. Yet compromise was fundamental to the creation of our Constitution and remains essential to the functioning of our federal system. That rejection of compromise often grows from misunderstanding. What, then, is compromise?

A Four-Letter Word

Scholars define political compromise as an agreement that has the purpose of accommodating conflicting views. This definition captures both the outcome of the agreement-seeking process as well as the process itself (Lepora, 2012; Spang, 2023). This definition will be our working model throughout this book. Yet more clarity is needed, because compromise is often confused with consensus.

These two terms are sometimes used interchangeably, since they are both solutions to disagreement. But the former

The Art of the Compromise

does not resolve the disagreement, while the latter does. Unlike compromise, consensus requires opposing parties "to change their minds on the controversial issue" (Spang, 2023). Under consensus, opposing parties come to agree with one another. By contrast, compromise does not end disagreement but channels it—each side yields part of its claim while holding to its convictions. Manon Wesphal (2017) states that a compromise settles the conflict but does not resolve the underlying disagreement, whereas consensus resolves the disagreement. Friderike Spang (2023) further explains that "compromise also differs from consensus in that the former characteristically involves a sense of regret or dissatisfaction."* She goes on to note that "parties to a compromise continue to believe that they are right and that the other party is wrong." At first glance, consensus might seem the nobler goal, but the reality is more complicated.

This discussion may lead one to believe that consensus may be more desirable than compromise—and perhaps this book should be titled *The Art of the Consensus*. Yet such a belief is not grounded in reality. As a practical matter, compromise is more feasible—and often more desirable—when it comes to dealing with disagreement in real life. Compromise, rather than consensus, can accommodate reasonable

---

*Many delegates at Philadelphia in 1787 shared that sentiment after a summer full of compromises to establish our Constitution. Even Benjamin Franklin, in his famous closing speech, confessed that he did not approve of the Constitution in every part but would support it for the sake of union. As Dennis Rasmussen notes, most of the Founders who lived into the nineteenth century grew disillusioned with the government they had framed, regarding it with "anxiety, disappointment, and even despair" (Rasmussen, 2021).

disagreements that are inevitable in a pluralistic society. Consensus may remain out of reach, but compromise still moves politics forward. Thus, compromise over consensus offers a more realistic path for democratic progress, given persistent disagreement.

This conviction shapes the chapters that follow. Over five chapters, I trace how the United States has drawn strength from a multitude of conflicting backgrounds—woven together by a common American Soul—to produce compromise solutions, often shaped by *integrative complexity*—a term that I define in a later chapter. Such solutions have enabled the nation to grow, adapt, and endure as the world's oldest and most resilient democratic republic. To frame the operation of compromise within our Constitution, I introduce two models: one depicts how the system strains under pressure, the other how the Republic works when functioning at its best.

Two-Party Compromise

To illustrate these dynamics, I often turn to diagrams. As a scientist and engineer, I often find that simple diagrams help clarify complexity. Throughout this book, I will refer to these visual models that map the operating conditions of the American political system. The diagram in Fig. 1 presents an abstract overview of the process. When democracy functions at its best, the system generates political solutions that reflect what author Jim Collins termed the "Genius of the And" (Collins, 2001). Collins' insights reflect the power of compromises.

To reach such compromises, the American system of government must work to *differentiate* the multitude of ideas expressed by the citizenry—represented in the diagram by small circles at the top of the figure—into two distinct sides of an

The Art of the Compromise

argument, shaped by the two-party system. Corralling people's individual thoughts into coherent political ideas resembles the task of herding cats. Citizens differ. We protest. And at times, we unfortunately riot. Yet these differences must not lead to anarchy.

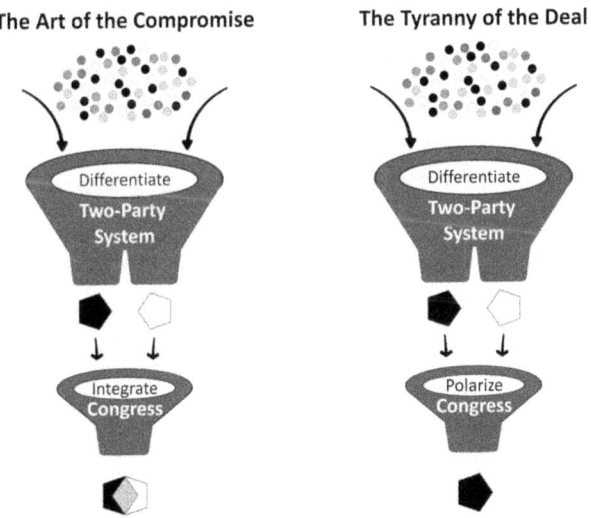

Figure 1. Conceptual models for the American political system. The left side illustrates optimal functioning, where differentiated interests are structured, integrated, and resolved through the Art of the Compromise. Policy emerges from shared understanding and institutional balance. The right side shows suboptimal functioning—what might be called the Tyranny of the Deal—where short-term bargaining replaces synthesis. Decisions are made outside the deliberative process, driven by transaction rather than transformation.

Therefore, the next step in the diagram gathers this diverse multitude into a coherent political form. The black and white pentagons symbolize two differentiated solutions—our two major parties—emerging from the clamor and diversity of citizen voices. Thus, out of the "Many" citizens' views comes a more cohesive and governable "Two" party solution.

Fear Not!

As the old saying* reminds us, "two's company, three's a crowd." Throughout the book, I argue the important value of a two-party system to enable compromise, and the virtue of two parties lies in their manageability. Two parties—rather than three or more—are well suited for channeling discord into a rivalry capable of sustaining republican order.

In the final stage of the diagram, the U.S. Congress serves as the integrating body that synthesizes the two competing visions into a *bisociated compromise*. This phrase captures more than a simple split-the-difference compromise. The term refers to a creative synthesis, where tension between opposing parties produces a third solution with elements of both. Later chapters will examine the term more thoroughly, but the six-sided polygon in the diagram previews the concept visually. This final shape symbolizes *integration*—a solution forged not through surrender, but through fusion.

This full process reflects the deeper structure of the American mind itself. The nation thinks in opposites—federal and state, liberty and order, large state and small state, left and right, blue and red, Democrat and Republican—and draws strength from the effort to reconcile them. When Congress

---

*The adage "two's company, three's a crowd" reaches back at least to the 1600s. John Ray's *Collection of English Proverbs* (1678) captured the thought as "One's too few, three too many." By the 1800s, several variants circulated—"two's company but three are none," "two's company but three's trumpery," and finally the familiar form, which appeared in America by the 1850s. Though often invoked in romantic settings, the underlying lesson extends beyond courtship. Two can create balance, but three often splinter coherence (Grammarist, 2019). In politics, the saying reminds us why a two-party rivalry, however imperfect, has proven more governable than a fractured field of many as in Europe.

The Art of the Compromise

achieves this synthesis, the result reflects what I call *The Art of the Compromise*. This art is rare, though not unreachable. Many of the most enduring political achievements in American history have emerged from bisociated compromises—solutions marked by depth, durability, and true integrative complexity.

The second illustration in Fig. 1 stands in contrast to the Art of the Compromise. The right side of the diagram reflects what Jim Collins has termed the "Tyranny of the Or," in which one side of an argument is selected, without integration or negotiation, over the other side. No compromise is achieved. In political terms, I refer to this failure as the *Tyranny of the Deal*—a deliberate allusion to Donald Trump's book *The Art of the Deal* (Trump & Schwartz, 1987).* Under this approach, one party imposes its preferred solution—essentially its *deal*—with no serious attempt to incorporate opposing views. Rather than aiming for a bisociated compromise that reflects shared governance, the process defaults to unilateral control. Neither compromise nor consensus. One side wins, and the other side loses.

The right-hand diagram represents this suboptimal condition of the American political system. A single party advances

---

*Donald Trump has said that *The Art of the Deal* ranks second only to the Bible among his favorite books (Scott, 2015). The book offers insight into his governing style. In 2016, George Wu, professor at the University of Chicago Booth School of Business, wrote a critical review describing Trump's dealmaking as "pugnacious" and grounded in a zero-sum mindset (Wu, 2016). That posture reflects the *Tyranny of the Or*—a win-or-lose approach that may hold in business negotiations but collapses in the context of congressional governance. I argue that this mindset is not just ill-suited for government but rather one of government's failure modes.

legislation unchanged by deliberation, bypassing the collaborative function of Congress. The black pentagon, representing one party's preferred outcome, moves through Congress without modification—unchallenged, undebated, and unbalanced. This version of lawmaking characterizes much of today's polarized environment. Congress, under such conditions, becomes paralyzed—unwilling or unable to integrate competing perspectives. The result is not a negotiated solution, but a partisan imposition masquerading as governance. Thereby, the Tyranny of the Deal replaces the Art of the Compromise.

The central thesis of this book is that the United States has built a democratic republic, grounded in the Constitution, capable of operating through the Art of the Compromise to generate resilient political solutions. These solutions are not ends in themselves; they are mechanisms that preserve the inalienable rights of life, liberty, and the pursuit of happiness. When the system functions as designed, it absorbs conflict, channels dissent, and produces durable outcomes.

However, when vigilance falters and polarization hardens, the machinery slips into the suboptimal mode of operation, the Tyranny of the Deal. Governance becomes conquest. Resilience gives way to resentment. Restoring the capacity for compromise must become a national priority. Without a renewed commitment to shared governance, the Republic cannot sustain itself.

Later chapters will examine how the American two-party system performs the intellectual heavy lifting required to distill the multitude of ideas, proposals, arguments, and grievances circulating across the broad and diverse population of *We, the People*. This system compresses pluralism of the Many into the Two, well-differentiated political viewpoints—Republican and Democrat—each with coherent, if imperfect, perspectives. That differentiation mirrors a familiar structure in the manner in which our human minds divide complex questions into binary form (Blachowicz, 1998).* In this sense, a nation of two parties reflects a people of two minds, an arrangement echoed in the way thought itself frames arguments through dual structures. Yet the American system is not the only way to translate pluralism into governance. Other democracies pursue the same task through a different architecture of parties.

Multi-Party Compromise

By comparison, the political processes of Europe often follow a multi-party model. The left side of Fig. 2 illustrates this approach. Like the American system, European democracies distill a multitude of public ideas, beliefs, proposals, and grievances into defined political positions. However, rather than channeling this diversity into two dominant parties, European systems assign those positions across multiple parties, each aligned with a narrower slice of the electorate. The task of integration then falls to the parliament, which must coalesce several platforms into a single governing agenda.

---

*Philosopher James Blachowicz explores this structure in *Of Two Minds: The Nature of Inquiry* (1998), arguing that human reasoning often proceeds through binary tensions—thesis and antithesis—before achieving resolution. This dynamic mirrors the structure of American political discourse and the role of bisociated compromise.

Fear Not!

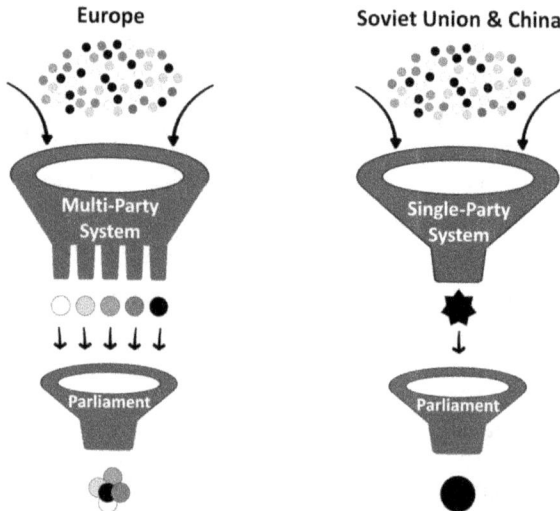

Figure 2. Conceptual illustrations of alternative political systems. The left model represents the European multi-party structure: high differentiation of viewpoints, but limited integration. Coalitions form after elections, often fragile and short-lived. The right model depicts a single-party system—such as the former Soviet Union or modern China—where integration is strong, but differentiation is suppressed. Debate is muted, dissent punished, and pluralism absent. Each system lacks the structural balance required for enduring synthesis.

Achieving integration under a multi-party model proves difficult. With more than two sides competing for influence, the resulting political solution often resembles a loose coalition rather than a cohesive synthesis. The diagram in Fig. 2 reflects this reality with a disorganized cluster of circles at the bottom—symbolizing a differentiated outcome that lacks true integration. As a result, multi-party systems tend to produce fragile coalitions, unstable governance, and short-lived policy alignment. We will explore these topics more in later chapters.

One of the key differences between the European and American models lies in where political synthesis occurs. In

The Art of the Compromise

most multi-party systems, the process of coalition-building takes place after the election, within the legislature itself. Party platforms may diverge significantly during the campaign, only to be rapidly stitched together in behind-the-scenes negotiations once the votes are counted. Integration becomes an elite exercise—reactive, opaque, and often unstable.

Whereas Europe relies on post-election stitching, America forces the stitching earlier. The two-party system compels integration before the vote is cast, at the boundary between the multitude and the major parties. The work of political consolidation happens before power is allocated, during primary campaigns, and during platform development. Citizens cast votes not merely for candidates, but for already-formed, broad-based coalitions, unlike European systems. This structural feature creates a stronger alignment between electoral mandate and legislative action. Though imperfect, this early-stage integration encourages compromise by requiring parties to accommodate dissenting factions before governing begins.[*]

---

[*]Political scientists Giovanni Sartori and Arend Lijphart offer contrasting but complementary analyses of democratic systems. Sartori argues that the structure of party systems and electoral incentives determines how ideas are filtered into governance. In *Comparative Constitutional Engineering* (1997), he emphasizes that coalition-building before elections—characteristic of majoritarian, two-party systems—yields clearer mandates and more stable outcomes than coalitions formed afterward in fragmented parliaments. Lijphart, in *Patterns of Democracy* (1999), provides a broader comparative study across thirty-six democracies, distinguishing between majoritarian and consensus models. While Lijphart acknowledges the inclusiveness of post-electoral coalition governments in consensus systems, he also recognizes the instability and policy fragility that often follow. Both scholars highlight a core structural insight: when political

Fear Not!

Political theorists have noted that systems that build coalitions before elections, like the American two-party system, tend to yield more durable, accountable, and publicly understood policies (Lijphart, 1999; Sartori, 1997). When integration occurs after the election, within a fragmented legislature like European multi-party systems, governance often becomes reactive and brittle. The American system, by demanding a coalition before elections, equips Congress to focus not on forming a government, but on forging compromises.

A parable may be helpful. Consider friends at a crowded table ordering one pizza together. In a multi-party world, each person champions their own topping—pepperoni, mushrooms, olives, pineapple. One party represents each topping. The friends quarrel until only plain cheese remains as a mutual consensus, safe for all but loved by none. Europe's multi-party systems thus tend toward consensus—cheese pizza—safe and uninspiring. By contrast, in a two-party world, the friends divide into Meat Lovers and Veggie Lovers, with passion coalescing into two parties. After a deliberative struggle, they settle on a compromise in a supreme pizza—sausage with peppers, mushrooms, and onions. The Veggie Lovers can pick off the sausage, the Meat Lovers can push aside the peppers, but the meal holds together. The pineapple vote is left behind. That is Compromise, richer than cheese alone, but disagreement persists.

---

integration occurs early—before power is allocated—governance becomes more durable, transparent, and accountable, which is the advantage of the American two-party system.

The Art of the Compromise

If multi-party systems drift toward bland consensus and two-party systems foster compromise,* the single-party system lies at the opposite end of the spectrum, depicted on the right side of Fig. 2. This model, exemplified by the former Soviet Union and present-day China, centers authority in a unitary leadership—typically embodied in the General Secretary—who provides a strong mechanism for political integration. Policies emerge with speed and coherence, backed by a centralized command structure. The General Secretary may choose pineapple topping without consulting Meat or Veggie Lovers.

The simple diagrams in Fig. 2 capture this spectrum—from the fragility of multi-party coalitions to the rigidity of one-party command. The left model represents the European multi-party structure: high differentiation of viewpoints, but limited integration. Coalitions form after elections, often fragile and short-lived. The right model depicts a single-party system—such as the former Soviet Union or modern China—where integration is strong, but differentiation is suppressed. Debate is muted, dissent punished, and pluralism absent. Each

---

*Scholar Arend Lijphart distinguishes between "majoritarian" and "consensus" models of democracy, the former associated with two-party systems and the latter with multi-party, proportional systems. In his book *Patterns of Democracy*, he argues that multi-party systems distribute power more broadly and therefore cultivate consensus through coalition and inclusiveness, while two-party systems concentrate responsibility and more often force adversarial compromise before elections (Lijphart, 1999). The distinction provides the theoretical scaffolding for my pizza parable. Multi-party coalitions often settle for the lowest-common-denominator cheese pizza, while two-party systems, though contentious, more often yield thicker compromises, like a supreme pizza carrying both meat and vegetables.

system lacks the structural balance required for enduring compromise.

Such coerced integration may appear efficient, but it strips away the very plurality that sustains democratic adaptability—if one even considers one-party systems to be democracies at all. The ruling party suppresses competing ideas and channels public discourse into a narrow ideological path aligned with state priorities. Political solutions exhibit high internal consistency but low adaptability. Innovation slows. Dissent becomes dangerous. The black circle at the base of the diagram represents this condition: full integration, achieved through the absence of differentiation.

Later chapters will examine how the health of a democracy depends on the dynamic balance between these two forces—differentiation and integration—and why resilient political solutions must begin with plurality and end in compromise. These models reveal more than regional differences; they expose structural tradeoffs. Multi-party systems push the work of differentiation too far upstream, asking elite party leaders to negotiate coalitions after the people have voted—cheese pizza. Single-party systems push integration too far downstream, forcing unity upon the public from above—pineapple pizza. The American system occupies a middle ground. Integration occurs at the threshold between the Many and the Two—where citizens themselves participate in forming broad, pre-electoral coalitions. This positioning reflects the *Genius of the And*. Differentiation is preserved, yet integration remains possible—supreme pizza.

The Art of the Compromise

In Limine*

The interesting magic of the American system lies in this paradox—that the Many and the Two find a way to share One Soul. That mystery is one we also uncover in this book.

In this revised and expanded edition, each chapter now includes charts and visual data that illuminate key arguments. These additions are not decorative. They ground the book's themes—dualism, conflict, and compromise—in historical patterns, demographic shifts, and legislative behavior. The aim is to make the argument not only felt and understood, but also seen. With these models in mind—each illustrating how differentiation and integration shape democratic systems—this book explores how America has become a nation of two minds, and why dualism in our political structure is essential—and should not be feared—to achieving the Art of the Compromise.

In Chapter 1, we explore the riotous nature of America—both past and present—that leads to events like January 6 and how we should not fear such moments, and yet we should not embrace them either. We are a nation of Many—many cultures, many heritages, many languages, many races, many religions, many colors, many philosophies, and, yes, many politics. Conflicts and even riots will arise. Chapter 1 argues that political riots like January 6, while alarming, are not an existential threat to American democracy. Rather, they are

---

* *In Limine* is a Latin legal phrase meaning "at the threshold." I use it here because it sounded just obscure enough to work as a chapter ending. For the record, the other chapters close with *In Sum* (summing up) and the last chapter with *In Totum* (the whole enchilada).

part of a long American tradition of passionate protest, even riotous dissent, tolerated and absorbed by a system designed for such disruption. The Constitution, particularly Congress, is structured to channel this pluralism into durable compromise.

That brings us to Chapter 2, where we seek to understand how this multitude can somehow unite—sometimes more successfully than at other times but unite nonetheless—into one nation. President Abraham Lincoln is the American hero who held our federal union together in the face of our most disunited time—the Civil War—to answer the question as to whether a government of the people, by the people, for the people, should perish or not from this Earth. Lincoln is our guidepost to move from internal conflict and dissent to a nation of one Soul. Lincoln delivered us across the Jordan River.

With this deliverance, we dig into Chapter 3 and examine the two-party system that emerged and stabilized after the Civil War. This structure performs the essential work of political differentiation. Unlike Europe's multi-party parliaments or China's one-party command, the American model compresses the Many into Two—conservative and liberal, Red State and Blue State, Republican and Democrat, left and right. This dualism is not a flaw, but a feature that enables clarity and contrast, allowing the system to identify the most salient tensions within each issue.

Then, the big step comes in Chapter 4, where we discuss the four-letter word "compromise," specifically bisociated compromise—a form of synthesis that transcends simple trade-offs. Rather than splitting the difference, bisociated compromise fuses opposing ideas to generate integrative, resilient political solutions. The chapter examines why such compromise is essential not only for legislative success but for the survival of democratic culture. Drawing on historical

The Art of the Compromise

examples and cognitive theory, the discussion traces how genuine compromise emerges through tension, not despite conflict, but because of it. The willingness to engage across divisions stands as one of the defining acts of American political character.

Finally, in Chapter 5, I turn inward. The chapter steps away from structural proposals and policy models to reflect on the human dimension of compromise. Through a more personal lens, I consider what it means to live with tension, to hold competing truths, and to pursue goodness in a fractured world. The concluding chapter serves not as a blueprint but as a meditation on the quiet resilience of those who keep showing up for the hard work of democracy. The goal is not merely to reclaim the Art of the Compromise in Congress, but to rediscover it in ourselves.

I invite the reader to join me in this book, which represents my deep dive into the current state of American politics—and my effort to restore faith in the enduring strengths and quiet goodness of our nation and its constitutional design. I write as a long-time conservative and Republican, shaped by the example of party stalwarts like Ronald Reagan and Dwight Eisenhower. I also confess to an awkward respect for figures often cast as villains within the party: Richard Nixon and Newt Gingrich.* I am not a Trump supporter, yet I am far from a Trump hater. I share these positions not to stake out partisan

---

*I understand why most folks vilify Nixon and Gingrich. I am not blind to their flaws, nor unsympathetic to their critics. Yet I hold a reluctant respect for their accomplishments—achievements often overshadowed by their downfalls, and rightly so. This respect does not excuse their conduct; it reflects a willingness to see the full, complicated arc of a political life.

ground, but to acknowledge the lenses through which I see—and to invite a conversation across the chapters that follow.

America stands again at a crossroads. We have faced hard times before. The challenge ahead is not new, but the stakes are high. The central argument of this book is simple: we must celebrate the power of two minds. We must reject *The Art of the Deal* and reclaim the Soul of a nation built on *The Art of the Compromise*.

So don't panic. Let us begin not with compromise, but with the riotous noise that defines us. In America, unity begins not in silence but in discord. To see how, we turn first to the Many.

CHAPTER 1

Out of Many

"OUT OF MANY, ONE," the phrase refers to the union of the original thirteen colonies—and by modern extension, the fifty states—into a single nation. Our journey to rediscover the Art of the Compromise begins here, with the Many, and that a functioning democracy can emerge not despite disagreement, but because of it. That unity and discord are not enemies of democracy, but co-conspirators in this wild—sometimes raucous—American experiment.

On August 20, 1776, Dr. Franklin, Mr. J. Adams, and Mr. Jefferson proposed the motto, *E Pluribus Unum*, as part of their design for the Great Seal of the United States (Deutsch, 1923). In time, the phrase appeared on coins and currency, official crests, and state documents. Yet its original purpose was never ornamental. It was explanatory—and aspirational. Out of many, one.

The words carried more than symbolism. They expressed the conviction that thirteen quarrelsome colonies could bind themselves into a single nation without dissolving their distinct identities. Unity would not mean uniformity. Factions would remain, interests would collide, voices would clash. The motto promised that out of the tumult of the Many, a durable One could still emerge. It is this paradox—the preservation of difference within a union—that gives *E Pluribus Unum* its lasting force.

Years later, during the Constitutional Convention, Dr. Franklin sat and often stared at George Washington's chair, its wooden crest carved with the figure of a half-sun. For weeks, he studied that sun without knowing whether it was rising or setting. At the close of the Convention, he stood and declared—with hope, not certainty—that the sun was rising. His hope rested not on unity of mind, but on unity of purpose.

Also, at the Convention was James Madison, who was known as the father of the U.S. Constitution, saw the raucous nature of democracy not as a flaw, but as a defining feature. He understood the political nature of men and the tendency for factions. In *Federalist No. 10*, he argued that a republic must extend its sphere so broadly that no single faction could dominate. In such a system, conflict would not vanish but could be managed. The structure, not silence, would keep the Union intact.

In America, the Many never melt away. We clang. We clash. We riot and yawp and shout—not to break the Republic, but to test the structure forged to withstand the blows. We organize. We shout, "Not my President," then shout the phrase again four years later. The noise may resemble disorder, but beneath the chaos lies feedback—a self-correcting pulse of a living republic. Not dysfunction. A raucous, partisan, self-critical republic may look like a crisis in motion, but the alternative is silence.

The Art of the Compromise

This chapter begins with a provocation that *We, the People*—the Many—should not compromise. We should not compromise our values, our morals, our religions, our voices, our politics, or our weirdness. That diverse multitude—the Many—is the essence of America. Yet as we will learn later in the book, Congress must compromise. Congress must distill the will of the Many into durable legislation and legitimate governance.

The heart of this book's argument is that structured compromise is essential—not from the People, but from Congress. *The Art of the Compromise* is not about the Many holding hands and singing *Kumbaya, my Lord*, but rather forging unity through disagreement, and then Congress must roll up its sleeves and hammer out solutions sharp-edged enough to matter.

Compromise is not a campfire chorus but a tension. Hammer and anvil. Push and pull. Give and get. Political compromise demands more than singing in unison. The Art asks us to sing in harmony while still holding our own note. In this light, we should not overreact to moments of civil unrest—even those as disturbing as the riot on January 6, 2021, which clearly represented a breach of democratic norms.

The American Constitution is structured to tolerate protest and even occasional riots, not because such events are good, but because they are byproducts of a vibrant pluralistic democracy. These events, while serious, should be viewed in the context of a resilient system built to contain the passions of the Many without breaking under those passions. We do not want a system of where no one cares. Yet if we strip away the passion entirely, we risk something worse than chaos: indifference and silence.

No One Cared

The Union dissolved. The President resigned. Almost no one cared.

One of the most powerful empires in the history of the world came to a surprisingly peaceful end with no fanfare, no bloodshed, no pomp, and no circumstance. An otherwise bland and unmemorable day closed with the flag of the union lowered from a perch atop the picturesque building known around the world. A smattering of pedestrians passed by and observed the occasion with a brief pause. The awkward moment was more reminiscent of a distant uncle's death than a powerful patriarch's demise. The world took little note nor long remembered what happened that day; the event has been mostly forgotten.

This description is not some dystopian future of America. The day was Christmas Day, December 25, 1991. The building was the Kremlin; the union was the former Soviet Union; and the president was Mikhail Gorbachev. In a brief 10-minute televised speech, Gorbachev announced the dissolution of his country. The weary Soviet President addressed his dying nation and resigned from his position as its leader, stating, "I hereby discontinue my activities at the post of President of the Union of Soviet Socialist Republics" (Gorbachev, 1991). With that statement, the once mighty empire—the Evil Empire, according to former President Ronald Reagan (Reagan, 1983)—faded away to become fifteen separate and independent states, no longer a single monolithic power. The Soviet collapse led to no riots, no protests, no outrage, no fracas in the streets, and no event like our January 6th. No one seemed to care enough to fight for the existence of the once vaunted union, the largest country in the world. No one cared about the demise of the Soviet Union. No one rioted.

The Art of the Compromise

Unlike Soviet founders Lenin and Joseph Stalin, Gorbachev was a unique leader in the 70-year line of the Soviets. He was willing to compromise to move his country—the large, diverse republic it was—forward into a more modern era. Yet the Soviet system was a rigid, single-party political system incapable of compromise. Since the fall of the Berlin Wall in November of 1989, the demise of Gorbachev's beloved empire was—unknown at the time but seen in the vivid hindsight of history—a question of when, not if. Under the pressure of a changing world, the Marxist–Leninist governments of the Warsaw Pact, of which the Soviet Union was the dominant figure, collapsed one by one. History's events gradually reduced the orbit of the Soviet influence to the immediate borders of the once mighty USSR (Kengor, 2021). Then, in March 1990, the snowball rolled over those borders (Siegelbaum, 2015). The union collapsed.

Gorbachev was pulled in two directions (Klein, 2016). On one side, the democratic reformers pulled toward greater freedoms and autonomy for the republics. On the other side, hardline conservatives pulled in the other direction to end the reforms, which they believed were causing the breakup of the union. Two directions, like Republicans and Democrats in the U.S., but unfortunately, their one-party system had no room for two factions, and left no room for Gorbachev's compromising path. In a few months, Gorbachev would give his Christmas farewell.

One party. One voice. No dissent. No compromise. That mantra worked for 70 years in the Soviet Union to transform an agricultural backwater into an industrial superpower, but ultimately failed to tolerate—let alone foster—the political creativity to move the large, diverse republic forward into the information age. The one-party system failed—and failed rapidly. No one cared when that system faded from history. In contrast, America makes noise.

The Riot

Here in the States, we do not go quietly or fade away. We yell. We argue. We chant. And, yes, we sometimes throw punches. We are a bit wild. Our strength as a nation is not our unity of ideas but our ideal of unity—Out of Many, One.

Unlike the last days of the Soviet Union, nearly every day in the United States, someone, somewhere, is protesting—Black Lives Matter, Earth Day, March for Life, Million Man March, National Pride March, Washington for Jesus, Occupy Wall Street. The parade of protests in America sometimes seems endless, with the Many expressing themselves vigorously. More precisely, according to Tommy Leung and Nathan Perkins, 42,347 reported protests occurred in the United States between January 2017 and January 2021 (Leung & Perkins, 2021). That's a lot of protests.

Tommy and Nathan are "engineers and scientists with a keen interest in civic responsibility and public policy," per their website CountLove.org. The pair met as left-leaning graduate students at the Massachusetts Institute of Technology, and in 2016, frustrated with Donald Trump's presidency, they began keeping a digital tally of American dissent. Their data indicate that, on average, nearly 30 protests, ranging from civil rights to immigration and from guns to the environment, occur each day across America. They use automated and semi-automated methods based on advanced machine learning techniques, such as natural language processing and artificial neural networks, to crawl local newspapers and television sites daily to gather their data.

The Art of the Compromise

The work of Tommy, Nathan, and others (Fisher et al., 2019) underscores the time-honored American tradition—since our nation's Founding—for citizens to express their grievances through protest. The protection of this tradition is codified in the First Amendment to the U.S. Constitution:

> *Congress shall make no law respecting an establishment of religion or prohibiting the free exercise thereof, abridging the freedom of speech or of the press, or the right of the people peaceably to assemble and to petition the Government for a redress of grievances.*

Notably, the amendment is careful to qualify with the adverb "peaceably," but Americans are not always obedient, and from time to time, protests turn to violence and thus become riots like January 6th.

Though distressing and hard to watch, riots are an essential yet unfortunate part of American history, as Paul Gilje documents in his book *Rioting in America* (Gilje, 1999). Like Tommy and Nathan at CountLove, Gilje has tracked the nation's habit of blowing off steam, documenting over 4,000 riots since 1776. That's an average of more than one per month—a staggering number. He readily admits his count is a gross underestimate that "does not come close to the total of all rioting" (Gilje, 1999). Leveraging Gilje's data, we can plot in Fig. 3 a bar chart of estimated riots using a loose categorization around major periods in American history.

Reflecting on his interest in rioting, Gilje recalls somewhat tepidly and somewhat nostalgically his experience growing up when his "father worked in a machine parts factory and belonged to a union that went on strike every few years" (Gilje, 1999). As a boy, Gilje witnessed the angst on his mother's face each time his father joined the picket line, knowing the danger that the strike could erupt into a riot. Yet he also experienced the contrasting attitude of his father, who seemed to enjoy the fellowship and ritual of the strike despite the looming threat of violence. Gilje's reflections are not unique and are a common framing in American union families.

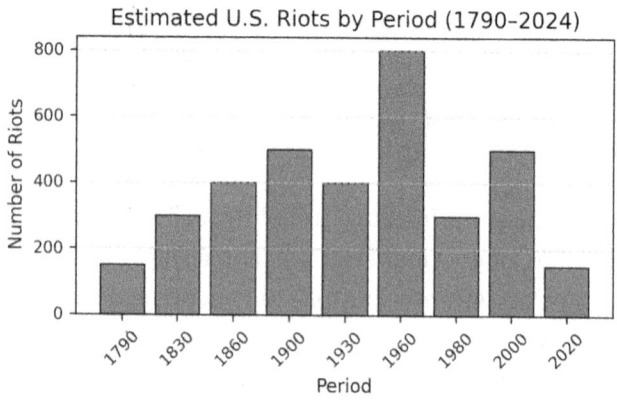

Figure 3. Estimated number of riots in the United States by historical period. Peaks align with major national crises: Civil War and Reconstruction (1861–1900), labor and racial tensions (1901–1930), and Civil Rights (1961–1980). Data source: (Gilje, 1999).

Through his personal experience, Gilje urges his readers to recognize and internalize that American protests include riots from time to time and "to see the troubled course of American history and to understand that the fragile gains of American democracy have come at a gruesome cost" (Gilje, 1999). Riots are an embarrassing, awkward, cumbersome, unfortunate, perplexing—yet necessary—aspect of American democracy.

We are a cantankerous people. We fight. Unlike the Soviets, we do not go gentle into that good night, whether we are Republicans, Democrats, right-wingers, left-wingers, Federalists, Anti-Federalists, Jeffersonians, or Hamiltonians. Our riotous nature is not flattering in comparison to the rest of the world. (See Fig. 4, which we will discuss more later.) We

The Art of the Compromise

protest, and from time to time, we fight. We rage, rage against the dying of the light*—whatever that light might be for our political grievances. If we as a people could avoid riots and subsequent violence and still maintain progress, that state of being would be most preferable. However, theory and practice are hardly good bedfellows.

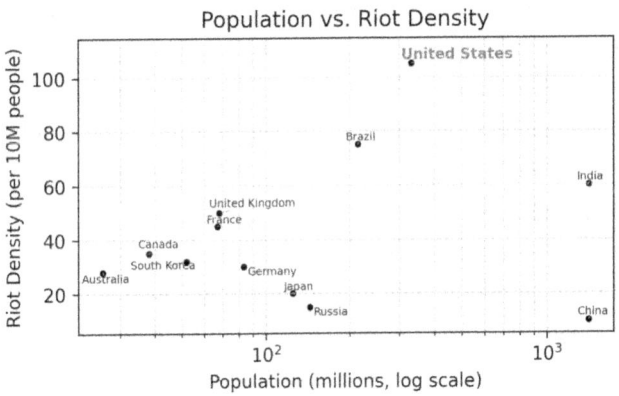

Figure 4. Riot density (per 10 million people per decade) compared to population. The x-axis is a log scale for improved visualization of the large populations in India and China. Data compiled from multiple sources (Fearon, 2003; Gilje, 1999; Marshall & Gurr, 2020; Sundberg & Melander, 2013).

So, the riot of January 6, 2021, should not be as shocking with the contextual evidence of Gilje's data, although when I first learned of the unfolding violence, I was indeed shocked.

---

*My apologies to the Welsh poet Dylan Thomas and his well-known 1951 villanelle, "*Do not go gentle into that good night.*" I am fond of the poem, and its defiant rhythm feels especially fitting in the context of this discussion.

I remember standing in an office hallway at work, leaning into the doorway of a colleague to watch the events of what was unfolding in Washington, DC, that day—the official day that a joint session of Congress was to certify Joe Biden over Donald Trump to be the next President of the United States.

While walking down the hallway, I heard an exclamation, "They've shot a police officer!" This startling news, which would prove later to be false, grabbed my attention, and I leaned into the doorway where the voice came from. A live stream from CNN was playing on the computer screen. "Trump is leading a coup on the Capitol!" my colleague shouted. The news shocked me. We spent the next few minutes discussing the situation, and he brought me up to speed on what was happening. I was appalled as the streaming news laid out that protesters had invaded the Capitol building and allegedly killed a police officer amid the mayhem.

David Boaz, executive vice president of the Cato Institute, a self-declared Libertarian organization but conservative-leaning think tank, explained that "what we saw on our television screens was a direct assault on the rule of law...freedom is fragile; we can't take it for granted."

As an American, I did not like what I saw on January 6. I could feel the fragility of our democracy. Yet Americans have never been easy to hush.

Raucous Americans

As jarring as January 6 was, Americans are no strangers to riots and political mischief, and the events of January 6 should not be held out as some appalling exception. Our unity as a nation has persisted through disorder. Our nation's birth is built on such dramatic protests.

The Art of the Compromise

Walt Whitman, the quintessential American poet, captured this uniquely American spirit in his poem *Song of Myself*, where he proclaims,

> *I too am not a bit tamed, I too am untranslatable,*
> *I sound my barbaric yawp over the roofs of the world.*

The January 6 rioters—and many untamed Americans before them—have sounded their Whitman yawp to be heard across the rooftops of the world.

The Boston Tea Party is no less of an instructive example of raucous Americans who needed to do a little yawping. Through our historical perspective of having successfully achieved independence from the British, we often retell the Tea Party more like a college prank than a radical act, which belies the true gravity and gravitas of the protest. In our present-day sugar-coated mythology, the Bostonians sneak aboard a few ships dressed as natives, dump the cargo of tea overboard, and thereby mock King George and his taxes without representation. America is born, and we exalt the Tea Partiers to folk hero status. Yet the reality of the Tea Party, much like the January 6 Capitol Rampage, had much graver consequences. We celebrate the Tea Party through the eyes of history as a glorious moment, but Colonial Americans, including George Washington, did not celebrate the event as we do today (Carp, 2010).

The Tea Party was a high-stakes political protest, much like the events of January 6. At Griffin's Warf in Boston Harbor in 1773, three ships, the Dartmouth, the Eleanor, and the Beaver, were docked and loaded with tea from the British East India Company. American Colonists were angry at the King for imposing "taxation without representation" on the imported tea, along with a long list of other grievances. On the night of December 16, a group of about 60 Colonists, members of the Sons of Liberty, led by Samuel Adams, disguised themselves in Native American dress and boarded the three ships. The Sons of Liberty was an underground resistance group, considered radical extremists and outside the mainstream of other American Colonists. While equating the Sons of Liberty to the Proud Boys or Antifa* is a bit over the top, the organization was made up of instigators and provocateurs who practiced extreme forms of civil disobedience. They would have been at home among the January 6th crowd.

They were more than innocent pranksters, and over the next three hours, they destroyed East Indian property and dumped 342 chests of tea overboard and into the Boston Harbor. These radical Colonists purposefully cut and split the chests of tea with their makeshift tomahawks to make sure the tea dissolved into the seawater. The chests held more than 92,000 pounds of tea—equal in weight to 45 Volkswagen 1979 Beetle automobiles—and had an equivalent dollar value of nearly $1,000,000 in today's money (Carp, 2010).

By comparison, one can hardly imagine celebrating and immortalizing a similar protest today where a costume-laden group climbs aboard a massive transport ship and pushes

---

*The Proud Boys is a far-right, neo-fascist militant group founded in 2016 by Gavin McInnes. The group emphasizes "Western chauvinism," opposes left-wing and progressive politics, and has frequently engaged in street violence and confrontations with anti-fascist protesters (Kriner & Lewis, 2021).

Antifa (short for anti-fascist) is not a centralized organization but rather a loose network of activists (often decentralized, locally organized) committed to opposing fascism, racism, authoritarianism, and far-right ideologies. The term "Antifa" functions both as a descriptor and a banner under which various anti-fascist actors operate without formal hierarchy (Vysotsky, 2020).

The Art of the Compromise

45 VW Beetles into the sea. Yet the damage to the U.S. Capitol building by the January 6 rioters, according to a May 2021 estimate by the Architect of the Capitol, approached $1,500,000 worth of repairs (2021). The Boston Tea Party was no small college prank, and most Colonists at the time—and in the years that followed—were appalled at the actions of their radical compatriots.

Though no one was hurt, the Tea Party was not an isolated act of political protest. Leading up to the night, the secretive Sons of Liberty harassed and bullied government officials throughout Boston. The Tea Party was the apex moment of their extremist violence. As the historian Jonathan Carp writes (Carp, 2010),

> ...the destruction of the tea was also the culminating act in a series of violent threats and deeds against friends of government in Boston. Bostonians intimidated importers and customs officers, threw rocks and shattered windows, printed death threats against the tea consignees, surrounded them at their homes and places of business, refused to allow the governor to give them armed protection, and effectively exiled them to a fortified island in the harbor.

Faced with these violent threats, the tea consignees and customs officials fled to Castle Island off the Boston shores. They fled out of fear for their lives in the bullying, thuggish environment. Our rose-colored glasses of nostalgic hindsight mask the bullying nature of the Tea Party. This clash between rough reality and comforting legend sets the stage for the myth that followed.

A Convenient Myth

In a somewhat eerie manner, Carp's description echoes the modern descriptions of how the January 6 rioters behaved both in the months leading up to the protests at the Capitol and during the event (Saric, 2022). To be clear, my comparison is not intended to elevate the status of January 6 to equal historical footing with the Boston Tea Party, but the intent is to compare the context and nature of riots to political protests in American history.

Essential to that comparison, the American colonists in 1773 were embarrassed that their fellow compatriots smashed windows and dressed like natives. The Tea Party, as a patriotic act, was not celebrated then as we do today. Our modern sensibilities are likely uncomfortable with the comparison to the clumsy January 6 riot. Yet the Sons of Liberty are more aligned with a radical viewpoint than our modern embellishments prefer.

In the aftermath of the Tea Party, the blatant destruction of British property outraged the British Parliament, but Parliament was not alone in condemning the clandestine acts. Many Colonists were equally outraged, which may be a surprising fact to our modern understanding of the Tea Party. While some Americans, like John Adams, who was a second cousin to the Tea Party leader Samuel Adams, reveled in the news that East India tea colored and caffeinated the Boston Harbor, others, like the venerable George Washington, condemned the act. Washington disapproved of Bostonians and "their conduct in destroying the tea," as he and other elites held private property to be sacrosanct (Carp, 2010). They saw the Tea Party as an act of vandalism by radicals outside the accepted norms of other Colonists. Washington went so far as to claim Bostonians "were mad." This sentiment finds echoes in modern elite responses to January 6.

The modern myth that Colonists viewed the Tea Party as a patriotic act that inspired the revolution is historically inaccurate. The men who threw the tea into the harbor that night

The Art of the Compromise

took great pains to keep their participation a closely guarded secret for fear of civil and criminal reprisals from the British and their fellow compatriots. Tea Partiers kept their identities secret long after winning independence, and after the threat of British reprisal abated (Carp, 2010). They feared prosecution from the British and persecution from their fellow Colonists. However, the Sons of Liberty in 1773 did not have smartphone cameras to document their actions, so British officials could not track down Samuel Adams and his treasonous band. Social media did not exist to expose the Tea Party participants to the Crown immediately.

Suppose the King and Parliament could identify the Bostonians and bring them to trial. The resulting show trials may have extinguished the flames of revolution before the American Cause ever took popular hold. America may have never been. Cable news also did not exist; thus, the views of elites such as Washington that mocked the tea rioters could not spread and magnify their ridicule. Digital connectivity has allowed the rapid spread of the most casual news. The times were different, and the reputation of the Tea Party Colonists survived the initial outrage by the British and their fellow Americans. Their acts of rebellion slowly transformed with the whitewashing of time to elevate to the historical myth of patriots rather than thugs.

The lesson of the original Tea Party is that protests and riots in America are an unfortunate—but a necessary—part of democracy, and it is difficult to discern in the moment whether they will result in positive or negative change. Riots are a warning sign that something is wrong in society. If we look deeper into the rioters of January 6, we will see they were not an organized horde armed and ready to mount a coup. Instead, they were a disorganized band of citizens who were disgruntled with the outcome of the election, with deep-seated resentments that were, unfortunately, fueled by Trump as a demagogue. Unlike Moscow on December 25, 1991, the rioters—misguided and misinformed as they were—cared about America, perhaps a difficult fact for some Americans to believe. Their story begins with people like Michael Sparks.

January 6

Like most rioters on January 6, Michael Sparks was an unlikely insurgent—an everyday American drawn into extraordinary events. As history would record, at 2:11 PM, Sparks climbed through a broken window and into infamy (Leatherby et al., 2021). On that overcast day, Sparks was the first man through the window on the northwest side of the United States Capitol Building, and a legion of protestors followed him. The protest, which began at a rally near the White House, became a riot at the Capitol. The riot, which lasted less than four hours, would eventually take on multiple names: the Trump Rampage, the Terrorist Attack, the Coup Attempt, the January 6th Insurrection, and other labels.

Yet the crowd was far from cohesive. The rioters were mostly typical Americans: a retired Air Force Reserve officer (Farrow, 2021), a Florida firefighter (Galbraith, 2022), two off-duty officers from Virginia's Rocky Mount Police Department (Weiner, 2022), a Messianic Rabbi (Davis, 2022), a Christian pastor (Reilly, 2022), a West Virginia state lawmaker (Raby, 2023), a New York City sanitation worker (Feuerherd, 2021), a two-time Olympic gold medalist (Sheinin, 2023), and Sparks, a sometimes auto mechanic from Kentucky. The rioters, predominantly white, male, and middle-class, spanned multiple states, occupations, and personal

The Art of the Compromise

stories about why they were at the Capitol that day, but they shared a common belief—Trump had been wronged.

Ben Hamilton, a former history teacher turned documentarian, was there too—not to riot, but to witness. Disenchanted with both political parties, Hamilton took a recorder and camera to Washington, D.C., intending to serve as a primary source for future generations. His goal, as he later described it, was not to be fair but to be accurate. In *Sorry Guys, We Stormed the Capitol* (Hamilton, 2022), Hamilton describes the day as it unfolded—not filtered by hindsight or political spin, but raw and in real time.

He saw what others missed. Like the 1773 Tea Party, January 6 had its costumes (Friedman, 2021). Some folks wore tactical gear. Others showed up in garb more suited for Halloween. Hamilton even interviewed the now-infamous "Shaman" in the bearskin hat. A photograph of the Shaman has become an iconic moment of January 6 as he stands defiantly in a Capitol corridor, glancing slightly upward and letting out a Whitman-like yawp (Sheinin, 2023). "These farcical cartoon characters have somehow taken ownership of the Capitol Dome," he wrote. "My government has been overthrown by an episode of *Monty Python*." And yet at the time, the Shaman seemed to Hamilton to be just one more oddly dressed MAGA fan, i.e., Trump's Make America Great Again slogan. How could he know this man would become the riot's reluctant mascot?

Many rioters were clad in standard winterwear—knit caps, down jackets, MAGA scarves. The tactical clothing, Hamilton and others noted, seemed more cosplay than coup. "Many of these people aren't serious about buying duty gear," one gear company CEO observed (Penzenstadler, 2021). "They're doing it for show." A USA Today journalist likened them to sports fans in team jerseys, except the "team" was the U.S.

military (Penzenstadler, 2021). The tactical dress, like the Native American dress of the Boston Tea Party, is a caricature. The writer Ben Sixsmith tweeted (Friedman, 2021), "It's like the Storming of the Bastille as recreated by the cast of National Lampoon's Animal House. These photos will outlive us all."

While some rioters did have ties to fringe groups, fewer than 15 percent had connections—loose or otherwise—to organized extremism. The FBI concluded that the riot was not an orchestrated assault but rather a spontaneous eruption of MAGA loyalists, more herd than army (Hosenball, 2021). Even an FBI informant embedded in the Proud Boys tweeted live during the breach (Hsu et al., 2023), "PBs did not do it or inspire. Crowds did, herd mentality. Not organized." Herd mentality is a less satisfying explanation than outright insurrection.*

Hamilton's recordings back that up. The people he interviewed throughout the day had different stories, different goals, and no coherent plan. The notion of a well-executed insurrection led by sinister masterminds does not square with what he saw—confusion, improvisation, delusion. For

---

*Journalist and author Gerald Posner has made similar observations in his two books on the respective assassinations of John F. Kennedy (Posner, 2013a) and Martin Luther King, Jr. (Posner, 2013b). In these books, Posner definitively lays out in each case that lone gunmen killed these greater-than-life men. He also explains that such simple explanations are not as satisfying as the grand conspiracy theories that revolve around these events. Our human minds crave explanations that match the magnitude of the events. Unorganized herds of costume-clad rioters are less satisfying an explanation than an organized extremist mob, dressed like an army. That narrative pulls more eyeballs to screens.

The Art of the Compromise

example, the infamous man with zip cuffs found them lying on a desk inside the Capitol. He did not bring them with him. The savage fire extinguisher murder of a Capitol police officer, reported breathlessly at first, was later retracted. The officer had died of natural causes (Cameron, 2022). This death was the only report of Trump supporters "killing" someone on January 6, even though it was an erroneous report. As Hamilton put it:

> ...*never bet on genius when stupidity explains just as well.*

Hamilton saw stupidity at every level: a mayor who rejected federal reinforcements, a president who whipped up a crowd then left them to wander, a police force that failed to coordinate, and a mob that believed simply entering the building would magically overturn the election. "A perfect storm of intersectional stupidity," according to Hamilton.

Yet that storm had unfortunate and dire consequences. The breach forced members of Congress to flee, and bomb squads had to sweep the halls. But by nightfall, the rioters had largely gone home. If this catastrophe were an insurrection, it came with a curfew. Social media—so vital to fueling their rage—began to turn against them. As texts and tweets poured in from friends and family across the country, the "epic" narrative unraveled. Hamilton noticed the mood change in real time. Rioters who earlier had spoken proudly now looked confused, sheepish. By the time he reached Union Station that night, a new script had emerged. Blame Antifa. Pride no longer filled the conversation among the rioters.

Still, the damage was done. America, with all our barbaric yawps, was embarrassed. Yet if there is any faint note to salvage, it lies in the contrast with the Soviet collapse. Our citizens, however reckless, were not indifferent. They cared enough—misguided as they were—to act.* As Gilje's work on American riots suggests, the January 6 rioters followed in the footsteps of a long tradition of interrupting the peaceful pulse of American politics. Around 4:00 PM, President Trump tweeted a message—with staccato verbiage that is a hallmark of Trump's weird egotism—to the costumed rioters (Leatherby et al., 2021),

> *I know your pain. I know you're hurt. We love you. You're very special. You've seen what happens. You've seen the way others are treated. I know how you feel, but go home, and go home in peace.*

By 6:00 PM, Capitol Police and National Guard units had cleared the Capitol of rioters (Leatherby et al., 2021).† Then,

---

*Let me be clear. To acknowledge their passion is not to defend their conduct. The rioters on January 6 were reckless, destructive, and often violent. As with Charlie Kirk's assassination and other tragic political moments, we can never condone violence. The January 6 rioters must face the punishment of the law. Yet apathy poses its own danger. The absence of civic energy, such as that seen in the Soviet Union's quiet dissolution, signals a democracy in decline. The American problem is not indifference but undisciplined fervor. Liberty without responsibility is untenable. The task of statesmanship is to channel that fervor into lawful, constructive forms.

†Despite false claims from conservative news outlets, court records and Department of Justice indictments confirm that many rioters on January 6 were armed (Nelson, 2022). Yet among the armed rioters—who were angry, agitated, and hell-bent (reportedly) on insurrection—none fired their weapons to kill. The only firearm death that day came from a U.S. Capitol Police officer drawing his service pistol and killing rioter Ashli Babbitt (Feuer, 2021). My goal here is not to minimize the severity of the riot, but to question the political language surrounding it—terms like *insurrection, coup,* and *domestic terrorism.* If insurrection or a coup d'état were the intent of the thousands of armed rioters dressed comically in military garb and other cartoonish regalia, a four-hour timeline and no weapons fired seems ineffective as a strategy.

The Art of the Compromise

by 3:24 AM, Congress had reconvened and confirmed Joe Biden's victory. The transfer of power held. The Republic stood. And as Jon Meacham reminds us of Jefferson's sentiment, "a little rebellion now and then is a good thing, and as necessary in the political world as storms in the physical." But the storm, it turned out, was mostly thunder and fog.

Shays's Rebellion

Was Thomas Jefferson serious? Did he truly believe that "a little rebellion now and then is a good thing"? If we hold his words up to the unsettling events of January 6, they demand a second look. Would Jefferson have cheered Michael Sparks crawling through a broken window or the self-styled Shaman posing in the Senate Chamber? Would he have heard a noble *yawp* or a dangerous clamor? To grasp Jefferson's frame of mind, we need to step back to the rebellion that inspired him to write those words. That rebellion was the 1787 farmers' uprising known as Shays's Rebellion.

Jefferson penned those words in a letter to James Madison on January 30, 1787 (Jefferson & Madison, 1995).* He was reacting to a series of riots—armed uprisings that spanned more than six months, far longer than four hours—that occurred in Massachusetts. He was in Paris at the time of the uprising, and

---

*Somewhat surprisingly, Jefferson's famous quote about rebellion is unrelated to the Boston Tea Party. He actually sided with elites like George Washington and Benjamin Franklin in condemning the destruction of private property, believing the Bostonians should be held accountable under local law. Still, in his pamphlet "A Summary View of the Rights of British America," Jefferson framed the Tea Party as a justifiable act of political protest (Carp, 2010).

Madison was in Virginia. Through multiple letter exchanges, Madison kept Jefferson abreast of the news on events known as Shays's Rebellion. In his letter, Jefferson expanded on his thoughts with these words (Jefferson & Madison, 1995):

> *Unsuccessful rebellions generally establish encroachments on the rights of the people who have produced them. An observation of this truth should render honest republican* governors so mild in their punishment of rebellions as not to discourage them too much. It is a medicine necessary for the sound health of the government.*

Jefferson was instructing his young protégé in his core belief that the power of government is not derived from its leaders but rather from its people and that rebellions are a signal from the people to their leaders that the government is intruding on their rights. Jefferson did not necessarily support Shays's Rebellion, but he was not condemning the uprising either.

This letter and Jefferson's sentiment at the time were considered radical. Jefferson held a deep belief, perhaps more so than other elites of the Founding Generation (Ellis, 2002), that the People had a right to express their grievances against their government—even if those grievances erupted in violence. Jefferson described such eruptions as a necessary medicine for American democracy, at least from time to time. That prescription was radical in his day and remains difficult to swallow in the aftermath of January 6.

In his 1787 letter, Jefferson counseled Madison on tolerance for riots and not harshly punishing the people

---

*Jefferson's use of the word "republican" refers to the form of representative government, not to the modern Republican Party.

The Art of the Compromise

participating. Jefferson felt that ordinary citizens needed to air grievances because he understood that the ordinary person was not as articulate as the elite and that the political expressions of the people needed an outlet before they could find their words and become articulate. While educated elites like Jefferson could express themselves in polished letters to reveal their convictions, Jefferson felt that vocal protests in the streets were necessary for the ordinary person to express their convictions, and those expressions might become violent, but they were still necessary.

Shays's* Rebellion was a notorious event from 1786 to 1787 that many feared, perhaps in exaggerated and dire terms (Richards, 2014)—as the possible end of the newly formed nation. Abigail Adams, who was with her husband, John Adams, in London at the time and who also frequently exchanged letters with Jefferson, was horrified by the reports she was receiving about the Rebellion back in her home state of Massachusetts. She had a very different take on the violence than her friend Jefferson. She feared a looming apocalypse, writing from London to Jefferson in Paris (A. Adams, 2010),

> With regard to the tumults in my Native State which you inquire about, I wish I could say that report had exaggerated them, it is too true Sir that they have been carried to so allarming a Height as to stop the courts of justice in several Counties. Ignorant, restless desperadoes, without conscience or principals, have led a deluded

---

*The possessive form of "Shays"—whether "Shays'," "Shays's," or even just "Shays"—has stirred ongoing debate among grammarians (2013). I follow the guidelines of the Chicago Manual of Style, which favors "Shays's," though I have no dog in the fight.

> *multitude to follow their standard, under pretence of grievances which have no existence but in their own imaginations.*

Her choice of language—ignorant, restless desperadoes—is striking, even for a woman of her stature and era. While she may seem unladylike by 18th-century standards, Abigail was never one to mince words, especially when writing to political peers. Her warning reveals how seriously she regarded the uprising—not as a noble rebellion, but as a dangerous contagion spreading through the Republic's fragile veins.

Unlike Jefferson, Abigail would have likely called January 6 a coup and blamed the rioters for the possible future downfall of our democracy.* While Jefferson was extolling the possible virtues of the men in the Rebellion, Abigail looked down on their ilk. Most historians agree (Ellis, 1997) that her fears, as well as the fears of her contemporaries, were an overreaction, and the more tempered reaction of Jefferson was—though unusual for the time—more clear-sighted. Jefferson was not blinded to the violence and was concerned about the unfolding events. In the opening of his letter to Madison (Jefferson & Madison, 1995), he wrote, "I am impatient to learn your sentiments on the late troubles in the Eastern states." While he promoted tolerance of protests, he was concerned that the events could go too far.

---

*Some observers argue that January 6 has marked the beginning of the end for American democracy, too (Pilkington, 2022). Abigail Adams may have felt similarly about Shays's Rebellion, and while Shays was the end of the Articles of Confederation, the event led to the creation of the U.S. Constitution. We can wish away January 6, or we can learn from it. The Founders chose to learn from Shays's Rebellion. Can we learn from January 6?

The Art of the Compromise

Shays's Rebellion involved an armed uprising in Massachusetts, which began in 1786 and carried through the winter of 1787. Several distressed farmers in western Massachusetts took up arms in protest against their eastern creditors, mainly in Boston. The farmers' anger was fueled by the injustice of a regressive state tax system and an out-of-touch state government that many farmers believed was no better than the former British rule (Richards, 2014).

The Rebellion carries the name of Daniel Shays, a former Continental Army captain who, at the time of the Rebellion, was a local farmer from Pelham, a hill town south of Shutesbury in Massachusetts. Shays was not wealthy but hardly at the bottom of the economic ladder. He and his wife, Abigail Shays, owned a small farm of about one hundred acres with a smaller portion under tillage, leaving enough pasture for one horse and a cow. Shays's farm was ranked in the second quintile of town assessments, and he was active on the Pelham Committee for Safety, where his distinguished service as a Revolutionary War veteran earned him respect from his fellow residents. Still, he was slow in joining the Rebellion that would take on his namesake. He was a reluctant and unlikely insurrectionist (Springfield Technical Community College, 2023), though history has worked hard to damn him (Zug, 2021). Shays and Sparks, if living in each other's era, may have well been neighbors in political thought, if not in geography.

Shays was committed to the cause that carries his name. At the time, he wrote of his intentions to "march directly to Boston, plunder it, and...destroy the nest of devils, who by their influence make the Court enact what they please, burn it and lay the town of Boston in ashes" (Black, 2018). In today's world, Sparks—or even Trump—might have tweeted something similar if he had been with Shays.

Shays's Rebellion and the Tea Party mirror the calamity of January 6, but they are not alone. Later generations would add their own chapters of tumult. Protests—and at times riots—have served as the unpolished voice of the Many in American democracy. Jefferson's warning about rebellions has echoed beyond his era, from the fields of Massachusetts to the streets of Chicago.

Chicago, 1968

"Hell, we couldn't agree on lunch," Abbie Hoffman quipped in response to allegations of conspiracy among the "Chicago Eight"—a succinct, if somewhat dismissive, retort aimed at Judge Julius Hoffman (Wiener, 2006).* The group of eight defendants, which included Abbie along with Rennie Davis, Dave Dellinger, John Froines, Tom Hayden, Jerry Rubin, Lee Weiner, and Bobby Seale, were on trial for collectively inciting a riot at the 1968 Democratic National Convention in Chicago (Wiener, 2006).

This riot, like the January 6 riot, led many Americans to question whether the democratic fabric of the American system of government was unraveling and pulling apart at the seams. Such disorganized protests, often misunderstood by elites, are frequently followed by overreactions, but they serve a function. While Hoffman and the others clashed with

---

*Despite sharing a name, Judge Julius Hoffman and Abbie Hoffman had no familial relation. During the trial, Abbie Hoffman mocked this coincidence, calling the judge "Julie." According to one account (Liebman, 2020), after Judge Hoffman clarified the lack of relation, there was a sarcastic outcry from the defense side, "Father, no!"

The Art of the Compromise

police outside, the conventioneers on the floor inside the International Amphitheater did not fare much better. The delegates to the Democratic Party scuffled amongst themselves over party business, prompting respected broadcaster Walter Cronkite to observe (Hendershot, 2018), "I think we've got a bunch of thugs here."

The Democratic National Convention would be a contested event, primed for dissent. Anti-war advocates throughout America took note, and protests gained momentum as organizers prepared to use the Convention as a national stage for opposition to the Vietnam War. A broad spectrum of protest groups and fringe factions—much like the splintered factions seen on January 6—began planning that summer to seize the moment and converge in Chicago for what they intended to be peaceful, non-violent demonstrations (Waxman, 2018).

The trial accused the eight defendants of conspiring to lead protest groups to Chicago for violent demonstrations. Yet as Abbie Hoffman quipped, they could hardly agree on lunch, let alone conspiracy. The ragtag band of youth that descended on the city in August 1968 was more like a disorganized herd of feral cats than a disciplined pride of dangerous lions. Though the youth shared an anti-war bent, they shared little else—different leadership, different agendas, and different approaches to protests. In short, they mirrored the disorganized MAGA crowd of January 6, except they wore different "uniforms," and no demagogue like Trump stood at their helm and barked orders to stoke the fire.

However, Chicago Mayor Richard Daley was not about to let a band of out-of-towners take over his city. Daley was an old-school politician with no qualms about employing strong-arm tactics to impose his will, and his will in the Summer of 1968 was for his city to be one of law and order (Gilje, 1999). Earlier that year, on April 4, riots had broken out on the West

Side of Chicago following the assassination of Martin Luther King Jr. Daley shocked reporters by stating that police had orders to "shoot to kill" arsonists and to "shoot to maim or cripple" looters (Briscoe & Olumhense, 2020). Though he would oddly deny these comments (Little, 1996)—despite being caught on camera—the words revealed his mindset. Daley was determined that anti-war protests would not spoil the Democratic Convention in *his* city for *his* party.

Daley's resolve extended to legal trench warfare over curfews and permits. Protest organizers clashed with city officials over permission to sleep in public parks and were repeatedly denied permits for rallies. In the end, Daley's office approved only a single protest permit, despite many requests (History.com, 2018). The Convention became a political disaster. Hoffman and the other protestors believed the public would side with them over Daley's bullying tactics. But they were wrong. Polls taken after the riots showed a clear majority of Americans supported Daley and his no-nonsense crackdown (Brown, 2016). Like January 6, many Americans believed our democracy had barely escaped disaster.

Yet unlike January 6, when the U.S. Capitol Police had insufficient resources to contain Sparks and the other rioters, Mayor Daley opted for overwhelming force. He deployed 12,000 Chicago police officers and another 15,000 state and federal personnel as a line against the anticipated 10,000 protestors. With this force amassed and Daley's incendiary "shoot to kill" rhetoric from earlier that year, a volatile clash was inevitable. The ensuing riots became known as the "Battle of Michigan Avenue" and played out on the nightly newscasts across America (History.com, 2018). Police severely beat and tear-gassed demonstrators as well as journalists covering the events. Daniel Walker, a Chicago attorney, described the confrontation as a "police riot" directed at the protestors (Little,

1996). Walker led a special commission appointed to investigate the protests, and one might wonder if Thomas Jefferson was whispering in Walker's ear, reminding him not to punish rebellion too harshly.

The trial of the Chicago Eight became political theater. Judge Julius Hoffman clashed with the defendants in a courtroom drama that came to symbolize the era's deep rifts over free speech and civil disobedience. Jefferson would have enjoyed the antics, though the glorification of Hoffman and the other rioters did not come until decades later. The juxtaposition of the 1968 Chicago riots and the 2021 Capitol riots is instructive, particularly when framed alongside Shays's Rebellion and Jefferson's admonishment for tolerance that "a little rebellion now and then is a good thing."

At first blush, the line between Jefferson's version of a rebellion and a treasonous revolt to overthrow the government might initially appear to be a fine line. Yet the heterogeneous assembly of the rioters on January 6, 2021, who seemed to think the event was a costume party, could hardly agree on lunch. They resembled a tantrum more than a revolution. By comparison, the rioters on Michigan Avenue in 1968 revealed that American citizens were not seeking to destroy our Constitution through a violent coup d'état but rather to remind the government that the people hold the power—a Jeffersonian reminder, loud and messy, for a little rebellion now and then. That loudness is no accident.

The Noise of Liberty

America feels uniquely loud, chaotic, and at times even violent in its politics because we are uniquely big and diverse. The data confirms this conclusion. Recall Fig. 4, which shows the United States outpaces the world in riot density. We experience more riots per capita than other nations.

The graphs in Figs. 5–7 provide a fuller picture. The United States is not just a large country, but we are also a highly diverse one. We are an outlier in population diversity. Using data from James Fearon (2003)and Alberto Alesina (2003), Fig. 5 shows that America stands alone as both a populous and highly heterogeneous country that has sustained democratic stability.* This combination of size and diversity places the U.S. in a category of its own.

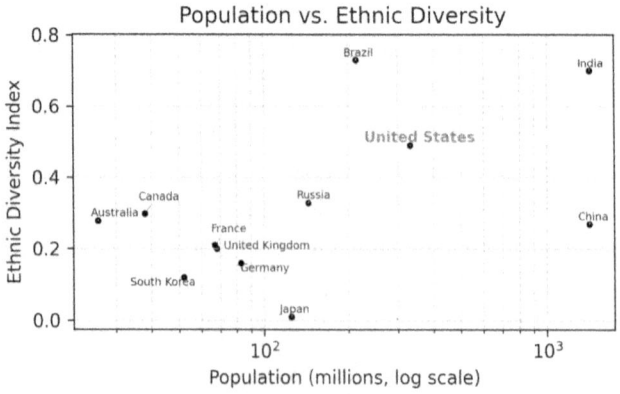

Figure 5. Ethnic diversity by population size across the selected countries. Data compiled from Alesina et al. (2003) and Fearon (2003). The U.S. has both a large population and ethnic diversity.

---

*Among the world's large and ethnically diverse nations, the United States stands alone as a stable, continuous democracy. While India and Brazil share comparable levels of population and diversity, both have experienced periods of democratic backsliding, institutional fragility, or military interference that compromise their classification as stable liberal democracies (Diamond, 2020; Varshney, 2003).

The Art of the Compromise

Such scale and diversity generate tension at the heart of American democracy—a tension James Madison intentionally built into the Constitution—whereby unity and multiplicity must dance in careful balance through a federal system. By comparison, small and ethnically homogeneous countries in Europe often achieve stability more easily but at the cost of less inclusion. Authoritarian regimes like China and Russia, meanwhile, suppress riots not through compromise but through force.

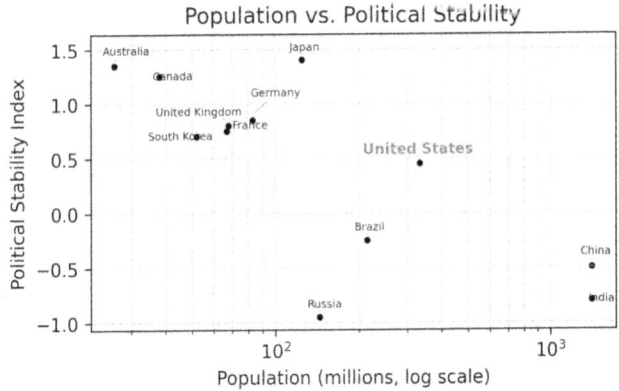

Figure 6. Political stability by population size across the selected countries. Data compiled from World Bank (2023).

The graph in Fig. 6 using World Bank governance indicators (2023) underscores the difference. Political stability is easier to maintain in smaller or more homogeneous states, but America has chosen the harder path. Our system tolerates disagreement and even invites conflict. The result: more noise, more friction, more visible clashes. Thus, more conflict per square mile and per citizen. Yes, as Fig. 7 shows through data from the V–Dem Institute's "Freedom of Expression" index (Coppedge et al., 2024), the payoff is more liberty.

The lesson is clear. The riot data in Fig. 4 should not be read as evidence of American failure. Quite the opposite. Taken together with the figures above, the data suggest that riots are distress flares in a system designed to channel conflict without collapsing. Jefferson reminded us that riots "generally establish encroachments on the rights of the people who have produced them" (Jefferson & Madison, 1995). The Boston Tea Party was a riot. So was Shays's Rebellion. The Civil Rights Act of 1968 was passed within days of the urban uprisings that followed the assassination of Dr. Martin Luther King, Jr. These moments are messy, even shameful. Yet they force reckonings. When other avenues feel closed, the Many turn to the streets. The question is not whether they should. The question is whether we listen.

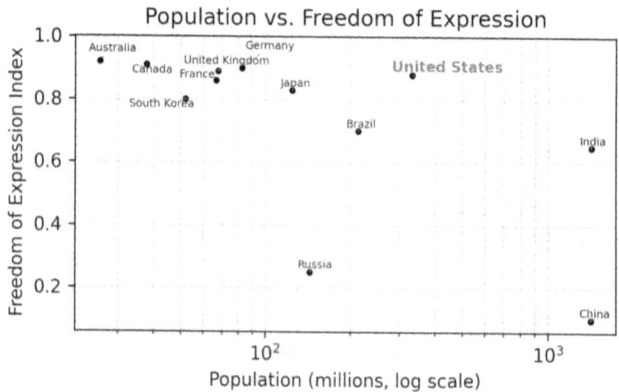

Figure 7. Relationship between population size and freedom of expression across selected countries. Data compiled from Coppedge et al. (2024).

The Art of the Compromise

Extend the Sphere

To understand how we got here—and why we have yet to fall apart—we need to read James Madison's argument in *Federalist No. 10*. Madison, perhaps America's first political scientist—if not history's first modern one—confronts the problem of factions* head-on. Rather than trying to eliminate factions, which would require eliminating liberty itself, Madison suggests something bold. He argues to let them thrive, and thereby dilute them and spread them out. In his words, "extend the sphere" (Hamilton et al., 2015). His logic is simple but profound. The bigger the republic, the more factions one will have. The more factions a nation has, the more difficult it is for one faction to gain majority control. Like big fish in a small pond, factions in a small polity can dominate, but in Madison's ocean of a continental republic, factions become just another ripple.

Madison's viewpoint was a major shift in political thought. A central tenet of classical republicanism was that public virtue—and public virtue alone—could restrain leaders from acting in the best interests of the Republic. The Founders believed that the new nation could subsist on public virtue by "relying on the self-restraint of those in power to act for the common good and not their personal interest" (Ricks, 2020).

George Washington embodied, as Ricks notes, this reliance on public virtue, but experience with the Articles of

---

*The term *faction* is not familiar to our modern ears. We would prefer the term *party*, or more precisely *political party*. Political factions and political parties are one in the same. When the Founding generation speaks of factions, they are in essence speaking of political parties.

Confederation as a governing system for the American republic proved that few others beyond Washington did. Few others then or now have lived up to General Washington's virtuous standard. The Founders were wrong as the Articles demonstrated, and the adroit Madison was one of the first to grasp this error in political thought. Public virtue was a weak foundation for a republic, particularly a large, diverse republic like the U.S. Madison, however, saw a different path—unique in history. Madison saw factions as a beast that could be tamed for the common good. Madison argued that (Ketcham, 1990)

> ...*all civilized societies are divided into different interests and factions, as they happen to be creditors or debtors—Rich or poor—husbandmen, merchants or manufacturers—members of different religious sects—followers of different political leaders—inhabitants of different districts—owners of different kinds of property &c &c.*

Madison was beginning to realize that factions were inevitable and natural—not unnatural as the Ancients taught—and that a new form of government was necessary where the vices of factions were not ignored or outlawed but rather balanced against one another.

At the time, Madison's insights were pure theory and untested. History has since vindicated his vision. The historical timeline* in Fig. 8 illustrates the contrast. The United States

---

*The data on conflicts is a compilation from a range of historical estimates, including Gilje's work (Gilje, 1999) on American riots and uprisings, regional war catalogs (Brecke, 1999), and supplemental databases on civil wars and internal armed conflict from the Uppsala Conflict Data Program (2017). Estimates are rounded by decade and focus on domestically-contained conflicts between organized factions or states and insurgent forces.

has experienced relatively few internal armed conflicts compared to Europe and China. Europe's curve surges with Napoleonic wars, revolutions, and two world wars. China's climbs with staggering bloodshed, from the Taiping Rebellion to the Cultural Revolution. The graph counts conflicts, but if measured by death toll, the divergence would grow even starker.

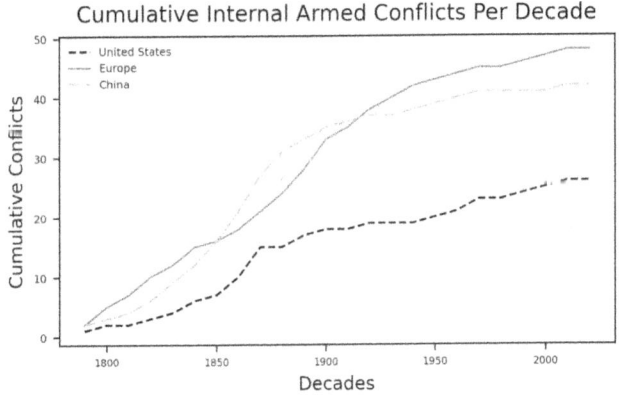

Figure 8. The cumulative total of internal armed conflicts within each region—the United States, Europe, and China—excludes wars fought outside the region, such as U.S. involvement in World War I or II. Data compiled from the Correlates of War Project (Singer & Small, 1994), the Uppsala Conflict Data Program (Gleditsch et al., 2002; Pettersson & Öberg, 2020), and Clodfelter (2017).

America's curve tells a different story. After the Civil War and the close of the Indian Wars that marked the end of westward expansion, the trajectory levels off. While Europe balkanized and China convulsed, American conflict did not disappear but transformed—shifting from interstate wars to intrastate unrest, from secessions to protests, from bullets to bullhorns. Madison was right. The structure held.

Madison foresaw that the problem of factions could not be solved by removing them. Nor could the problem be solved by scolding them, as Washington attempted in his Farewell Address. In that address, he writes at length to warn the young nation "in the most solemn manner against the baneful effects" of factions (Christmas, 2017). Madison argues for a structural and institutional system that would not eliminate factions—that would be "worse than the disease"—but one that would pit faction against faction. He goes on to explain in *Federalist No. 10.* that "the latent causes of faction are thus sown in the nature of man" and that individuals have a "zeal for different opinions concerning religion, concerning government, and many other points" and that human passions, have, in turn, divided mankind into parties, inflamed them with mutual animosity, and rendered them much more disposed to vex and oppress each other than to cooperate for their common good.

So, Madison took a system—based on human nature—that amplifies voices and disagreements, and then stretched that system geographically so wide that no single voice could drown out the rest. Madison proposed to turn a handful of feuding states into an extended sphere. He thus built a political marketplace robust enough to contain chaos without collapsing. Unlike Europe or China, America, with Madison's guiding hand, has traded riots—Chicago in 1968 and the Capitol in 2021—for wars.

So yes, the United States is noisy. Yet that noise is not dysfunction but rather the sound of feedback. Madison designed our system not to prevent conflict, but to channel it. To hear it. And when Congress is at its best, it responds—not with

The Art of the Compromise

force (as in China or Russia) or with farce (as in Brexit or Chamberlain's "peace for our time"*), but with compromise. As the data shows, we are the only large, diverse, democratic republic to have sustained our form of government this long (nearly 250 years), without periodic revolutions, dictatorships, or collapse. That result is not luck. That's Madison's design. That's the Art of the Compromise—turning the Many into One, again and again, without breaking the whole.

In Sum

We began this chapter with a simple Latin phrase: *E Pluribus Unum*—Out of Many, One. That motto is not a statement of what we are but a declaration of what we strive to become. At the heart of the American experiment is a structural tension designed by Madison. We are a large, diverse republic forged in compromise and sometimes tempered by conflict. Madison understood this tension. He foresaw that factions were not a structural flaw to be stamped out, but a human condition to be managed. Not a software bug, but a hardware feature. His answer was not to shrink the sphere of political life, but to extend it—widen it so broadly that no single faction could dominate, and each faction would be forced to contend with

---

*British Prime Minister Neville Chamberlain, facing Adolf Hitler's demands for the Sudetenland (part of Czechoslovakia), agreed to Hitler's terms in the 1938 Munich Agreement—without Czechoslovakia even at the table. Chamberlain returned to London and declared he had secured "peace for our time." Within a year, Germany invaded Poland and triggered World War II (Gilbert, 2014). Chamberlain's 1938 proclamation is the archetype of political farce masquerading as diplomacy.

one another. That feature, he argued, was the only way to preserve liberty in a democratic society. Extend the sphere.

The historical data across the U.S., Europe, and Asia bear this result out. The United States endured thousands of riots, protests, and moments of civil unrest. Yet aside from the great rupture of the Civil War, the nation has not fractured into warring states or spiraled into recurring civil wars. Where Europe Balkanized and China convulsed, American conflict has remained only loud enough to be heard but not so violent as to shatter the Union. That resilience is no accident. It reflects constitutional design—Madison's design. Our system was built to absorb stress through representation rather than revolution—through compromise rather than collapse.

This chapter and this book do not ask each citizen to compromise. That burden belongs to Congress. Compromise belongs not in private citizen quarrels but beneath the dome of the Capitol, where power must meet principle and where, in Madison's words, the passions of the People are to be refined and cooled. As Jefferson observed, the common man may not always express himself with polish, but a representative can shape that raw civic instinct, translating frustration into law, rather than allowing that anger to fester in the streets. Only then can the work of politics clear the space for citizens to gather, not in conflict, but in common life.

With that said, protests and riots are not an outcome we should seek or celebrate, but neither should we fear or overreact to them. Recall the words of activist H. Rap Brown, "Violence is as American as cherry pie" (Brumback, 2019). America's Whitman-esque yawps may be jarring, but they are preferable to Europe's wars of mass killing (World War I and II, or more recently, Ukraine) or China's authoritarian silencing of dissent (massacre at Tiananmen Square or Uyghur Muslim repression in Xinjiang). In the U.S., the rule of law

The Art of the Compromise

must remain paramount, but we must learn to punish the crime and not the cause. We must hold protestors and rioters accountable, but we must not make them unforgivable. Punish the act, not the soul.

So yes, the United States is noisy, untamed, and often messy. Yet that noise is not dysfunction, but rather feedback. The American yawp is the music of a free people working out the tension, turning the discord of factions into the rough harmony of self-governance—the sounds of a nation working through growing pains, not collapsing under them. The clamor echoes across time from tea crates splashing into Boston Harbor to Shays's pitchforks raised in western Massachusetts; from 1968 police batons on Michigan Avenue to the 2021 fury at the Capitol steps. Each riot, each rupture, reminds the Republic that power does not rest quietly. When the system works, when Congress listens, when Compromise prevails, we become again what we have claimed to be: Out of Many, One.

In the next chapter, we explore the Civil War—a moment that nearly shattered the Republic. Recall the conflict data in Fig. 8. The Civil War in this graph marks a sharp peak, after which the U.S. curve flattens. Violence gives way to stability. Once we had shaken the unsettled itch for disunion from our veins, we entered the longest stretch of internal peace in modern times—more than eight score years and still counting. Yet we still had to pass through that fire. We had to suffer before we could cross the Jordan, and in the end, that moment revealed the depth of America's Soul as a nation and the enduring strength of our Union.

Noise can become something more. Discord can test a Union's bones beyond protest—driving it to the brink of fracture. To see how the Republic survived its darkest hour, we cross the battlefields of civil war and stand beside Lincoln, who held the Many together through fire.

CHAPTER 2

Into One Soul

THE AMERICAN CIVIL WAR nearly broke us as a nation. Almost two percent of the American population died in that bloody conflict, more than all other American wars combined. Brother against brother in a struggle for the very Soul of America. The war revealed the terrible cost of disunion, yet it also reinforced a simple truth of our constitutional order. Congress cannot abandon an argument. Representation requires persistence. When the votes fall against a faction, the duty is not to leave the chamber—secede from the Union—in protest but to remain, to contend, and to seek resolution within the bounds of law.

Would a government of the people, by the people, for the people endure or perish? The stakes were high, and an untested President in the unheralded Abraham Lincoln, a backcountry lawyer from Illinois, would stand in the gap and attempt to bridge the enormous divide separating the rebel South and the Unionist North. Ultimately, Lincoln and the North prevailed, but the victory came at a great cost. The American Soul was deeply wounded. Yet our Creed that "all men are created equal" loomed large, urging us toward our better angels and into one Soul.

What's at Stake?

So what's at stake today as we struggle toward *E Pluribus Unum*? What's at stake as the Many strive to become One? What's at stake as faction faces faction and each raucous generation yawps? What's at stake when protests devolve into riots and when states threaten to leave the Union?

What is at stake? Our American Soul.*

Yes, it's a bit corny and sentimental, but our national Soul is at stake. As Jon Meacham, the Pulitzer Prize–winning journalist and presidential biographer, writes in his book *The Soul of America* (Meacham, 2019), the battle is for "the better angels of our nature"† to win the day and for our national Soul to tilt towards progress. We must recognize that our Soul as a

---

*Can a nation have a soul? As Elliot Cohen reflects (Cohen, 2020), the ancient philosopher Plato introduced the idea in his Socratic dialogue *The Republic* that a nation could have a soul. He argues that a soul infuses the state in the same manner that a soul infuses an individual. "Must we not acknowledge," Plato said (Plato, 2007), "that in each of us there are the same principles and habits which there are in the State; and that from the individual they pass into the State?"

†Meacham quotes Abraham Lincoln in his first inaugural address as he took the reins of the Presidency at the dawn of the Civil War. Lincoln desperately wanted to avoid armed conflict, so he ended the address with this plea: "I am loath to close. We are not enemies, but friends. We must not be enemies. Though passion may have strained it must not break our bonds of affection. The mystic chords of memory, stretching from every battlefield and patriot grave to every living heart and hearthstone all over this broad land, will yet swell the chorus of the Union, when again touched, as surely they will be, by the better angels of our nature." This eloquent passage has flowed down through history and into Meacham's book.

The Art of the Compromise

nation—like the soul of a person—is not fixed. A soul can rise or fall, be noble or base, stand with hope or shrink from fear. A century later, standing on the steps of Lincoln's own memorial, Dr. Martin Luther King, Jr. clarified our national Soul once again and declared a dream rooted in the same Creed. "I have a dream," he proclaimed, "deeply rooted in the American dream." In that moment, the call to unity, equality, and justice came not from law, but from the Soul itself. King's dream was not new—it was an echo, a reprise of what Lincoln had once asked the nation to become.

As Meacham writes, the Soul of our nation is "the vital center, the core, the heart, the essence of life." Heroes and martyrs "have such a vital center," but poignantly, "so do killers and haters." So, is the Soul of America good or evil? A hero to its citizens and the world? Or a villain cloaked in stars and stripes? The answer is neither final nor guaranteed.

Our task, then, is not to declare ourselves righteous, but to keep the darker side of our nature at bay. We must draw out the better angels of our character. This balance, as discussed in the previous chapter, depends more on a large, diverse republic than on any other form of government. A small one, as James Madison warned, will not do. To secure liberty and prevent tyranny, we must "extend the sphere" across a broad territory. We must disperse factions, limit abuses of power, and foster a unified identity. Yet to remain fractured as the Many without ever becoming One is to invite ruin, as the Soviet Union discovered. The Soviets were Many but had no Soul.

Madison understood what was at stake. "We must not shut our eyes to the nature of men," he said, "nor to the light of experience" (Ketcham, 1990). In *Federalist No. 51*, he wrote (Hamilton et al., 2015), "If men were angels, no government would be necessary." Conversely, in speaking to the Virginia Convention in 1788, he warned that if men are evil (Ketcham, 1990), "we are in a wretched condition," and "no form of government can render us secure." Therefore, we need guideposts to keep our Soul on track, to elevate our national character, to subdue the evils of human nature, and to anchor our aspirations for a more perfect Union.

One such guidepost is our national Creed. As Americans, we know our Creed well. We can recite it by heart: *All men are created equal.* This Creed feeds our Soul and is the essence of the American experiment in self-government, though we have often failed to live up to it. We know this historic line thanks partly to the eloquence of Dr. King and his dream. King's struggle to bend our national Soul toward the good (Jones & Connelly, 2012)

> ...to speed up that day when all of God's children, black men and white men, Jews and Gentiles, Protestants and Catholics, will be able to join hands and sing in the words of the old Negro spiritual:
>
> Free at last! Free at last!
> Thank God Almighty, we are free at last.

Dr. King spoke these words on August 28, 1963, in one of the most impressive orations in history. In his brief 17-minute speech, he set out to call for an end to racism in America from the steps of the Lincoln Memorial in Washington, DC. His soul-stirring speech is best appreciated in video or audio form, as the written text of this book does little to communicate the powerful force of Dr. King's "I Have a Dream" speech. His signature cadence, groomed through years of service in a Baptist pulpit, compels each listener to marvel at the artistry of his delivery as he shook the American Soul that August day through the aspirations of our Creed.

In the book *Behind the Dream* (Jones & Connelly, 2012), Clarence Jones, who co-wrote the famous speech with Dr.

The Art of the Compromise

King and served as a close confidant, relates how a remarkable shift occurred during the middle of the speech. Witnesses say that Dr. King paused for a moment and, during that brief silence, Mahalia Jackson, a gospel singer who was standing a few feet from the podium and a good friend to Dr. King, called out, "Tell 'em about the 'Dream,' Martin, tell 'em about the 'Dream!'"

Unknown to his audience,* Dr. King unceremoniously departed from his prepared text after her urging and carried the audience into history. In historical footage of the event, one can see that Dr. King no longer glances down at the podium at this point in the speech. He is no longer referring to his notes, which Jones so carefully crafted. He, at this point, is beginning to riff extemporaneously. He is now calling up a lifetime of speeches and injustices to urge his audience—and the collective American Soul—to live out our Creed.

Jones recalls his thoughts in his book as he witnessed this transition and realized King was starting to improvise, "These people out there today don't know it yet but they're about to go to church."

And so they did.

I still have a dream. It is a dream deeply rooted in the American dream.

I have a dream that one day this nation will rise up and live out the true meaning of its creed.

---

*Jones reports that not many people heard Mahalia, but he found out years later that Senator Ted Kennedy was one of the few people near the podium who did listen to her, and of course, the one person that mattered most, Dr. King.

Into One Soul

> *We hold these truths to be self-evident, that all men are created equal.*

That speech etched Dr. King's 'Dream' and the words of our Creed into our national memories. Yet the gap between the ideal and reality persisted, and still does to some extent.

Meacham takes up this tension, arguing that the American Soul operates best not when seeking greatness or perfection but rather when we seek progress over perfection. He writes (Meacham, 2019):

> *I have chosen to consider the American soul more than the American Creed because there is a significant difference between professing adherence to a set of beliefs and acting upon them. The war between the ideal and the real, between what's right and what's convenient, between the larger good and personal interest is the contest that unfolds in the soul of [America].*

This tension is not new. The riot of January 6 and the other tumultuous events noted in the previous chapter are not unprecedented. Our nation has survived some pretty tough times. Meacham reminds us that the politics of fear often battle against the politics of hope.

Meacham expresses deep concern over Donald Trump's reaction to the 2017 Charlottesville rally when white supremacists marched and Heather Heyer, a young counter-protester, was killed. In response to her death, Trump's response to blame "many sides" that day blurred moral lines. Meacham calls out Trump for his disturbing quote and questions how reasonable citizens could find more than one side to a conflict between neo-Nazis and conscientious Americans, like Heyer, who stood against them. Trump's inability or unwillingness to recognize the racist tone of his words is more than troubling.

Leadership matters. In other dark times in American history, presidents such as Ulysses S. Grant, Theodore

The Art of the Compromise

Roosevelt, Woodrow Wilson, Franklin D. Roosevelt, Harry S. Truman, Dwight Eisenhower, and Lyndon B. Johnson have pulled the nation up. And when presidents were not up to the challenge, citizens such as Frederick Douglass, Elizabeth Cady Stanton, Susan B. Anthony, Sojourner Truth, Booker T. Washington, Alice Paul, and Dr. King stepped forward and pulled our Soul to the good.

So, what's at stake when Shays challenged the status quo? Sparks crawled through a Capitol window? Hoffman defied Daley? Or Trump belittled Heyer? The Soul of America is at stake. We have no guarantee whether hope or fear will prevail. A back-and-forth battle at a national level occurs each day in America. Meacham nudges us to remember that for "all of our darker impulses, for all of our shortcomings, and for all of the dreams denied and deferred, the [American] experiment begun so long ago, carried out so imperfectly, is worth the fight."

History reveals what should have been obvious—the enslavement of one race by another was evil, and the South was wrong; the denial of suffrage to women was unjust, and the suffragettes were right; the destruction of native peoples was a national sin, and Jackson was wrong. Our Soul bears scars. Yet as Meacham and others have reminded us, the American experiment—despite our flaws—has built a strong track record (Wilstein, 2021) "to replace fear with hope and then to reverse injustice and expand equality." We have yet to achieve perfection, yet our system of government somehow tilts toward progress and our better angels, guiding us toward a more perfect Union.

The Civil War was the crucible that set our course. That war showed us what was at stake and what could be saved. The American Soul—scarred but intact—unites the Many as One. In that unity, we begin again to live out our Creed. Yet that unity came at a terrible cost, paid not by speeches or mottos but by ordinary citizens who bled and died to prove it real.

Why Did Americans Fight?

The causes of the Civil War are well known, but beyond the causes, why would Americans fight? Why would ordinary citizens endure what would become America's bloodiest conflict? Because Lincoln asked them to fight? To save the Union? To end slavery? What, exactly, would compel a foot soldier from the North to risk life and limb for the Union? He could have easily stayed home and let the South go. One can understand why a Southern soldier would take up arms to protect his homeland from an invading force, but what would motivate Northern men to go South?

The unprecedented violence pitted brother against brother in the battles of Shiloh, Antietam, Chickamauga, Spotsylvania, and—the most shocking of all—Gettysburg. Over 620,000 men died in the Civil War. By comparison, 58,000 Americans died in the Vietnam War. The scale of sacrifice required is hard to fathom. Why did Americans fight? The death toll is staggering, as shown in Fig. 9, which gives context to other American wars and their death tolls. Each number is more than a statistic. The bars in the graph are a measure of what a people are willing to endure to preserve an idea larger than themselves.

So, again, why fight? Why preserve the Union? If we fight against kings, against fascists, against communists, for ideals with hundreds of thousands of military deaths, why would we fight against each other with far greater bloodshed?

After Gettysburg, President Abraham Lincoln answered that question with the most succinct, grand, and impactful political oration in what has become known as the Gettysburg

The Art of the Compromise

Address. He answered the "why" not just for his own generation, but for generations to come. Lincoln delivered a profound and timeless message.

In his book *Start with Why* (Sinek, 2011), best-selling author Simon Sinek argues that great leaders inspire action by starting with purpose, by answering the question of "why." People need to know why something matters. Why something is important. Sinek identifies two predominant ways leaders influence human behavior: inspiration and manipulation. Inspiration taps into a person's heart and mind, creating an internal drive and motivation to act. Manipulation, by contrast, coerces a person through fear or force. A leader inspires. A demagogue manipulates. Lincoln inspired. As Lincoln instinctively knew, inspiration was the better option. Inspiration is empowering, and manipulation is babysitting.

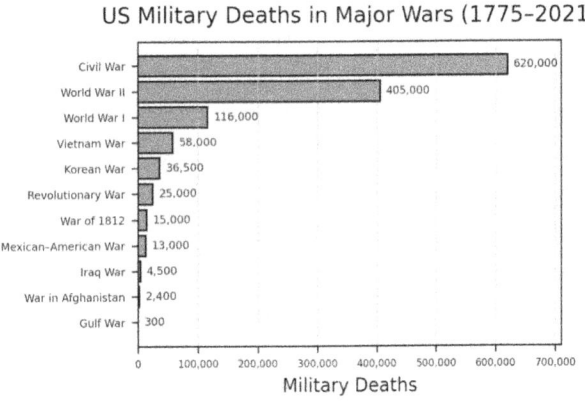

Figure 9. The Civil War remains the deadliest conflict in our history, claiming over 620,000 lives, more than both World Wars combined. That number represents more than just the scale of the war. That number also speaks to the strength of the idea of why Americans fought, why brothers would kill brothers. Data compiled from (2022).

Into One Soul

Lincoln did not manipulate the North into war. He did not bully soldiers into sacrifice. Instead, through his Gettysburg Address, he offered a moral vision—a reason to fight. He inspired the North to push on to preserve the Union. Lincoln defined what's at stake when faction faces faction, when rioters yawp, when Dr. King riffs his Dream. Lincoln's Gettysburg Address answers what's at stake and explains why the American Soul matters.

For such a profound speech, one would hope that the audience on that historic day would have recorded for posterity what Lincoln said. Unfortunately, like many great moments in history, few could foresee that this moment would be so meaningful, and the actual words Lincoln spoke are not directly archived. Unlike Dr. King's "Dream" speech, no television cameras or tape recorders were available to preserve the moment.* And so, historians have had to do some sleuthing to uncover the actual words spoken. Five known copies of the speech exist in Lincoln's handwriting, and each copy has a slightly different wording (George, 1990). The "Bliss" copy, named after Colonel Alexander Bliss, is widely accepted as the most authoritative. This version appears on the walls of the Lincoln Memorial in Washington, DC (George, 1990) and thus is the one I quote in this book.

Lincoln stood on November 19, 1863, beneath a gorgeous blue sky. A brisk air with a temperature of 52 degrees Fahrenheit mocked the solemn occasion (Jacobs, 1919). Lincoln took the podium at Gettysburg following Edward Everett, the

---

*Thomas Edison invented his phonograph in 1877 (Pretzer, 2002), unfortunately, 12 years after Lincoln's death. As a result, we have no recordings of Lincoln's voice or his Gettysburg Address.

The Art of the Compromise

main speaker that day. Lincoln put on his steel-rimmed glasses, glanced down at his notes, and spoke to both the crowd and history.*

Four score and seven years ago our fathers brought forth on this continent, a new nation, conceived in Liberty, and dedicated to the proposition that all men are created equal.

Now we are engaged in a great civil war, testing whether that nation, or any nation so conceived and so dedicated, can long endure. We are met on a great battle-field of that war. We have come to dedicate a portion of that field, as a final resting place for those who here gave their lives that that nation might live. It is altogether fitting and proper that we should do this.

But, in a larger sense, we can not dedicate—we can not consecrate—we can not hallow—this ground. The brave men, living and dead, who struggled here, have consecrated it, far above our poor power to add or detract. The world will little note, nor long remember what we say here, but it can never forget what they did here. It is for us the living, rather, to be dedicated here to the unfinished work which they who fought here have thus far so nobly advanced. It is rather for us to be here dedicated to

---

*The voice I hear in my ear of Lincoln is actor Robert Barron from the 1989 teen comedy flick *Bill and Ted's Excellent Adventure*, which tells the story of two hapless American teens traveling through time in a desperate attempt to pass their final high school history exam. Barron is tall and gaunt with an unusual and original timbre, and his vocal overtones give color and personality with an ever-so hint of Katherine Hepburn's iconic tremor. Since we have no recording of his voice, Barron is my preferred rendition. However, some evidence in contemporary descriptions of his voice offers a less flattering account of Lincoln's voice (Barsanti, 2020). Those reports describe a high-pitched and perhaps even "shrill" voice. A far cry from the deep, commanding tones we often imagine booming throughout Gettysburg.

Into One Soul

> the great task remaining before us—that from these honored dead we take increased devotion to that cause for which they gave the last full measure of devotion—that we here highly resolve that these dead shall not have died in vain—that this nation, under God, shall have a new birth of freedom—and that government of the people, by the people, for the people, shall not perish from the Earth.

The speech consisted of just 275 words—depending on which of the five copies one considers more authoritative—and lasted little more than two minutes. In just ten sentences, Lincoln articulated, through his lifetime of preparation, the same conclusion he had shared months earlier with one of his cabinet members that the central idea of the Civil War was "the necessity that is upon us, of proving that popular government is not an absurdity" (Goodwin, 2009).

People need reasons. We need meaning. Lincoln delivered those reasons over and over again with each progressing line of the Gettysburg Address. He did so in a manner that was accessible and understandable to ordinary Americans. The Civil War, he explained, was not a war of Northern aggression. Soldiers from the North were not marching into Dixie to be bullies. No. On the contrary, Lincoln explained the war was a test of democracy, of whether a nation "so conceived and so dedicated [could] long endure." The men of Gettysburg gave the ultimate sacrifice that "this nation might live."

His words did not stop at Gettysburg. They echoed across the Atlantic. Lincoln also framed the why as a global referendum on democracy itself, making the conflict resonate beyond American borders. European governments, especially Britain and France, watched closely. Both nations relied heavily on Southern cotton for their textile industries, which gave them an economic incentive to consider recognizing the Confederacy. At the same time, widespread antislavery sentiment among European publics—particularly in Britain—made overt support for the Confederacy politically dangerous.

By casting the war as a test of democracy and, after the Emancipation Proclamation, as a struggle over slavery, Lincoln altered the calculus for Europe. Recognition of the Confederacy would mean backing both rebellion and human bondage; restraint meant giving democracy a chance to prove its strength. To liberals across Europe, the Union's survival promised that republican self-rule could endure. To monarchs, its failure would confirm that large republics inevitably collapsed under their own divisions.

Thus, the world was watching. And at Gettysburg, Lincoln gave not only Americans but all peoples a reason to believe the Union was more than a convenient clustering of states. The Union stood as a moral proposition, a sacred cause—a government of the people, by the people, for the people—worth the blood, the pain, and the sacrifice. Lincoln insisted that the Union was more than a legal contract. Northern soldiers marched and died to prove that the cause was indivisible.

Perpetual Union

"If there was any constitutional issue resolved by the Civil War," wrote Supreme Court Justice Antonin Scalia in 2006, "it is that there is no right to secede." Scalia's comment responded to an unlikely letter from Dan Turkewitz, a screenwriter working on a political comedy about Maine seceding from the U.S. to join Canada (Jones, 2010).

On a whim, Turkewitz wrote to the nine Justices, asking for their thoughts on secession. "I come up a bit short in the art of Supreme Court advocacy," he admitted, "but if you could spare a few moments on a serious subject that is treated in a comedic way, I'd appreciate your thoughts." Only Scalia replied. His response went straight to the heart of the matter. Was the Union perpetual? Is the American Soul unbreakable? Scalia emphatically said yes—our Union is enduring.

Historian Kenneth Stampp has asked the same question in more formal terms, "Did the [Constitution] create a union of sovereign states, each of which retained the right to secede at its own discretion? Or did it create a union from which no state, once having joined, could escape except by an extra-constitutional act of revolution?" (Stampp, 1978). That phrase "extra-constitutional act of revolution" is longhand for civil war.

The Soviet Union was not a perpetual union. Neither is the European Union. Member states in both cases have exited—sometimes with fanfare, sometimes with a shrug. The USSR fragmented in the 1990s, and the UK's Brexit became a global punchline. Yet in the United States, the Civil War resolved this question once and for all. Our Union is unbreakable. Once a state joins, there are no takebacks. No lawful secession is possible, which is the point. A lasting union demands that disputes be resolved within, not apart. That structure binds not only geography, but a soul—our American Soul.

Critics like law professor Mary Anne Franks warn of a "cult of the Constitution," where Americans treat the document less as law and more as scripture (Franks, 2019). Jefferson had a similar worry, noting that some viewed the Constitution like the ark of the covenant—too sacred to be touched (Jefferson, 1816). Yet Madison, who once dismissed a Bill of Rights as a parchment barrier, came to embrace its emotional power (Feldman, 2017). The Founders chose pen

The Art of the Compromise

and parchment not for efficiency, but reverence.* Logic rarely stirs the soul. But a sacred script? That inspires the minority to rise when logic says surrender.

Perpetuity is hard to explain in practical terms. The concept does not feel as tangible as a flag or a boundary. Yet a perpetual union—unlike a union of mere convenience—carries a deeper sense of shared responsibility. Citizens begin to look beyond their state lines—to think about national duty, sacrifice, and common good. By contrast, a looser union, where exit is a ready option, invites self-interest. When quitting is easy, commitment is shallow. Such a casual union encourages each member to look inward first.

We see this casual dynamic in the EU today. Member states face domestic pressures that pull them away from collective action. As Helen Thompson observed in *Foreign Affairs* (Thompson, 2018), the EU "has always struggled to accommodate the democratic politics of its members."

---

*Despite the ready availability of printing presses—Franklin himself made his living in the trade—the Founders chose to record the nation's foundational texts by hand. The Declaration of Independence, for example, was engrossed in 1776 by Timothy Matlack, whose fine script remains the version displayed in the National Archives Rotunda (Coelho, 2013). In 1787, the Constitution was handwritten by Jacob Shallus, assistant clerk of the Pennsylvania General Assembly, who completed the 4,000-word document across four large sheets of parchment in roughly 40 hours for a payment of $30 (Rosenblatt, 1987). Shallus made several small errors, which he noted and corrected directly on the final sheet. When Congress passed the Bill of Rights in 1789, engrossing clerks William Lambert and Benjamin Bankson prepared the official handwritten copies sent to the states for ratification (Woodard, 2011). These acts of manual transcription were not driven by utility but by ritual—the deliberate use of pen and parchment conferred solemnity, permanence, and emotional gravity (Kurlansky, 2016).

Into One Soul

Writing amid the eurozone debt crisis, she noted that the EU lurches from "crisis after crisis with no lasting solution." One can little wonder why the UK chose the easy route—Brexit—over the hard work of building a stronger union.

In America, the permanence of the Union means that running away is not an option when times get tough. The states are bound together and must work through conflict, not flee from it.* When one state faces a hurricane or economic collapse, the others show up—not perfectly, but consistently. That shared bond is what a perpetual union demands—a commitment to the whole, not just concern for the part.

President John F. Kennedy captured this spirit in his 1961 inaugural address: "Ask not what your country can do for you—ask what you can do for your country." Kennedy's words are a call to service, sacrifice, and national identity. In the EU, people first identify as Greek, German, or French. In the U.S., we first identify as Americans. That shift in identity—anchored in a Constitutional permanence—makes all the difference.

The South, in 1860, was unwilling to make that shift. Southern leaders rejected Lincoln's election, not because he broke the law, but because he broke their control. They had long dominated the Union's highest offices and were willing

---

*In *Hamilton's Blessing* (Gordon, 2010), John Steele Gordon recounts how Alexander Hamilton championed the federal assumption of state debts incurred during the Revolutionary War. The issue was highly contentious, but Hamilton offered a counterintuitive insight that "a national debt, if it is not excessive, will be to us a national blessing." He further argued, "It will be a powerful cement to our union." This moment stands as an early example of the binding force of a perpetual union.

The Art of the Compromise

to remain so long as they were in charge. Once outvoted, they walked. Like a child storming off the playground, the South refused to play if they were not in control. They rejected the majority's will, the very foundation of a representative democracy. The South was not bullied. They were spoiled.

Adlai Stevenson,* Illinois governor and two-time presidential candidate, made this point powerfully on November 19, 1951, the 88th anniversary of the Gettysburg Address (Holzer, 2009). Stevenson, who grew up in Illinois, revered Lincoln—Illinois' most favored son—and used the occasion to explain *why* the Union was worth preserving

> Lincoln saw the war in its global dimensions...the Confederate states had rejected two fundamental precepts of democracy. First, in refusing to accept him as their President...they had violated the first rule of democratic government, the obligation of a minority to abide by the result of an election...
>
> Second, in making slavery the foundation stone of their new government, the Confederacy was renouncing the doctrine of the equal rights of man in favor of the creed of the master race, an idea that Lincoln abhorred.

Stevenson's words struck a chord with his audience, who had just defeated Nazism. He reminded them that Gettysburg was more than a battlefield—it was the front line in a global

---

*An interesting historical aside is that Adlai Stevenson later served as U.S. Ambassador to the United Nations during the Cuban Missile Crisis in 1962. In an unforgettable exchange, Stevenson demanded that the Soviet Ambassador Valerian Zorin confirm whether the USSR had installed nuclear missiles in Cuba. When Zorin refused to answer, Stevenson famously shot back (Prosser, 1963), "I am prepared to wait for my answer until hell freezes over, if that's your decision." The moment became iconic.

fight for human dignity and democratic government. Americans were not just dying for the Union. They died for the revolutionary idea that free people should govern themselves—just as they had at Bunker Hill and Yorktown. Stevenson's speech dismantled the two common defenses of the Confederacy. First, that the South had a right to secede, and second, that the war was not about slavery. On both points, he was right to be blunt. The South left because they had lost control, and the war was indeed about slavery.

Modern apologists may cloak the cause in vague terms—states' rights, tradition, economics, Southern pride—but the Confederate constitution makes no such attempt. Like a guilty man who cannot stop talking, the Confederacy dedicates five different sections in its constitution to slavery. Drafted and ratified within a week of Lincoln's inauguration, the document mirrors much of the U.S. Constitution except that the infamous document explicitly protects slavery.

Whereas the U.S. Constitution famously and awkwardly avoids the word "slavery," the Confederacy embraced the term. The word *slavery* never appears in the United States Constitution of 1787. The framers used indirect phrasing such as "other persons" or "persons held to service." By contrast, the Constitution of the Confederate States of America (1861) mentions *slavery* explicitly ten times, making the protection of human bondage central to that document's design. The Confederate charter prohibited any law "denying or impairing the right of property in negro slaves," required federal protection of slavery in the territories, barred member states from abolishing the practice, and forbade foreign importation of slaves while guaranteeing its perpetuation at home.

The omission of the word "slavery" in the U.S. Constitution was intentional. As James Madison explained during the Constitutional Convention, he thought "it wrong to admit in the Constitution the idea that there could be property in men" (Ketcham, 1990). The South had no such scruples. Its founders wrote a document that enshrined slavery without hesitation. That blunt fact alone collapses the apologists' fragile pretense that slavery was incidental to the war.

The Civil War was about slavery. The slaveholding states saw their grip on power weakening, and Lincoln's election confirmed the shift. Rather than accept the democratic outcome, the South chose disunion and war, not the North.

The Writing on the Wall

The South did not secede merely because Lincoln won the presidency. The South seceded because it lost political control. The South left the Union because slaveholding elites lost the power to control the federal government, losing the presidency, losing Congress, and seeing the Supreme Court slip away. The South saw the writing on the wall, and rather than stay and govern under majority rule, they took their ball and went home. The South only liked democracy when they could call the shots.

For much of the early Republic, the South held sway. Despite having a smaller free population, the slaveholding states exercised enormous influence through a series of structural advantages. Chief among them was the Three-Fifths Compromise, which allowed slave states to count three out of every five enslaved persons toward their congressional apportionment and electoral votes. This count was no small matter. The enslaved, who had no vote, artificially inflated Southern power for decades (Ricks, 2020).

The Constitution's design gave the South a long runway. The Senate, with equal representation per state, gave even the smallest slaveholding state a veto over national policy. Early on, the presidency was dominated by Virginians and Southern allies. The Supreme Court leaned South, too, culminating in the disastrous Dred Scott decision of 1857 (Burger, 1995).

Yet history and the numbers did not stand still. Population growth in the North—driven by immigration, industrialization, and urban expansion—reshaped the balance of power. As shown in Fig. 10, the free states surged ahead in sheer population during the antebellum decades. That growth translated into more representatives in Congress, more electors in the presidential Electoral College, and a louder national voice for free labor.

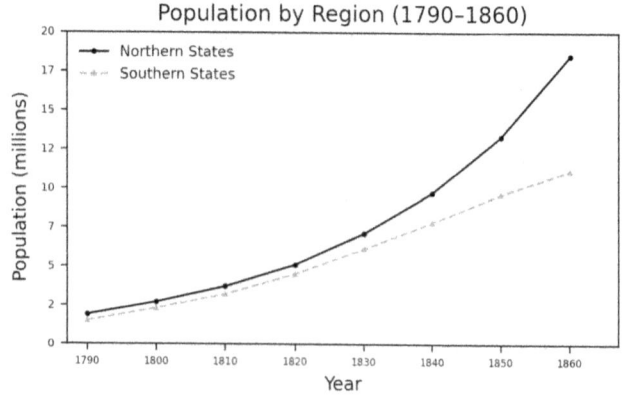

Figure 10. The South remained a minority in total population, and an even smaller minority in free population. Yet for decades, this minority controlled much of the federal government. Data compiled from the U.S. Bureau of the Census (1976).

The story was not demographics alone. New free states joined the Union one after another, each carrying its own delegation to Washington. The graph in Fig. 11 traces that slow but relentless arithmetic. Decade after decade, the free states stacked higher, while the South could add only so many slave states before exhausting the frontier. The tilt became

The Art of the Compromise

unmistakable. By 1860, the Union's political ledger revealed a Northern majority entrenched not only by numbers but by the map itself. The South's grip on national power, once secure, had slipped away.

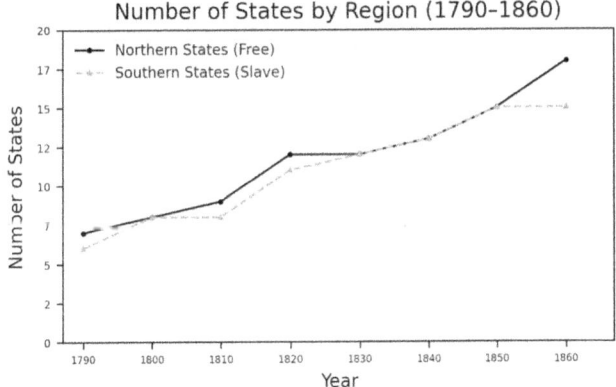

Figure 11. Number of Northern and Southern States. Early compromises, like those in 1820 and 1850, kept a regional balance in the Senate. But this equilibrium was temporary and increasingly untenable. Basic admission dates for states and their classification as free or slaveholding compiled from Leubsdorf et al. (2023).

The graphs tell the story. As the population gap widened, congressional power tilted northward. In the House of Representatives, Fig. 12, the free states surged ahead. Despite repeated efforts to maintain parity in the Senate, Fig. 13—pairing each new free state with a slave state through the Missouri Compromise*—the North's advantage became

---

*The Missouri Compromise of 1820 first formalized the practice of pairing one free state with one slave state to preserve the balance

Into One Soul

undeniable. The Electoral College followed suit. By 1860, the South could no longer muster the votes to elect a president of their choosing. The chart in Fig. 14 lays bare that steady erosion, as parity slipped year by year into Northern dominance.

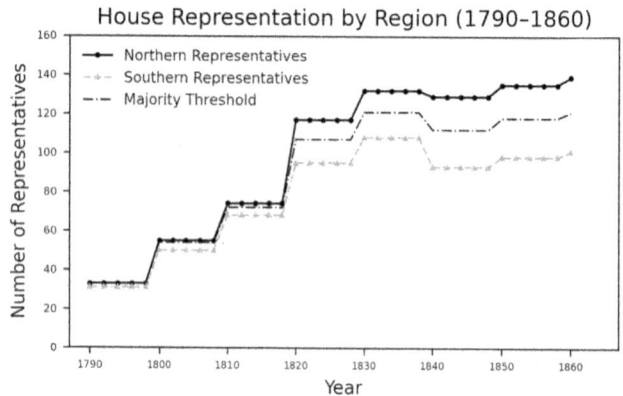

Figure 12. House Representation by Region. Despite structural advantages, the South could not hold its ground forever. The population growth of the North translated into political dominance in the House. Apportionment data and sectional alignment for antebellum Congresses (Martis & Rowles, 1989).

Then came Lincoln. He won the presidency without a single electoral vote from the South. Not one. That outcome shattered the illusion of Southern control. They had been outvoted, and they chose not to abide by the verdict of majority rule.

---

of power in the Senate, and this "balance rule" continued informally in later decades (McPherson, 2003).

The Art of the Compromise

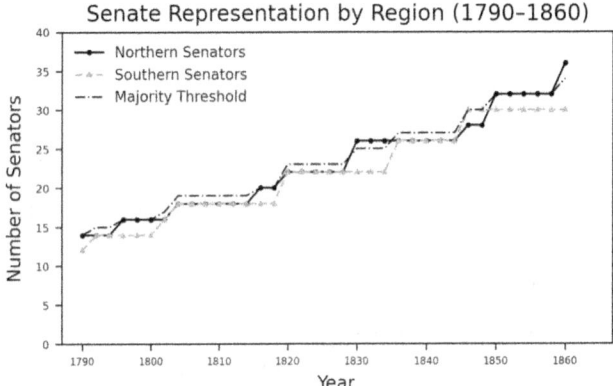

Figure 13. Senate Composition by Region. The Senate, once the South's safe harbor with near equal representation split between the two regions, began to lean North. The game was changing, and the South knew time was running out. Apportionment of Senate seats by state and party, from which regional counts can be inferred (U.S. Senate, 2002).

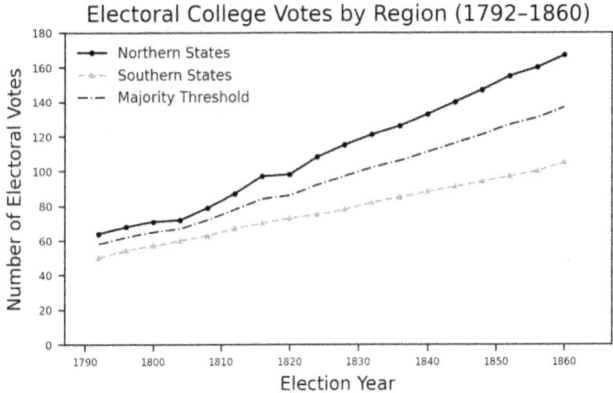

Figure 14. Electoral College Votes by Region. By 1860, the North had the numbers. The Electoral College was no longer a firewall, but rather a mirror of political reality. The primary source for official historical Electoral College vote distributions (2023).

Even the Supreme Court, once the South's bulwark, was slipping away. As shown in Fig. 15, the balance of appointees—and the even Chief Justice's chair—began to edge beyond the South's majority grip. By 1860, with aging justices on the bench, Southern leaders could see that Lincoln would soon hold the power to appoint new members, and likely a new Chief Justice as well. The *Dred Scott* ruling, intended as a crowning triumph for the slaveholding class, proved instead to be a final gasp (Varon, 2008). Chief Justice Roger Taney, who delivered that infamous opinion, still presided at age eighty-three during the 1860 election. His years made the stakes clear: the next president would name his successor. The curve in Fig. 16 shows Lincoln's breakthrough on the presidential scorecard, a victory that would also tip the Court toward the North.

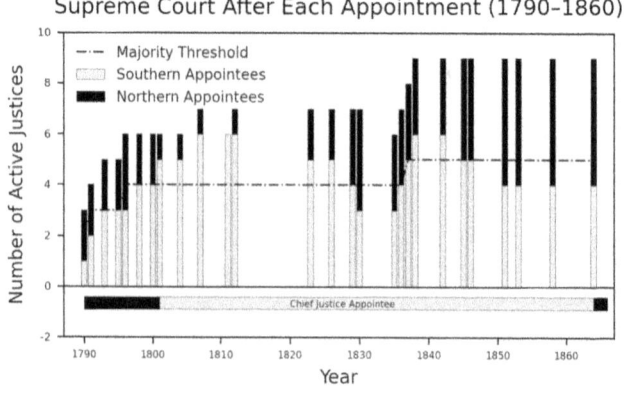

Figure 15. Supreme Court Justices by Region of Origin. Southern dominance in the judiciary reached its peak with Chief Justice Taney, spanning from 1836 to 1864. Yet that dominance was on borrowed time. Lincoln's presidency would change the Court's trajectory. Data compiled from Urofsky (1994).

The Art of the Compromise

Taney, a Maryland slaveholder himself, was no neutral umpire—he regarded Lincoln's rise with disdain and saw federal power as a shield for slavery rather than a sword for freedom. His opinion in Dred Scott stripped Congress of authority to limit slavery's spread and branded Black Americans as forever without rights, "which the white man was bound to respect" (Simon, 2006). Time was running out. The odds favored Lincoln to shift the Court's direction for decades to come. Southern leaders saw the aging Taney for what he was: a final line of defense, soon to fall. Indeed, Lincoln would appoint five justices in total, including Taney's replacement, Samuel Chase (Goodwin, 2009).

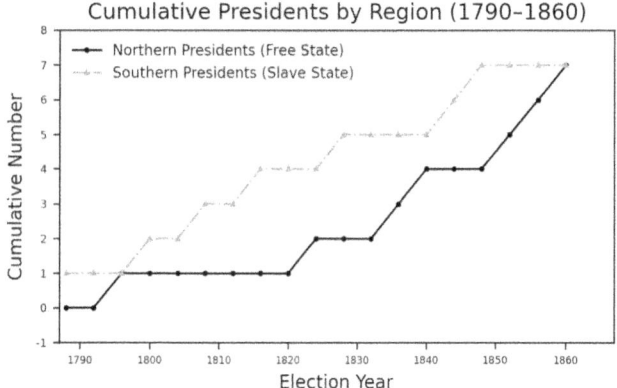

Figure 16. Presidents by Region. The presidency had long been a stronghold of the South. Lincoln's election brought parity—half from the North, half from the South. The cumulative importance of the presidency is one of trajectory rather than overall influence. Data compiled from Woolley and Peters (1999).

The South saw the future, and they wanted no part of it. They spoke of states' rights, of sovereignty, of honor, and of tradition, but what they really wanted was control, something they no longer had. Contrary to Lost Cause mythology, the

South was not overtaxed by Northern aggression (DiLorenzo, 2020). Yes, the economic imbalance between the North and South was an issue, but the North was not overtaxing the South as some folks have claimed.

The graph in Fig. 17 shows that Northern states paid the lion's share of federal taxes through tariffs and customs duties. The effective per capita tax burden was consistently higher in the North. Still, Southern leaders felt encircled—culturally, politically, and economically. In some ways, they were right. The Constitution had protected the minority interests of the South for decades. Madison had worked hard to construct the Constitution to protect such minority factions. Yet the immoral institution of slavery could no longer survive the growing majority that opposed this institution, and the South could no longer abide by the democratic majority.

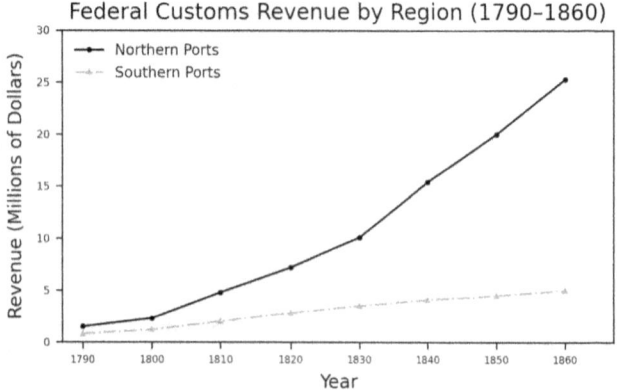

Figure 17. Federal Customs Revenue by Port Region. Federal taxes came primarily from tariffs at ports. Northern ports—especially New York—generated the lion's share of revenue. Southern ports contributed far less, even as they demanded more political power. Data compiled from primary sources for customs receipts by major port cities (McCulloch, 1864) and Gallman for the economic context (Gallman, 1960).

The Art of the Compromise

The South did not fear tyranny. They feared democracy. For the first time, the votes no longer favored them. They were no longer the ruling minority.

They were outnumbered.

They were outvoted.

They were outmaneuvered.

And so, they left. They did not leave because they were oppressed. They left because they were losing power, as the data demonstrates. The system still worked; it just no longer worked for them. This rebellion was not one born of desperation but rather a tantrum dressed in gray. The tide turned, and a new President stepped forward to face the South.

Since the secession of South Carolina in December of 1860, the seceding states had started to seize federal forts and arsenals and to build a military. Lincoln responded to these actions in his inaugural address by stating his intentions to "hold, occupy, and possess the property, and places belonging to the government and to collect the duties and imposts" but he promised that "there will be no invasion—no using of force against, or among the people anywhere." As historian Ludwell Johnson notes (Johnson, 1960), this phraseology could mean all things to all men—a Lincoln specialty.

Before 1869, no legal document or court ruling explicitly forbade a state's secession from the Union, and no legal document or court ruling explicitly allowed a state to do so either. The question was left ambiguous. At the nation's founding, however, the idea of a permanent union was unambiguous.

The full title of our first governing framework—often abbreviated to the Articles of Confederation—was actually the Articles of Confederation and *Perpetual Union* (my *emphasis* added). Article XIII of that document left no doubt that the "Union shall be perpetual" (Stampp, 1978). That phrase, often forgotten today, was a guiding star for the Founders. Yet when

Into One Soul

Madison and the delegates met in Philadelphia to write the Constitution, the word "perpetual" disappeared. The Constitution made no direct claim to indissolubility. No article, clause, or phrase said outright that the Union could not be broken. That omission has raised eyebrows ever since.

Why did Madison leave the phrase out? In his writings, he clearly expressed the need for the permanence of the Union. Yet Maidson did not believe that permanence came from a word or a phrase. Madison did not believe in paper promises. Madison grasped that permanence came from structure. Madison believed the Union would be held together not by decree, but by design. Madison foresaw a system of shared powers, competing interests, and representative compromises. Still, the absence of the printed word left a rhetorical gap. One that Abraham Lincoln would eventually fill.

As author Elisabeth Varon documents in her book *Disunion!* (Varon, 2008), when the initial euphoria of the nation's Founding faded, and the Republic began to confront the fate of slavery, arguments around secession and disunion began to unfurl, starting in earnest around the 1830s when the nullification controversy[*] in South Carolina moved the calls for

---

[*]In another historical irony, the demagogic presidency of Andrew Jackson served to dampen the drumbeat of nullification and, thus, disunion temporarily. Nullification is a discredited legal doctrine whereby states can arbitrarily nullify or strike down and ignore federal laws. President Jackson, who was generally in favor of states' rights, vehemently disagreed, however, with this doctrine, and in an incisive, coherent, and comprehensive proclamation on December 10, 1832 (Stampp, 1978), he outlined his position as (Mullin, 2023)"I consider, then, the power to annul a law of the United States, assumed by one State, incompatible with the existence of the Union, contradicted expressly by the letter of the Constitution,

The Art of the Compromise

disunion forward. These arguments, of course, reached a crescendo in 1860 with the election of Lincoln.

By the time Lincoln took the oath of office in 1861, seven states had already seceded. Mississippi, January 9; Florida, January 10; Alabama, January 11; Georgia, January 19; Louisiana, January 26; Texas, February 1, 1861 (DiLorenzo, 2020). Each had walked away after Lincoln's election, unwilling to accept the results of a democratic process that they no longer controlled. War was not yet inevitable, but it was close.

And so, on March 4th, Lincoln made his way to a small table on the square platform constructed out from the East Portico of the Capitol and delivered his first inaugural address (Goodwin, 2009). The Washington Monument in the distance was only partially built. The symbolism was not lost on the crowd in attendance that day. The country—like the landmark—was incomplete. Lincoln spoke plainly. With lawyerly precision and constitutional care, he addressed the looming crisis:

> *I hold that in contemplation of universal law and of the Constitution the Union of these States is perpetual. Perpetuity is implied, if not expressed, in the fundamental law of all national governments. It is safe to assert that no government proper ever had a provision in its organic law for its own termination.*

Lincoln did not mince words. Our Union was binding and irrevocable. He then turned to the historical record.

---

unauthorized by its spirit, inconsistent with every principle on which It was founded, and destructive of the great object for which it was formed..." He went on to say, "Disunion by armed force is treason." Jackson's leadership would forestall secession for another 30 years.

> *The Union is much older than the Constitution. It was formed, in fact, by the Articles of Association in 1774. It was matured and continued by the Declaration of Independence in 1776. It was further matured, and the faith of all the then thirteen States expressly plighted and engaged that it should be perpetual, by the Articles of Confederation in 1778. And finally, in 1787, one of the declared objects for ordaining and establishing the Constitution was "to form a more perfect Union.*

If perfection were the goal, one can only assume a perpetual Union. Perfect implies permanence.

Lincoln's argument was simple, elegant, and grounded in the lived experience of the Republic.* If the Constitution created a "more perfect union" than what came before, then this new document could not possibly permit disunion. If the original Articles said the Union was perpetual and the Constitution was an improvement upon the Articles, then the Union was still perpetual—only better. If a state could simply leave because of a lost election, then the entire experiment in self-government and democracy would be a sham.

Lincoln's argument would not remain rhetorical for long. Eight years after his speech, the Supreme Court affirmed his position in *Texas v. White* (1869), declaring that the Union was "an indestructible union, composed of indestructible states." The Court ruled that individual states had no right to unilaterally secede, cementing Lincoln's logic as legal precedent. His words, once contested, had become constitutional doctrine (Stampp, 1978).

---

*Lincoln would echo much of Andrew Jackson's nullification argument during his inaugural.

The Art of the Compromise

Lincoln then delivered the line that drew the moral and constitutional line in the sand.

> *You have no oath registered in heaven to destroy the Government, while I shall have the most solemn one to preserve, protect, and defend it.*

Lincoln makes a powerful statement about his constitutional authority that, unfortunately, foreshadows the war to come. He then turned to reconciliation. He closed not with fire, not with defiance, not with hatred, not with hubris, but with grace.

> *We are not enemies, but friends. We must not be enemies. Though passion may have strained it must not break our bonds of affection. The mystic chords of memory...will yet swell the chorus of the Union, when again touched...by the better angels of our nature.*

Forty days later, on Friday, April 12, 1861, cannon fire rang out at Fort Sumter. The war had begun. The sun Franklin once declared as rising now stood obscured by cannon smoke. Yet Lincoln, in his restraint and resolve, refused to let the sun set. Lincoln had not declared war, but rather Southern leaders rejected the very notion of a perpetual, democratic union. The South was no longer in control, and like a spoiled child, they had decided to take their ball and leave. Lincoln had asked them to stay. They chose to leave. He had reminded them that the Union was older than the states, that the Union's legitimacy was rooted in history, sacrifice, and common cause. He argued for the continuity of the American project—not in defiance of the Constitution, but in fulfillment of it.

After being sworn in, President Lincoln and now former President Buchanan returned down Pennsylvania Avenue past the Willard Hotel, this time bound for the White House.

Little did Lincoln know that his inaugural pledges and political wordsmithing would be tested sooner rather than later.

First Shot

Lincoln believed that Fort Sumter in South Carolina and other forts, such as Fort Pickens in Florida, were secure in federal hands and adequately supplied for the foreseeable future. He did not anticipate an immediate challenge to his inaugural pledges. On the morning of March 5, the day after the inaugural, Lincoln would learn profoundly disturbing news (Goodwin, 2009).

Major Robert Anderson, the commanding officer at Fort Sumter, had sent a letter[*] to Lincoln stating that the troops garrisoned at Fort Sumter could not hold out for more than four to six weeks without reinforcement and assistance. South Carolina had blockaded the harbor, and Fort Sumter ran low on supplies (Barsanti, 2020). Anderson estimated that a force of not less than twenty thousand "good and well-disciplined men" would be necessary to relieve and reinforce Sumter (Current, 1963). One day into his official duties as President of the United States, Lincoln consulted General Winfield Scott, who recommended the fort's surrender and evacuation of the troops. Lincoln's firm language and vow to "hold, occupy, and possess" in his inaugural faced a challenge. Barely sworn in, Lincoln was between a rock and a hard place. He

---

[*]Major Anderson had sent the letter on February 28, 1861, and it arrived at the White House on inauguration day, March 4, and Lincoln would see it on his desk the first thing the following day, March 5.

The Art of the Compromise

had to decide whether to send reinforcements with warships to fight through the blockade and hold the fort or to abandon the fort altogether. The first option would break his pledge to "not assail" his fellow countrymen—not a good way to start an administration—but the second option was none the better—humiliation in both the eyes of the North and the South. The South was in rebellion, but no shots had yet been fired, and no civil war existed. War was, however, imminent, and the question that remained was who would be the aggressor. Who would fire the first shot? Lincoln made no rash decisions and took no hasty actions. He carefully weighed the options and diligently stepped through significant decision-making efforts. First, he met with Gustavus Fox, a former Navy officer who had developed an ingenious plan to reinforce Sumter. Lincoln liked the plan and had Fox share it with his cabinet. Next, he called his cabinet together and asked them to commit in writing a response to the following question: "Assuming it to be possible to now provision Fort Sumter, under all the circumstances, is it wise to attempt it?" Finally, he gathered intelligence with "boots on the ground" to understand the political forces at work in South Carolina.

Lincoln sent Fox to meet with Major Anderson directly and discreetly for intelligence by using Fox's connections in South Carolina to gain entry to Fort Sumter. Lincoln also sent Stephen Hurlbut, a native South Carolinian and a trusted colleague from his lawyer days to visit Charleston and gauge the Southern stronghold's sentiment. Reporting to Lincoln on March 25, Fox returned and confirmed that Anderson and his men may be able to last until April 15. Fox also confirmed the feasibility of his plan to reinforce Sumter.

On March 27, Hurlbut returned with even more dour news. The "bonds of affection" that Lincoln spoke about in his inaugural no longer existed among either South Carolinians or Charlestonians, and Hurlbut noted (Goodwin, 2009) that "no attachment to the Union" existed with "positively nothing to appeal." Hurlbut reported that a separate Southern nationality was an "established fact." The winds of Compromise were not blowing in the South. On March 29, Good Friday, Lincoln called a critical cabinet meeting to review the intelligence from Fox and Hurlbut and to take the pulse of the cabinet members. The meeting also included recommendations from General Scott.

The time for a decision had come, and after this meeting, Lincoln set in motion a modified plan for Fox's resupply. No reinforcement would occur, only resupply, and communications would be sent to the South Carolina governor conveying Lincoln's intentions "to provision the fort peaceably if unmolested."

This clever solution to Lincoln's conundrum between a rock (fire the first shot and start a war) and a hard place (surrender the fort and walk away in humiliation) found a middle ground where resupplying without reinforcement projected a clear peace mission, while holding the fort projected apparent strength. Lincoln understood the Art of the Compromise. Unlike the Articles of Confederation, the Constitution gave Lincoln and Congress the authority to use force to bring the rebellious states into submission, but Lincoln understood that our "better angels" should not fire the first shot, nor should they walk away from danger in disgrace. After March 29, Lincoln put into motion a plan that balanced between these two

The Art of the Compromise

positions and, in the end, would demonstrate the South as the actual aggressor in the secession conflict.*

At 4:30 AM on April 12, the commanding officer, Pierre Gustave Toutant–Beauregard,† of the Southern forces that encircled Fort Sumter in Charleston harbor, commanded his soldiers to open fire.‡ Major Anderson and his small garrison of sixty men returned the volley, and the Civil War began.

---

*Some scholars have argued that Lincoln did not intend peace in his alternative plan to war. As historian Ludwell Johnson writes (Johnson, 1960), such scholars argue, "Lincoln deliberately provoked the Confederates into firing the first shot as the only possible way out of an otherwise insoluble political dilemma." Johnson, however, demonstrates quite the contrary: the South, led by Jefferson Davis, fell into a delusional echo chamber whereby they could only see war in each decision made by the North and Lincoln. The South was operating in an information-poor environment where "an atmosphere already thick with suspicion and distrust" became a self-fulfilling cycle where war with the North seemed inevitable.

†Beauregard, who graduated from West Point in 1838, was a student of Anderson, who taught Beauregard in his artillery class.

‡A Virginian, Edmund Ruffin, fired the first shot at the fort (Ruffin, 1977). Ruffin is an interesting character in the history of the Civil War. He was a popular (at least in the South), semi-crazed secessionist (Barsanti, 2020). Born in 1794, Ruffin was 67 when he pulled the lanyard of a 64-pound Columbiad cannon aimed at Fort Sumter to fire the first shot (Mitchell, 1961). He had traveled from his home in Virginia to South Carolina to enlist in the Palmetto Guard. He reveled in the battle against Sumter and was reportedly the first to enter the Fort after it fell. Ironically, Ruffin published a futurist novel in 1860 entitled "Anticipation of the Future," in which he unknowingly foreshadowed the Civil War and an attack on Fort Sumter as the opening battle of such a war. He was deeply troubled after the Civil War ended, and on June 18, 1865, he took his own life (Petersburg Express, 1865).

General Beauregard was acting under orders from the new Southern capital in Montgomery, Alabama,* to attack Fort Sumter before Fox could arrive. The Confederates had intercepted the plans for Fox's resupply and intended to usurp the mission (Goodwin, 2009). Major Anderson and his men held out for 34 hours but ultimately succumbed to the Confederate onslaught and surrendered to General Beauregard. The South had fired the first shot, and Lincoln responded with a proclamation calling for the raising of a 75,000-man militia "to suppress" the secession acts of the South and "to cause the laws to be duly executed." Lincoln notably did not call on Congress to declare war on the seceding states. Doing so would have recognized the Confederacy as a legitimate nation rather than an internal rebellion.

In the proclamation (Lincoln, 1953), Lincoln had noted that the acts of the rebelling states—seizing forts and arsenals, including Fort Sumter, that were the property of the Union—had gone beyond the ordinary powers of the government and were "too powerful to be suppressed by the ordinary course of judicial proceedings, or by the powers vested in the marshals by law." Lincoln emphasized that the extraordinary measure to raise a militia was the next step in Constitutional authority "to maintain the honor, the integrity, and the existence of our National Union, and the perpetuity of popular government; and to redress wrongs already long enough endured." Lincoln spoke directly to the rebelling states to "command the persons composing the combinations aforesaid to

---

*The Southern capital would later move to Richmond, Virginia, after Virginia seceded to join the Confederacy in reaction to Fort Sumter.

disperse and retire peaceably to their respective abodes within twenty days from this date."

Lincoln and the North would need four long years and, unfortunately, many thousands more lives to deliver on this proclamation. On April 9, 1865, Confederate General Robert E. Lee surrendered his army to Union General Ulysses S. Grant at Appomattox Court House in Virginia. Lee's surrender marked the beginning of the end of the Civil War (Davis, 1957). The last battle was fought at Palmito Ranch, Texas, on May 13. Lincoln would not see this formal end as the assassin, John Wilkes Booth, a Southern sympathizer, would place a forty-four-caliber derringer in the back of Lincoln's head at Ford's Theater and shoot the unsuspecting President (Goodwin, 2009). Lincoln would die from this gunshot wound the following day. The Civil War was over. Lincoln and the North preserved the unbroken Union. Yet cannon fire alone could not bind the nation's Soul. For that, the law itself had to be reborn.

Fourteenth Amendment

The first shot at Fort Sumter settled nothing by itself. The outbreak of war forced the Union to declare whether the great experiment could hold together (McPherson, 2003). Yet once the guns fell silent, a harder truth waited in the rubble. Force alone could not weld the Many into One people. If the nation was to survive, we needed more than a battlefield victory. We needed a constitutional Soul strong enough to keep states from unraveling that victory.

James Madison saw this danger long before it spilled into blood. He argued at the Constitutional Convention of 1787 that the states—left unchecked—would chip away at national unity (Feldman, 2017). Local factions, petty legislatures, backroom bargains—these acts were the small minds of nullification that would someday grow into disunion (Feldman, 2017). Madison's solution was clear. Give Congress a "Federal Negative"—the power to veto state laws that threatened the Union or the rights of its people (Feldman, 2017).

Madison lost that fight. The delegates refused to grant Congress so sweeping a power, fearing another British Parliament in disguise (Rakove, 1998). Instead, the delegates settled on the Supremacy Clause, a principle without clear enforcement. Into that vacuum, nullification took root (Varon, 2008). John C. Calhoun gave the idea its teeth during the Nullification Crisis of 1832 (Freehling, 1992). Later, Southern leaders twisted Madison's *Virginia Resolutions* into a justification for resisting federal authority, a reading Madison himself rejected late in life (Ketcham, 1990).

The Civil War settled secession by force, but the war did not fully settle the idea that a state could ignore or block national law whenever it wanted. That idea—the claim that states could pick and choose which parts of the Constitution to follow—needed more than military defeat to disappear. We needed a clear constitutional rule to say, once and for all, that federal law was supreme and that each American's rights came first, no matter which state they lived in. The Founders, led by Madison, had argued about how to achieve federal supremacy, but they never finished the job.

Fortunately, after the Civil War, the Fourteenth Amendment came into play. Ratified in 1868, right after the smoke cleared, this amendment did not just confirm freedom for people who had been enslaved. The profound addition rewrote the basic relationship between the federal government and each individual American (Foner, 2019). The Due Process and Equal Protection Clauses within the amendment state that the rights promised in the Constitution were not up

The Art of the Compromise

to the states to grant or take away (Ricks, 2020). These rights now ran straight from the national government to the citizen, binding our Soul into one national unity. This direct national government was Madison's motivation in proposing the Federal Negative, and with the 14th Amendment, his idea was rejuvenated.

This new amendment meant no governor, state legislature, or local sheriff could fence off individual rights to suit local politics or prejudice. If a state passed a law that trampled a person's basic freedoms, the federal courts could step in and strike it down. That shift—putting each citizen's rights on *national* ground instead of local ground—was the piece Madison had hoped for back in Philadelphia with his Federal Negative, but that he did not get at that time (Feldman, 2017). A war, unfortunately, was necessary to prove his point, and the Fourteenth Amendment to make the concept stick (Curtis, 1986).

Madison's negative never became a statute. Yet over time, the courts assumed the burden he once placed on Congress. The 14th Amendment slept for decades, but in the early 20th century, the amendment stirred awake. Through a concept known as "selective incorporation," the Supreme Court gradually applied the Bill of Rights to the states (Perry, 2001). The First Amendment, the Fourth, the Sixth—piece by piece, the nation's guarantees reached down to each county courthouse (Ricks, 2020).

The graph that appears in Fig. 18 traces that arc in stark numbers—for over a century, with scarcely a case testing the First Amendment. For the first hundred years, the prevailing consensus held that the Bill of Rights bound only the federal government, not the states or localities. The modern habit of invoking a "First Amendment right"—or any other right under the Bill of Rights—is, in truth, a twentieth-century embodiment of what had long remained little more than words on

Into One Soul

parchment. In Madison's language, no Federal Negative existed before the Fourteenth Amendment. Then, a steady rise with the Fourteenth in place—the legal story of Madison's Federal Negative reborn by judicial hand. With this rise, the connective tissue of the one American Soul was growing stronger. Citizens no longer felt a simple bond to their state, but a larger bond to the U.S.

The Fourteenth Amendment finished what the first shot of the war began. The amendment buried nullification not by force but by text and verdict. This powerful addition to the Constitution gave the country a single constitutional floor beneath each citizen's feet and reminded us that some principles stand above. Rights, once secured, are not local options.*

Madison did not live to see this final piece fall into place. Yet in the legal architecture that rose from the War's ashes, his signature remains. Liberty is too precious to leave at the mercy of local power. Madison's Federal Negative lives on—

---

*The Fourteenth Amendment's rebirth of Madison's dream—the idea that federal power must stand guard over state excesses—laid the constitutional bedrock for the modern civil rights movement a century later. By weaving the Bill of Rights into state law through the doctrine of incorporation, the amendment gave civil rights leaders and ordinary citizens alike a federal shield against local segregation and injustice. As legal historian Michael Klarman writes, "The Fourteenth Amendment became the primary constitutional weapon wielded by the Supreme Court to strike down state-enforced segregation and discrimination" (Klarman, 2004). Without this reborn Federal Negative, Brown v. Board of Education (1954) and the Civil Rights Act of 1964 might have found no footing. In *The Bill of Rights: Creation and Reconstruction*, Akhil Reed Amar contends that incorporation through the Fourteenth Amendment ultimately achieved Madison's original vision—providing national safeguards for individual liberty against the dangers of local majoritarian abuse (Amar, 1998).

not in Congress, but—in the courts and in the quiet faith that the Union's Soul still holds.

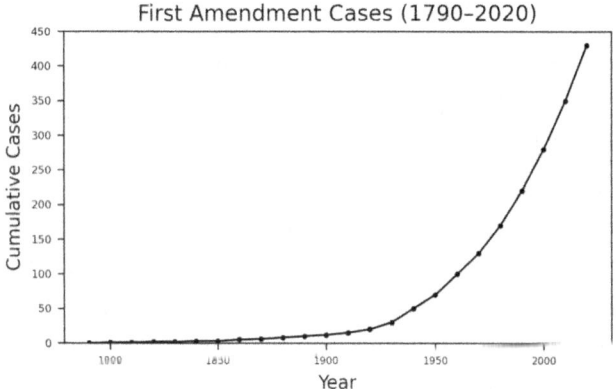

Figure 18. First Amendment Cases Reaching the Supreme Court. For generations, the First Amendment bound only Congress, but through the Fourteenth Amendment and the courts' incorporation, the amendment now binds each level of American government—not just the national but also the state and local governments (Perry, 2001). The steady rise in cases marks the moment the Union's promises truly became national—one Soul.

Set of the Soul

The Soul is a fitting metaphor, and one of my favorite poems is by Ella Wheeler Wilcox, an American poet born just five years after Appomattox. In *The Winds of Fate*, Wilcox gives us the image of two ships caught in the same wind but bound for different shores. The difference in the ships' journeys is not the gale but the set of their sails (Wilcox, 1916):

> *One ship drives east and another drives west*
> *With the self-same winds that blow;*
> *'Tis the set of the sails*
> *And not the gales*
> *That tells them the way to go.*

Into One Soul

> *Like the winds of the sea are the winds of fate*
> *As we voyage along through life;*
> *'Tis the set of the soul*
> *That decides its goal*
> *And not the calm or the strife.*

Wilcox's words remind us that for each storm we face—nullification, rebellion, riot, war—what matters most is the set of our Soul. The American Soul gives our republic its course, not the calm or the strife.

The ability of a sailing ship to move against the wind seems impossible at first glance. A boat cannot sail directly into the wind, but it can make headway in an upwind direction by tacking. This maneuver, fundamental to a seasoned sailor, shifts the boat's bow through the wind so that the sails catch the wind at an angle, usually about 45 degrees off the wind's direction.

From above, a sailboat tacking upwind carves a clear zigzag across the water, edging closer to the windward destination with each careful pivot. Each tack demands a fresh set of sails. The rigging must adjust with each turn to catch the wind just right. Sailing downwind is easy—one sail setting and the breeze does the rest. Yet upwind sailing is an art. This art takes skill, patience, and an unshakable sense of where one means to go. For a good skipper, the wind's push is not a limit, but a challenge.

Wilcox's lines hold up because they speak to this truth. The course is not set by the gale, but by the soul. Her metaphor holds for nations as well as people. The American Soul must tack into the winds of history. Our sails must be trimmed and reset each time the storms change direction—Shays's, 1968, January 6. If not, we drift.

Lincoln grasped this ability to sail into the winds of politics better than most. In his inaugural, he offered a steady hand to

The Art of the Compromise

a divided Union. At Gettysburg, he gave us the "why" for our sacrifice. Lincoln reminded us that our Soul must steer toward the Creed we claim—all men are created equal—and when storms of hate and faction threaten to blow us off course, we need leaders to steer us. We need Lincoln. We need Dr. King.

Our Soul turns the abstract promise of the Creed into something real. When rightly set, this Soul makes us wince at old injustices—slavery, segregation, second-class citizenship. The American Soul stirs that sick feeling when we know our actions fall short of our Founding words. The wind may blow where fate wills, but 'tis the set of the Soul that keeps us true.

In Sum

We as a nation almost ceased to exist. The Civil War nearly broke us. Yet we emerged from that crucible a different country—scarred, yes, but better for the sacrifice. We had begun to shed the sin of slavery, and the Union—the uniquely American experiment in popular self-government—had not perished from the Earth.

Lincoln grasped what was at stake when so many others had not. In December 1862, a month before he signed the Emancipation Proclamation, he sent Congress a message that still echoes today (Holzer, 2009):

> *In giving freedom to the slave, we assure freedom to the free—honorable alike in what we give, and what we preserve. We shall nobly save, or meanly lose, the last best hope of Earth.*

Lincoln knew that the struggle was not just about territory, tariffs, or the abstract right of secession. The Civil War was about power and principle. The South, cornered by its own numbers, could see the writing on the wall. The graphs in this chapter bear that out. Figure by figure, we see how the South

Into One Soul

lost its grip on the three branches of government: losing population share, losing seats in the House, losing the balance in the Senate, losing the Electoral College, and losing even the once-friendly bench of the Supreme Court. These losses were not abstractions; rather, they were hard truths that made the moral question of slavery unavoidable.

When the South could no longer win by the ballot box, it picked up its ball and went home, seceding from a democratic game it no longer controlled. The South did not secede because the North bullied them through overtaxation by tariffs or tyrannized them by some distant capital. The South seceded because they were losing. They seceded because the tide of numbers, votes, and moral courage was overtaking them at last.

Yet when the cannons cooled and the battlefields lay quiet, something remarkable rose from the ashes. The Fourteenth Amendment finished what the first shots of the War began. This powerful amendment transformed the Creed—*all men are created equal*—from parchment poetry into constitutional muscle. The amendment buried the old ghost of nullification by anchoring each American's rights in a single national guarantee. This addition to the Constitution told the nation that certain truths are not up for local tinkering or factional veto. Some things—like equality under law—stand above.

Madison, who had once dreamed of a Federal Negative to check state excesses, did not live to see this final safeguard. Yet in the Fourteenth Amendment and the long arc of constitutional law that flows from this change, his logic survived. Liberty would not rest on the shaky ground of local permission but would stand on a national floor. A stronger Union—one Soul, bound tighter than before. Lincoln's words still bind us, if we let them. *The last best hope of Earth* was never just a boast. The poetic phrase is a reminder that our American

The Art of the Compromise

experiment depends on the set of our national Soul. The winds of history will shift—factions will rise, storms will come, but as Wilcox's poem reminds us, *'Tis the set of the Soul that decides its goal, not the calm or the strife.*

The Union endured because Lincoln refused disunion. The same lesson applies within Congress itself. A minority cannot retreat from the table, nor can the majority abandon its opponents to silence. The Civil War taught—at terrible cost—that political responsibility means staying in the argument until the Union, and the Soul of the republic, finds its course.

Progress over paralysis.

Compromise over chaos.

Dialogue over departure.

Responsibility over retreat.

Engagement over evasion.

From that hard-earned lesson flowed the next challenge. With the Union saved in blood and principle, the question turned practical. How could so many voices keep contending without tearing the house apart again? America's answer was not to muzzle factions but to shape them into two enduring parties that give our discord form and direction. In the next chapter, we will see how this imperfect tool holds opposing truths in tension to keep the contradictions of the Many alive without breaking apart the Soul.

CHAPTER 3

Of Two Minds

"We may, therefore, experience a duality of consciousness—be more acutely 'of two minds'" writes philosopher James Blachowicz. In his 1998 book, *Of Two Minds: The Nature of Inquiry*, Blachowicz explores how we humans solve problems and expand our knowledge through an inner dialogue—what he calls our "inner speech"—that helps us discover, create, and solve the puzzles of our world (Blachowicz, 1998). The writer Jonah Lehrer, in his book *How We Decide*, describes this dialectical thinking as the mind "arguing with itself" (Lehrer, 2010).*

---

*Lehrer was publicly discredited in 2013 after revelations of falsification in his published work. Following an internal review, Houghton Mifflin Harcourt withdrew *How We Decide* from bookstores. Although the full review was never released, reports suggest sloppy journalistic practices—chiefly plagiarism—rather than flawed scientific claims (Alter, 2016). Skepticism toward the author is warranted, but dismissal of the work in full would be premature. Much of the

Of Two Minds

The dialogue within our minds is between two sides—not three, four, or five, but two. Whether by the direct hand of God or the invisible hand of evolution, this two-sided dialectic has become the pinnacle of creative reasoning on Earth. The human mind can differentiate and distill many possible solutions, parameters, conditions, factors, and possibilities into an inner dialogue between two opposing sides, and we do this remarkable work with little to no conscious effort. The human world around us—airplanes that defy gravity, poems that bring tears, medicines that cure diseases, machines that move mountains, stories that move souls—testifies to the power of the mind's two-sided approach to solving problems.

James Madison argued that ambition must be made to counteract ambition. The two-party system performs that function in practice, turning faction into friction, and friction into force. A republic of Many cannot survive by silencing differences. The strength comes not from suppressing division, but from structuring difference—channeling opposition into form. Like the mind, the American system differentiates and distills a multitude of challenges into a dialogue between two competing coalitions: Republicans and Democrats. One might assume that other democracies in the modern world have adopted a similar two-party approach. Yet they have not.

Some democracies, such as Mexico and Japan,* follow de facto one-party rule, where a single political party dominates

---

book still offers useful insights and a thoughtful synthesis of decision science.

*Political scientist Marjorie Randon Hershey notes that Mexico and Japan are not strict one-party systems like the former Soviet Union or present-day China (Hershey, 2017). Instead, these democracies have slipped into extended periods of one-party rule through a government policy. Other democracies, especially in Europe, have multi-party approaches where three, four, or more political parties wrangle endlessly over competing ideas. Unfortunately, one-party systems offer little to no differentiation, and multi-party systems are not as well-suited for integration into workable compromises.

Thus, a puzzle exists. The U.S. has no formal rule dictating a two-party system or even the existence of parties at all. This puzzle—why the United States has only two major political parties despite no formal rule requiring them—was my own starting point for this chapter and, in many ways, for this entire book. I kept wondering how a nation as large and diverse as ours could distill countless competing ideas into just two sides, and was that distillation a good thing? That curiosity led me to thinkers like Blachowicz and Lehrer and, eventually, to the insight of F. Scott Fitzgerald.

F. Scott Fitzgerald

In his 1936 essay "The Crack-Up," F. Scott Fitzgerald wrote that "the test of a first-rate intelligence is the ability to hold two opposed ideas in the mind at the same time, and still retain the ability to function" (Fitzgerald, 2009). Fitzgerald's wisdom is that holding both sides—Red–Blue, Republican–Democrat, North–South, Conservative–Liberal—is the

---

confluence of circumstances rather than a dictum of political governance. James Madison would argue that such an imbalance reflects a structural failure—one large faction dominating where healthy competition should thrive.

essence of intelligence, and tolerating paradox is essential to clear thinking.

Science writers now suggest that Fitzgerald's paradox—balancing contradiction without collapse—may be the ultimate benchmark for artificial intelligence. A machine that could pass that test might claim kinship with human cognition (Sonderegger, 2018). Yet computer algorithms today fail. They cannot sustain two opposing "thoughts" without freezing into error. A program must exist in one decision state or the other; it cannot linger in between, without succumbing to the Blue Screen of Death.* The human mind, however, does so as a matter of course (Fernyhough, 2016).

Fitzgerald's insight also applies to the practical world of debate. Consider the high school Debate Clubs, where the bright students gathered. These contests have served as cerebral training grounds for critical thought (Jones, 1994). The premise is simple but demanding: participants have to be ready to argue either side of a resolution, regardless of personal conviction (Bartanen & Littlefield, 2013). At the flip of a coin, a student might defend a proposition or dismantle it. The exercise requires mental agility, a readiness to shift frames without losing coherence. Whether in the design of AI, the ritual of Debate Club, or Fitzgerald's own reflection, the mark of a first-rate intelligence lies in perceiving potential truth on both sides of a contradiction.

---

* The "Blue Screen of Death," once unique to Microsoft Windows, has become a universal icon for a total computer system failure (Himanen, 2010). To Microsoft's chagrin, the phrase now describes any fatal system error across the computing world.

The Art of the Compromise

Similarly, I argue in this book that the mark of a first-rate political system is the ability to simultaneously hold two opposed ideas in the public sphere and still retain the ability to govern. This ability is the essence of the American two-party system. Unlike the Soviet or Chinese political systems, where the diversity of political ideas must coalesce behind a single party—the public sphere entertains only a single viewpoint—or unlike the European model, where diverse ideas rarely coalesce and remain scattered across multiple parties—a cacophony of various viewpoints overwhelms the public sphere—the American two-party system focuses public debate into the two sides of an issue—and only two sides.

The two political parties dichotomously carve out their positions around issues. Like a high school debate, one party takes the affirmative position, "yes," and the other takes the negative, "no." The single party of the Soviet or Chinese systems, conversely, has only the "yes" side, while the multi-party systems of Europe have many sides: "yes," "no," "maybe," "sometimes," "only on Tuesday," and a myriad of other viewpoints. The single-party systems hold only one side of a debate in the public sphere—Fitzgerald would likely be unsatisfied—and the multi-party systems juggle multiple sides of the discussion—the crippled mind of the Biblical "I am Legion" comes to mind.* The former is efficient but lacks

---

*In the Christian Bible, Jesus encounters a man in the country of the Gerasenes, possessed by a multitude of demons. When asked his name, the man replies, "My name is Legion, for we are many" (Yancey & Stafford, 2024c). Perhaps aware of this parable, Fitzgerald chose to speak of two opposed ideas in the mind—never three, four, or a legion of conflicting voices. Cognitive research suggests that our minds employ dialogical thinking, an inner

diversity, while the latter sustains diversity but cripples decision-making. The Soviets and Chinese have little trouble imposing decisions (Mitter & Johnson, 2021), and the Europeans struggle to agree on anything (De Vries, 2020).

Political parties in America, on the other hand, come in twos. As we will see, this two-party system has dominated American politics for nearly two centuries. When the nation was founded, George Washington believed political parties to be antithetical to the Republic (Christmas, 2017), but James Madison contrarily believed that "in every political society, parties are unavoidable" (Kurland & Lerner).

Madison's view won the day, and the two-party system emerged organically, though never intentionally planned. In a 2012 interview with *Esquire*, Bill Clinton reflected on this unconventional American habit of being "of two minds," looking back on the first term of the Obama presidency. Clinton said (Pierce & Warren, 2012):

> *Americans—not just starting thirty years ago but going back to the beginning, when we were rebelling against King George—we've always been of two minds about the government...It was supposed to give us enough government to do whatever we needed to do...but keep us from having too much so as to choke us off in terms of either our liberties or economic freedom.*

"Of two minds" is the fabric of the American system of government. Strangely, the U.S. Constitution does not

---

conversation between two sides when making decisions (Fernyhough, 2016). When too many voices intrude on that dialogue, the result is confusion or paralysis, perhaps like the Gerasene man's torment.

The Art of the Compromise

mention political parties or explicitly define mechanisms for a two-party political system. Yet the emergence of two parties is the linchpin that has kept our large, diverse Republic together. This chapter reveals the hidden hand that has nudged our nation towards two parties, and we will see why the two-party system—as opposed to a single- or multi-party system—is crucial to our past success as a nation and our future progress. One feature locks this hidden hand in place—the Electoral College.

Electoral College

"I think it needs to be eliminated," said Hillary Clinton of the Electoral College (Merica, 2017). "I'd like to see us move beyond it, yes." She made the comment in a 2017 CNN interview with Anderson Cooper. Clinton had just lost the presidency to Donald Trump, and in her memoir, *What Happened* (Clinton, 2017), she listed abolishing the Electoral College among many explanations for her defeat.

Her book offers a litany of finger-pointing at various political actors she blamed for her loss, ranging from former FBI director James Comey to Russian President Vladimir Putin to fellow Democratic candidate Bernie Sanders to third-party candidate Jill Stein to even former President Barack Obama. Her comment to remove a Constitutional element in the Electoral College stands out.[*] While Clinton's motives come across

---

[*]Edward Klein, former editor-in-chief of the *New York Times Magazine* and contributing editor to *Vanity Fair*, wrote *Unlikable: The Problem with Hillary* in (2015), a year before her loss to Trump. Klein is a long-time antagonist of Hillary Clinton, having written several books that cast her in an unflattering light. He once published a

as sour grapes, her comment has had some staying power with editorials and special interests. A 2020 Gallup poll (Brenan, 2020) indicated that three in five Americans also favored amending the Constitution to replace the Electoral College.

The danger in misreading this apparent popularity is clear once we unpack the partisan split: 89 percent of Democrats favor abolition, standing with Clinton. In comparison, far fewer Republicans, at 23 percent, support amending the Constitution. This wide disparity in partisan viewpoints is a warning that the motives for change are more likely suitable for one party over another rather than good for America as a whole. They reflect not the spirit of compromise and consensus that shaped the Constitution but rather the raw whims of pure democracy, the Founders feared. The knee-jerk reaction to eliminate the Electoral College does not reflect the Art of the Compromise.

The Electoral College is a perplexing instrument in the Constitution. The particulars of the quirky twist for selecting Presidents require explanation, and the convoluted mechanism confuses many voters. If one is like me, one had to dust off lessons from my middle school civics class to unwind the nature of the Electoral College. In 2016, Clinton beat Trump in the popular vote by nearly three million votes, while Trump beat Clinton in the Electoral College vote—and thus won the Presidency—with a majority of 306 pledged electors

---

column recounting her private use of harsh profanity—words like "cocksucker," "motherfucker," and "bullshit." Despite Klein's fixation on Clinton's personal failings, his core thesis—that her political downfall owed much to her unlikeability—remains persuasive in light of her post-election blame game.

The Art of the Compromise

out of 538 (DeSilver, 2016).* Clinton won the popular vote; Trump won the Electoral College vote.

This inversion of the popular vote relative to the Electoral College has happened five times in our nation's history: Andrew Jackson lost the Presidency to John Quincy Adams in 1824, Samuel Tilden to Rutherford B. Hayes in 1876, Grover Cleveland to Benjamin Harrison in 1888, Al Gore to George W. Bush in 2000, and Hillary Clinton to Donald Trump in 2016. See Fig. 19, which covers the modern two-party period from 1860 to 2020.† As of 2024, the other 54 of the 59 total Presidential elections have had the popular vote in sync with the Electoral College vote. These numbers reveal that, although we like to think of the inversion as a rare event, in almost 10 percent of our Presidential elections, the Electoral College winner is not the popular vote winner.

The event is not as rare as our intuition leads us to believe, and calls for reform of the "evils" of the supposed relic from the Founders—such as the self-serving calls from Clinton—have occurred more than occasionally and are not new. Before jumping into the deep end and ditching the Electoral College based on these numbers, we would be wise to consider the sustained success of our Presidential system over those 59

---

*The final Electoral College vote in 2016 differs slightly from the pledged numbers due to "faithless" electors—members who do not vote for the candidate they pledged to support. This quirk deserves deeper exploration than I offer here. For a thorough treatment, see Robert Alexander's *Representation and the Electoral College (2019)* or Tara Ross's *Why We Need the Electoral College (2019)*.

†By 1860, with Lincoln's election, the two-party structure was effectively locked in, cementing the Republican Party as the principal rival to the Democrats, a configuration that endures to this day (Burnham, 1970; Key, 1955; Sundquist, 2011).

elections and nearly 250 years, despite the occasional quirk with this popular vote inversion.

John F. Kennedy, a Democrat stalwart and hero of the Clintons, had a more sober view of the Electoral College than Clinton. In 1956, then-Senator Kennedy took a long-term view when yet another Electoral College reform plan was circulating through Congress that year. Such reform plans come and go with the regularity of fashion trends.

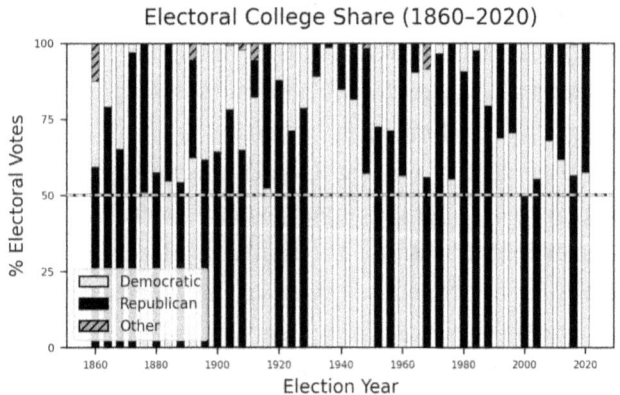

Figure 19. Presidential elections from 1860 to 2020 showing the Electoral College shares per candidate stacked vertically for each election. The largest vote getter is at the bottom, and the least is at the top. In each election shown, the winner secured more than 50% of the Electoral College vote, even in years when no candidate received a majority of the popular vote. This chart illustrates how the Electoral College produces a clear, decisive majority outcome where the popular vote might not. Data compiled from Kalb (2015) and Leip (2025).

Gary Bugh estimates in his book *Electoral College Reform: Challenges and Possibilities* (2016) that at least 772 amendments have been introduced since 1789 (almost four proposals each year) to abolish or change the Electoral College. None has passed. Senator Kennedy looked beyond this fad

The Art of the Compromise

and took the viewpoint of a sage to oppose the reform. "It is not only the unit vote for the Presidency we are talking about," Kennedy said in 1956 when talking about the Electoral College, "but a whole solar system of governmental power. If it is proposed to change the balance of power of one of the elements of the solar system, it is necessary to consider the others" (Kennedy, 1956).

Kennedy referred to the "unit vote," also known as "winner-take-all," meaning that whichever presidential candidate receives the most votes in a state also wins all of that state's Electoral votes. The unit vote is not a Constitutional rule, but as Robert Alexander and Tara Ross point out in their respective books, the practice has become inseparable from the Electoral College. Kennedy's comment reflects how the system's operation has not been fixed by design but has instead evolved organically.

Scholar Judith Best notes, "Our method of selecting a president is not entirely what the Framers of the Constitution envisioned in 1787. It has changed and developed in several ways, but it still is compatible with and supportive of the American idea of democracy" (Best, 2004). Kennedy focused on what served the nation; Clinton focused on what secured her own victory. Kennedy did not want to change the Electoral College or the evolved mechanism of the unit vote. Such perspectives distinguish the statesman Kennedy from the politician Clinton. As Senator Lloyd Bentsen might say, "Hillary is no Jack Kennedy."[*]

---

[*]During the 1988 presidential campaign, Senator Dan Quayle, the Republican vice presidential nominee, faced Senator Lloyd Bentsen, the Democrat, in a single televised debate. Vice presidential debates

Kennedy recognized the cascading domino effects across the inner connections and entwined interdependencies of the Electoral College to the broader American political structure. The narrow objective touted by Clinton and others in the quest for reform is usually a desire to achieve a purer democracy, where the call for "one person, one vote" is portrayed as a violation by the Electoral College. These critics are correct. The College does not follow pure democracy objectives.

"The political slogan 'all power to the people' is not one our Founders would have endorsed. Their slogan," writes scholar Judith Best, "was 'all power to no one,'* not even the numerical majority" (Best, 2004). The College follows

---

rarely matter much, but this one, writes Noah Bierman of the *Los Angeles Times*, "would go down as the most memorable in decades— a pop culture moment...because Bentsen landed a zinger that devastated Quayle and helped cement his reputation as a lightweight" (Bierman, 2016). Quayle, deflecting questions about his age—41 at the time—often compared himself to JFK. When the topic came up live, Bentsen was ready, "I served with Jack Kennedy. I knew Jack Kennedy. Jack Kennedy was a friend of mine. Senator, you're no Jack Kennedy." The line stung but did little to change the election outcome. It lives on as a political meme.

*Many folks are surprised to learn that "one person, one vote" is a relatively recent concept in the American system. On March 26, 1962, the Supreme Court issued its landmark ruling in *Baker v. Carr*, establishing that principle for the first time (Smith, 2014). Author J. Douglas Smith chronicles this little-known case—far less famous than *Roe v. Wade* or *Brown v. Board of Education*—and its political consequences in *On Democracy's Doorstep*. Before *Baker*, legislative boundaries in many states, especially Tennessee, where the case began, had gone unchanged for decades despite huge shifts in population. As urban populations grew while rural areas stagnated, the plaintiff argued that Tennessee's legislature unfairly favored rural voters. The imbalance meant roughly one-third of the state's mostly rural, white voters controlled two-thirds of its Congressional delegation.

The Art of the Compromise

republican—the political philosophy and not the party—objectives. Republicanism—again, the philosophy, not the party—is representative government by proxy. In contrast, a pure democracy has each citizen voting directly on each issue for themselves without intermediary representatives. The Electoral College is a republican mechanism.

Again, scholar Judith Best offers an interesting turn of phrase: "The infrastructure of the entire government is federal. No national governing decision of any kind in this country (including the ratification of the Constitution itself) has ever been made by adding votes across state lines" (Best, 2004). While the mathematical equality of one-person-one-vote has a nice ring to our democratic ears, the Founders rejected such mechanisms in favor of more republican approaches, such as the Electoral College.

The Founders studied democracies and their failures throughout history, and they discovered that pure democracies struggle to operate at the sizable geographic scale at which the United States operates. Pure democracies with one-person-one-vote break down at large scales. The Founders "opposed the uncompromised concentration of power," as columnist Author Cyr wrote in 2020, and the Founders, through the Constitution, set up a "complex network of institutions in which none was dominant, actually or potentially, by design" (Cyr, 2020). The Electoral College is a continuation of this network theme. The fact that we even talk about Red States and Blue States today is proof that indirect representation—geographically anchored and filtered through the Electoral College—still shapes our Republic's politics. Yet critics argue that a popular vote would better reflect the will of the people.

The Popular Vote

Lawyer and author Tara Ross, in *Enlightened Democracy: The Case for the Electoral College* (Ross, 2004) reviews the College's historical origins and convincingly argues why the Founders' 18th-century solution remains essential to our 21st-century republic.* In the foreword to Ross' book, the conservative columnist George Will states that the primary function of the Electoral College is to ensure that our system elects a President by a majority vote, not a plurality. Few American presidential elections have ever achieved a majority in the popular vote.

While five elections have had an inversion of the popular vote relative to the Electoral College vote since 1824 (when the popular vote was first fully recorded and reported), 19 elections have had the election or re-election of the President with a majority of the Electoral College vote but a mere plurality of the popular vote. See Fig. 20, which again illustrates the modern two-party period beginning in 1860 and shows the popular vote share across elections. In many contests, no candidate crosses the 50 percent threshold—the lower bar in each stacked pair remains below the majority line.

Thus, in 40 percent of the Presidential elections since 1824, the President has been elected with less than a majority of the popular vote, but the Electoral College gave these Presidents a majority of electoral votes. The chart in Fig. 21

---

*A common argument against the Electoral College is its age. Yet should age not be a strength? The wheel is among humanity's oldest inventions, and no one questions its usefulness. Age, by itself, is a weak argument.

The Art of the Compromise

combines the insights from Fig. 19 and Fig. 20 to emphasize the no-majority popular wins and the popular vote inversions. Bill Clinton, for example, never received a majority of the popular vote in either of his elections in 1992 or 1996. He won only through the Electoral College. The Electoral College balances the national popular vote of the people with the regional preferences of each state in a unique framework that harkens to the Great Compromise of a bicameral legislature, with the House representing the people and the Senate representing the states.

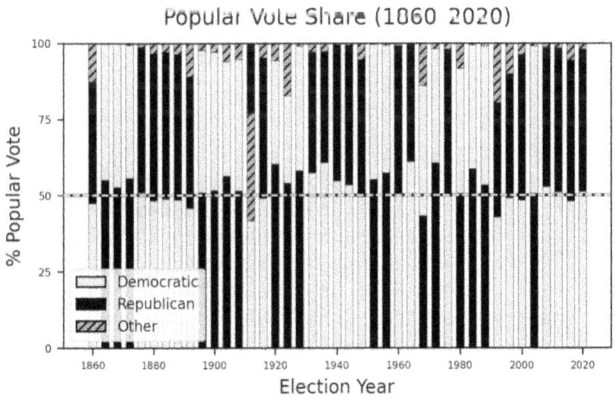

Figure 20. Presidential elections from 1860 to 2020 showing which elections resulted in a popular vote plurality (no candidate received more than 50% of the vote). The vertical bars are stacked by total votes, with the bottom bar representing the candidate who received the most votes. If that bar does not reach the 50% dotted line, then no majority winner exists. About one-third of these elections produced a President without a popular majority, illustrating how often the popular vote alone fails to deliver a clear mandate. Data compiled from Kalb (2015) and Leip (2025).

In 1992, Ross Perot won nearly 19 percent of the popular vote but carried no state and won no Electoral votes (McGee, 2020). By contrast, Bill Clinton won 43 percent of the popular

Of Two Minds

vote and captured nearly 70 percent of the Electoral votes, a whopping majority, perhaps even a mandate. The Electoral College rewards candidates with broad geographic and popular support.

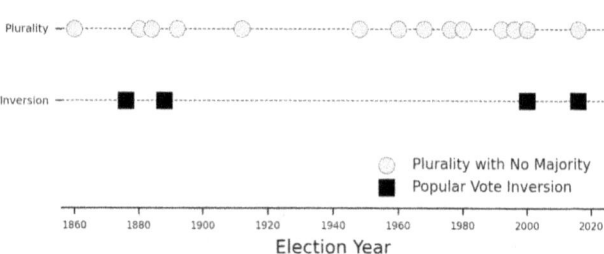

Figure 21. Presidential elections from 1860 to 2020 showing two key outcomes: when no candidate won a majority of the popular vote (plurality wins, top row) and when the Electoral College result did not match the popular vote winner (inversions, bottom row). The top row highlights elections where the President took office without most voters' support. The bottom row shows the rare instances where the College overrode the popular vote. Together, these outcomes reveal how the Electoral College transforms narrow or split votes into a clear national result, grounded in a majority selection process.

To win the College, a candidate cannot only be popular but must do so across multiple states. If we take Hillary Clinton's advice for a majority of the popular vote to dictate the Presidency, some scholars would argue that most of Perot's popular vote would have swung towards George H. W. Bush (the father, not the son), the Republican candidate in 1992. The Clintons could have faded into the footnotes of history with Bush achieving victory in a head-to-head runoff, though the what-ifs are complicated (Collins, 2019). Such runoffs are

The Art of the Compromise

necessary in a plurality system if majority rule becomes the foundation of Presidential elections.*

A common counterpoint contends that runoffs are unnecessary if a candidate secures a "super plurality." In Bill Clinton's case, one might reasonably suggest a 40-percent threshold would have prevented a runoff in 1992. Yet this counterfactual assumes rules can shift without altering voter behavior. As Tara Ross observes, new rules change how voters behave, especially strategic voters.† In the Perot example, more voters might have shifted to Perot if they knew a super plurality carried weight. In 1992, many commentators believed a vote for Perot was "wasted" because it helped Clinton. Under a super plurality scheme, however, voters might have cast their ballots differently—perhaps narrowing Clinton's margin and forcing a runoff.

This brings the irony into focus. Hillary Clinton's call to abolish the Electoral College—after losing the popular vote—overlooks how that same system cleared a path for Bill Clinton's win in 1992. The irony is thick.

---

*The Electoral College requires a majority vote of electors to select a President. If no candidate reaches a majority, the election goes to the House of Representatives, as it did in 1824 when Andrew Jackson lost to John Quincy Adams.

†Strategic voters may not choose their true first-choice candidate (Ross, 2004). Instead, they cast ballots to block an unwanted outcome when their preferred candidate cannot win. Such strategic voting is rare—or even non-existent—when two parties dominate.

The Three-Body Problem

Kennedy's solar system analogy now looms large. In physics, scientists have struggled for centuries with the "three-body problem"—the unpredictable orbits created when three celestial bodies interact (Musielak & Quarles, 2014).*

Physicists can construct a mathematical model to explain the inner connectedness of two celestial bodies—say the Sun and the Earth, for example, but if we include a third body—say the Moon or, in political terms, Ross Perot—into the model, scientists struggle to construct a mathematical model that predicts how three bodies interact together with their mutual gravitational interactions, as described by Newton's theory of gravity. Without a sufficient model, scientists cannot predict the behavior of celestial bodies interacting with one another through their respective gravitational forces, and small changes and perturbations have unpredictable consequences. If we throw in a fourth body, the modeling problems become even more complex and daunting.

The American electoral system may not be as complex as the inner workings of God's celestial universe, but the system is nonetheless complex. As Kennedy noted, changes—even small ones—are difficult to predict. Abolishing the Electoral College is not a small change, and abolishing it could lead to unpredictable changes—changes that may have meant Bill Clinton might have remained Governor of Arkansas in 1992.

---

*The concept is known in physics as the general three-body problem (Musielak & Quarles, 2014). For readers with a physics bent, Musielak and Quarles (2014) offer a clear review of its definition and a survey of both historical and modern developments.

The Art of the Compromise

Tara Ross further addresses the arguments for and against the Electoral College and refutes movements towards a national popular vote to replace the College. For those who believe the Electoral College is a relic of the past, I recommend reading Ross' book with an open mind and heeding Kennedy's advice. As she states in her book (Ross, 2004):

> The Founders did not create a system of checks and balances in the Constitution because they were worried about inadequate access to news or because the Internet hadn't been invented yet. They created constitutional protections because they knew that freedom would need to be protected from the flawed and imperfect nature of human beings. These concerns are as valid today as they were in 1787. The world may have changed, but the humans in it have not.

Ross argues that the same flaws—ambition, greed, and faction—still threaten self-government today.

> Ambition, power, and greed are still dangerous to self-government. Minorities still need to be protected. Rhode Island and Delaware are still smaller than their neighbors, and they still have unique interests that should be represented in the federal government. Moderation and compromise among federal officials and candidates are still beneficial. Americans still need a President who represents the variety of subcultures, regions, and industries that span the nation. The Electoral College ensures that presidential candidates develop a national base. They can't win if they are relying too heavily on specific regions or special interest groups.

With this impassioned plea in her book, Ross implores those "who are willing to look a little deeper" to understand the Electoral College better and thereby become defenders against the dangerous efforts to replace it.

While the ambition and greed of Trump are well known, Clinton's more subtle ambition and greed to change the

Electoral College to suit her election interests are not the statesman quality of Kennedy. The central theme of Ross's arguments is that the Electoral College is essential to forming and sustaining our strong two-party system. If we move away from the Electoral College, we will likely erode our two-party system and thus destroy our large, diverse republic. The Electoral College is the invisible hand that has formed and sustained the two-party political system of the United States and created the longest-lasting democracy in history.

We should not simply change the system because Clinton did not win. Nor should we change it because Trump won. Trump is no saint on the subject of the Electoral College either. In 2012 (Wang, 2016), Trump famously tweeted that "the electoral college is a disaster for a democracy!" Four years later, he conveniently flip-flopped after his 2016 victory when he tweeted, "The Electoral College is actually genius in that it brings all states, including the small ones, into play. Campaigning is much different" (Prokop, 2016).

Trump, too, has a self-serving view of the Electoral College because, without it, he easily loses the popular vote to Clinton. When we look at the 2016 election, we typically think of the breakdown in votes for Clinton, nearly 65.8 million, and for Trump, almost 62.9 million, a margin of almost three million in favor of Clinton (DeSilver, 2016). Supporters for change point out that Clinton won more votes and that this margin is significant. Three million votes question the legitimacy of Trump's Presidency.

In isolation, three million is a large number, but such calculus ignores that more than 62.9 million Americans voted for Trump, and over six million additional Americans voted for other third-party candidates such as Jill Stein—another Clinton nemesis. Thus, nearly 68.9 million Americans voted against Clinton, a margin of almost three million more votes

The Art of the Compromise

against her. The logic that the Electoral College should be changed because a three-million vote margin tainted Trump's Electoral College victory would equally apply that a three-million vote margin against Clinton would taint her popular vote. Clinton's plurality, with a three-million-vote deficit of a majority, fails a similar legitimacy test.

Clinton might have won a runoff against Trump, but again, such rules would have meant her husband would not have won in 1992. Without Bill Clinton winning, she would likely not have even been a candidate in 2016. "Oh, what a tangled web we weave," to quote Sir Walter Scott[*]—fitting words for the hidden forces that twist party fortunes.

Party Realignment

The Electoral College and the unit vote work as the quiet gears that scholars often name as the invisible hands shaping America's two-party system. Critics claim these parties stand frozen, stuck in old ruts and unable to adapt. That view misses the living reality. Republican and Democratic coalitions do shift—slowly, but steadily—shedding old ideas and absorbing new ones. This slow realignment is the core of the Art of the

---

[*]Sir Walter Scott wrote this famous line in his poem *Marmion*, published in 1808 (Scott, 2018). The complete phrase is, "Oh, what a tangled web we weave when first we practice to deceive." The quote illustrates how a single dishonest act can trigger a domino effect of complications that spiral out of control. My intent here is not to suggest that Hillary Clinton acted dishonestly, but rather to show that retroactively applying her wish to abolish the Electoral College would have created its own chain of unintended consequences, potentially including Bill Clinton never being elected in 1992.

Compromise and explains how two political giants keep a restless electorate stitched together.

Political scientists call this process *electoral realignment* (Ginsberg et al., 2019). Over time, realignment shifts the bedrock of each party—coalitions break apart, core ideas migrate, new issues enter, old ones fade. Since 1860, America has seen multiple major realignments that have remade the map of party loyalties again and again.

The figures that follow, Figs. 22–29,* trace this winding dance across American life. Each line on these charts—foreign policy, civil rights, immigration, regulation, trade, federal power, populism, culture—reveals how the two parties coil and uncoil like living snakes. They do not break and splinter into dozens of new factions as in Europe's multi-party systems. Instead, they shed old skins and grow new ones to adapt and survive.

The Civil War realignment established the Republican Party as the party of the Union and abolition, Fig. 27 (Key, 1955). By 1896, Republicans had shifted to become the party of business, Fig. 25, and industry, Fig. 26, while Democrats gathered rural populists, Fig. 28, and the agrarian South (Burnham, 1970). The New Deal and FDR upended this balance once more, pulling urban workers and immigrants, Fig. 24, into the Democratic fold (Sundquist, 2011). The civil rights battles, Fig. 23, of the 1960s fractured that coalition,

---

*These charts begin in the year 1900, when systematic data on issue alignment became more reliable. The Republican and Democratic parties assumed stable, enduring forms only after the Civil War and the late 19th-century realignments. Earlier data exist and generally follow the same trends, but the patterns are less distinct and harder to disentangle with confidence.

The Art of the Compromise

sending many Southern conservatives to the GOP (Black et al., 2009). The conservative realignment, Fig. 29, of the Reagan era brought suburban voters, evangelicals, and free-market champions under the Republican umbrella (Beck, 2003).

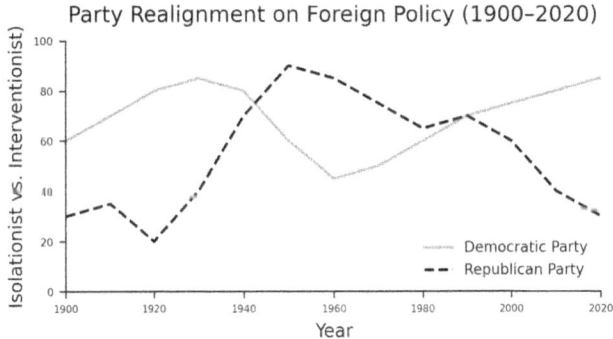

Figure 22. Party realignment on U.S. foreign policy, 1900–2020. Republicans shifted from isolationism to Cold War internationalism, then returned toward isolationist themes in recent decades. Democrats have largely held a multilateral, pro-engagement stance throughout. Data adapted from Ginsberg et al. (2019), Mead (2013), and Paterson et al. (1995).

This reshaping does not stop with economics or geography. Voters today might be surprised to learn that the Republican Party once stood as America's anti-war party, Fig. 22. In the early 20th century, Republicans called for isolationism, disarmament, and staunchly opposed entering World War II. Democrats, by contrast, led America into major conflicts under Wilson, Roosevelt, Truman, and Johnson. Republican presidents then ran on anti-war themes and oversaw American withdrawals from Korea and Vietnam.

By the century's end, both parties had shifted once again. Republicans increasingly favored foreign interventions—leading the Gulf Wars and Afghanistan—while Democrats leaned toward a smaller military footprint. These reversals on foreign policy reflect a broader tidal motion: over decades, the parties have swapped positions on urban elite support, religious identity, and cultural divides. This motion runs on an approximate fifty-year cycle (Ginsberg et al., 2019).

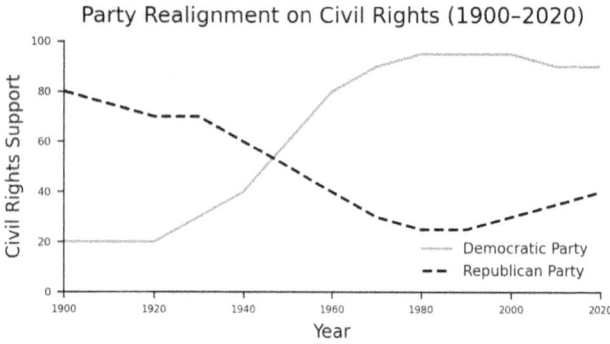

Figure 23. Party realignment on civil rights, 1900–2020. This chart traces how Democrats moved from defending segregation to championing civil rights, while many white conservatives shifted to the GOP. Data adapted from Sundquist (2011), Black et al. (2009), and Ginsberg et al. (2019).

Multi-party systems present voters with a wider spectrum of options, but rarely generate synthesis. Coalitions often form after elections, not before. Compromise arrives late, fragile in construction, and easily undone. In contrast, the American two-party system forces coalition-building ahead of elections—within primaries, conventions, and internal debates. Each party must blend discordant views into a common platform before facing the electorate. Failure to do so invites defeat. That pressure to unify early produces stronger outcomes and reveals the trade-offs made along the way (Sartori, 1997).

The Art of the Compromise

When coalitions fracture under a multi-party system, a successor party often rises from the split. The shell remains, but a new flag is raised, a new name adopted, a new identity constructed. European party systems adapt by shedding skin, casting off the past in search of a better fit, and in the process, sacrificing institutional continuity. Parties come and go like fashions, their fleeting cycles undermining lasting staying power.

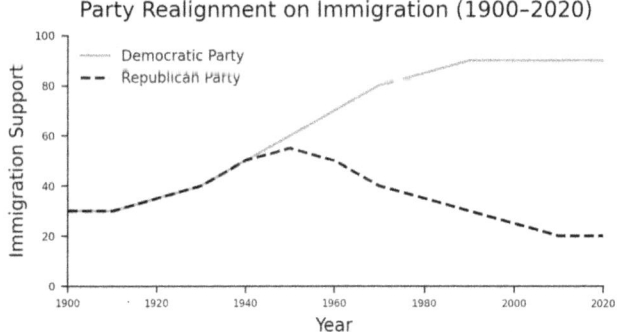

Figure 24. Party realignment on U.S. immigration policy, 1900–2020. Democrats shifted from early restrictionist positions to strong pro-immigration support, while Republicans moved from mid-century openness back toward restrictionism in recent decades. Data adapted from Ginsberg et al. (2019) and Tichenor (2002).

In America, the shell survives. Names rarely change. Institutions remain. Conflict is absorbed rather than expelled. The American party system forces reinvention from within. Factions must fight for dominance inside a common tent, not outside the party. Realignment happens not by rupture, but by redefinition. The shell holds because institutional memory persists—staff remain in place, donor networks stay intact, procedures require no retraining. A party rebrands from the inside—often clumsily, sometimes violently—but the infrastructure endures.

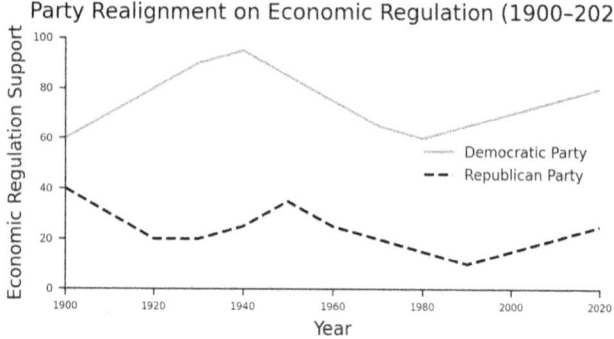

Figure 25. Party realignment on economic regulation, 1900–2020. Democrats historically backed progressive regulation, peaking with the New Deal, while Republicans shifted decisively toward deregulation and free-market policies after 1980. Data adapted from Ginsberg et al. (2019) and Skowronek (1982).

This ability to adapt without splitting explains why realignment reinforces party longevity rather than extinguishing it. In the United States, adaptation unfolds under familiar banners—Republican and Democrat—generation after generation. Such continuity remains rare in the democratic world. The defining feature is not merely the number of parties, but the fact that those parties endure—coiling, shedding, and twisting through history without fracturing into shards. That peculiar durability—like two snakes wrestling but never dying—prepares the ground for what comes next.

The deeper question is not how the parties change, but why they survive. That puzzle opens the next chapter: the power—and paradox—of America's two-party system.

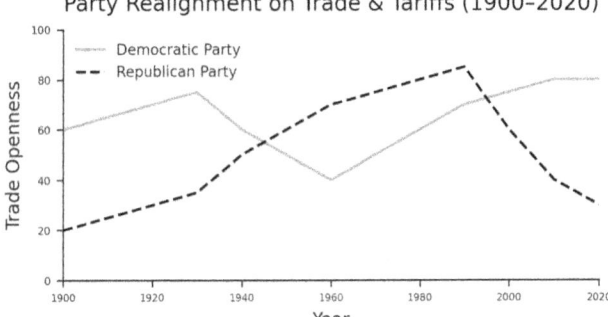

Figure 26. Party realignment on U.S. trade and tariffs, 1900–2020. Republicans shifted from early protectionism to mid-century free trade, then back toward protectionist rhetoric in recent decades. Democrats moved from promoting open trade for agrarian exports to supporting regulated free trade with labor protections. Data adapted from Ginsberg et al. (2019) and Irwin (2017).

Why Parties Endure

The Founders, especially George Washington, did not trust political parties and feared that factions—as they called them—would tear the young republic apart. They dreaded the "religious wars" (Christmas, 2017) that organized parties might spark. The Constitution omits any mention of parties not because the Framers were naïve but because they had seen parties fracture Britain's monarchy and breed corruption. In their view, a genuinely democratic republic would rise above factions.

Of Two Minds

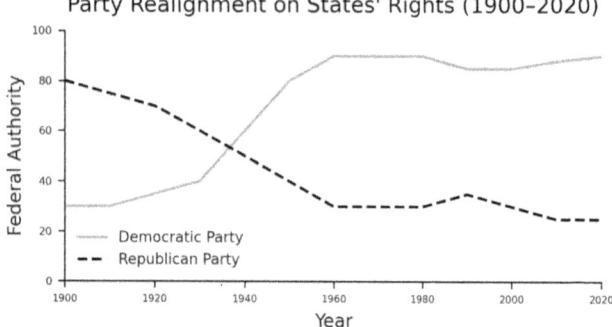

Figure 27. Party realignment on federal power vs. states' rights, 1900–2020. Democrats shifted from defending states' rights to championing strong federal authority, while Republicans moved from supporting federal supremacy during Reconstruction to defending states' rights from the New Deal onward. Data adapted from Ginsberg et al. (2019) and Sundquist (2011).

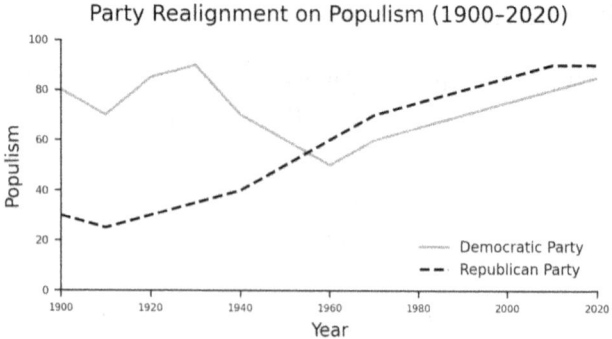

Figure 28. Party realignment on populism, 1900–2020. Democrats shifted from early populist roots to a mid-century elite focus, then revived progressive populism in recent decades. Republicans moved from representing business elites to embracing cultural populism in the late 20th century, culminating in the Trump-era surge. Data adapted from Ginsberg et al. (2019) and Kazin (1998).

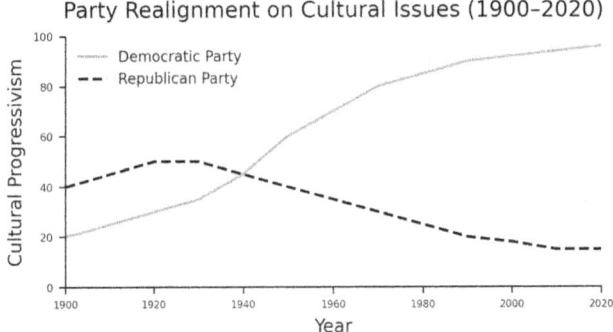

Figure 29. Party realignment on cultural issues, 1900–2020. Democrats shifted from traditionalism to strong progressivism on civil rights, gender, and identity. Republicans moved from early progressive reforms to a sustained defense of cultural conservatism. Data adapted from Ginsberg et al. (2019) and Kazin (1998).

The Founders were wrong. Their efforts to exclude parties from American democracy failed, and that failure proved fortunate. Political parties serve a vital role. They act as recognizable brands that lower the information costs for voters. Without parties, each voter would need to investigate each new candidate from scratch (Hershey, 2017). Parties give voters a reliable shortcut—a signal of where a candidate likely stands. The endurance of the United States as the world's most significant and longest-running democracy testifies to the power of these political brands.

Beyond anecdotes, the scholarly record shows how parties shape national success. Political scientist Marjorie Hershey (2017) documents how parties organize, recruit, and simplify democracy's chaos. More recently, Gerald Gamm and Thad Kousser examined each U.S. state from 1880 to 2010 and found that competition between strong parties improves economic and social well-being. They concluded that a healthy two-party rivalry is "central to the rise of the

American state and the flourishing of the American people" (Gamm & Kousser, 2010).

Despite frustrations with partisan bickering, parties are not the root of most modern dysfunction. Political scientist S.C. Stokes reminds us that "political parties are endemic to democracy" (Stokes, 1999). They are not written into most constitutions, yet they emerge naturally wherever free people organize.

The practical work of parties goes far beyond slogans. They recruit candidates, manage primaries, vet nominees, register voters, and get out the vote (O'Neill, 2017). Once in office, parties help elected officials coordinate and pass legislation—a difficult feat in a nation as vast and diverse as the United States. As Gamm and Kousser write, "the collective action necessary to pass [legislation] and put [it] into effect requires strong party organizations" (Gamm & Kousser, 2010). Long-lasting parties sustain the infrastructure that collective action demands. By contrast, parties that rise and fall with the shifting winds of political trends—as in many European multiparty systems—struggle to build and maintain such enduring institutional strength. Scholars find that new parties in Western Europe often last only 20 to 40 years before dissolving, merging, or rebranding (Bolleyer, 2013; Mair, 1990).*

Parties offer not only a *spatial* capacity to stitch together local efforts coast-to-coast but also a *temporal* capacity—

---

*Italy's political scene is the classic cautionary tale. Since the fall of the Christian Democrats in the early 1990s, parties have formed, fractured, and rebranded so often that some folks joke Italy holds elections mainly to rename parties rather than to govern (Pasquino, 2014).

The Art of the Compromise

linking generations under the same banner. The Democratic Party has existed since 1828; the Republican Party since 1854 (Christmas, 2017). Lincoln, FDR, JFK, and Reagan have passed, but their echoes shape today's debates. Continuity lends stability.

That continuity also demands Compromise. A party's machinery pressures members to align and coordinate. Discipline sometimes holds—consider the Republican Party's decades-long effort to reshape the Supreme Court (Zelizer, 2018). Yet discipline sometimes fractures, as seen when the Tea Party rose within the GOP in 2009, testing its boundaries and forcing internal compromises.

This balancing act is what sets large two-party systems apart from fragile multi-party coalitions. Small single-issue parties can splinter and fade with the political winds. By contrast, large parties must absorb clashing interests—merging them into one name, one umbrella, one *brand*. Multi-party systems, by contrast, show voters each crack. When disagreements emerge, splinter parties break off and form instead of compromising within the existing ones. The American two-party system masks these fissures behind big tents.

Without this masking function, small parties remain pure but brittle. They encourage extremes because compromise is optional—members can bolt and form new parties when compromise fails. Extremists can find shelter more easily in fragmented systems. Extremists struggle in large political parties.[*]

---

[*]The rise of extremists like Bernie Sanders (Klein, 2019) in the Democratic Party and Donald Trump—especially Trump (Harvin, 2023)—in the Republican Party are counterexamples of the moderating influence of America's two large political parties (Drutman,

Large parties force internal negotiation and reward coalitions broad enough to win. This built-in moderation is a hidden strength.

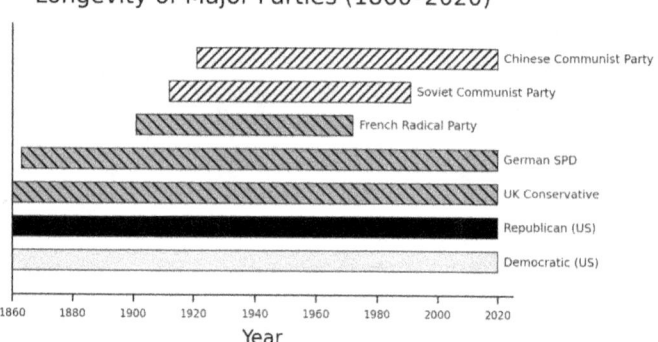

Figure 30. Longevity of major political parties across the globe from 1860 to 2020. This timeline compares the exceptional durability of the U.S. Democratic and Republican parties with major European and Communist parties, illustrating how only a few have maintained continuous dominance for over a century. Party dates adapted from Caramani (2017).

That strength is why major parties endure despite single-issue splinters that come and go. The Democratic Party, nearly two centuries old, is the oldest active political party in the world. The Republican Party is close behind, lasting more than 160 years and ranking just after Britain's Conservative Party, founded in 1834 (Christmas, 2017). Figure 30 shows

---

2018). While columnist Lee Drutman is pessimistic about the future of our two-party system to moderate extremism—he feels "we just got lucky" over the past 200 years of our Constitutional democracy—his insights are important not for his conclusions but for the symptoms he lists.

The Art of the Compromise

how unusual this durability is. Multi-party democracies rarely sustain dominant parties for generations. Communist systems maintain longevity only because their single party *is* the state.

E.E. Schattschneider wrote in 1942, "Modern democracy is unthinkable save in terms of parties" (Schattschneider, 1942). Therein lies the paradox the Founders missed. Parties divide, but they also unite. Partisan conflict can break a nation—as the Civil War showed—but healthy partisanship creates choice, competition, and the space for new ideas.

Madison never used the word "party" in *Federalist No. 51* (Madison, 2016), yet the famous phrase that he wrote, "Ambition must be made to counteract ambition," finds a living expression in our two-party system. He meant the branches would check each other, but the same principle holds true. One dominant party, as in the former Soviet Union or present-day China, leaves no rival force to restrain power. Too many parties, as in the democracies of Europe, scatter ambition so thinly that no single faction can build enough power to be worth checking. Two parties—our peculiar American balance, thanks to the Electoral College—gather just enough power to govern and enough to stand as rival guardians against each other.[*]

---

[*] "Ambition must be made to counteract ambition" stands among the most quoted lines in *The Federalist Papers*. Many read Madison's phrase as genius confined to balancing the branches alone. Yet the deeper brilliance connects *Federalist No. 10* and *Federalist No. 51*. A republic must extend the sphere to multiply factions, yet still channel rival ambitions into forces strong enough to check each other. The American two-party system became that unexpected vessel. The parchment framed the idea—parties gave the idea life.

The result is not static harmony but a perpetual contest. Like two prizefighters circling in the ring, each party is forced to regroup, adapt, and re-enter the fight when knocked down. Out of this rivalry comes the tension Madison trusted to keep ambition honest. One party smothers the counterweight. Many dissolve it. Two carry it forward—holding the ring, sustaining the battle. Such rivalry becomes Madison's *Federalist 51*, alive in practice.

This combative rhythm carries beyond politics into the American character itself. Walt Whitman captured the American habit of contradiction in *Song of Myself*:

> *Do I contradict myself?*
> *Very well then I contradict myself,*
> *(I am large, I contain multitudes.)*

Whitman's line speaks to the American mind but also to its parties—sprawling contradictions under one banner. This sprawling tension is no flaw. It sets the stage for something deeper: the ability to argue, distill, and integrate opposing ideas. The two-party system does not just hold factions together—it creates a durable vessel for what cognitive psychologists call integrative complexity to flourish.

Two enduring parties give Americans a stable framework for separating ideas, testing them, and weaving them into workable solutions. The core of how a healthy democracy manages conflict and compromise.

Integrative Complexity

At the heart of the Art of the Compromise is what psychologists call "integrative complexity," the mental habit of pulling opposed ideas into a stronger whole (recall Fig. 1). Integrative complexity describes how individuals process

The Art of the Compromise

information and make decisions. Political and social psychologists use the term to study the cognitive style behind human thinking—not the content of thoughts, but the mental process that holds opposing ideas and works to resolve them.

Peter Suedfeld and Philip Tetlock, in their 2014 summary article, show how integrative complexity is widely used to study leadership, diplomacy, conflict resolution, and decision-making (Suedfeld & Tetlock, 2014). In this book, I use the same idea as a practical framework for how compromise keeps American democracy strong.

Formally, integrative complexity means the mental capacity to develop and hold opposing ideas even amid ambiguity—and then to synthesize those tensions into a coherent solution. Crucially, this capacity involves more than choosing one side over the other; true complexity produces a synthesis stronger than either idea alone—what one might call an outside-the-box solution. Jim Collins, in his book *Good to Great*, describes such synthesis as the "Genius of the And." Great leaders refuse the easy either–or choice. They hold both dimensions—purpose and profit, continuity and change, freedom and responsibility—to find solutions that unite the extremes (Collins, 2001). The "Genius of the And" and high integrative complexity both aim for solutions that merge multiple dimensions into something novel.

Consider Abraham Lincoln as a statesman who exemplified the "Genius of the And." The synthesis remains easy to miss, in part because the path was subtle, improvised, and forged under pressure. From the outset, Lincoln framed his case not as a fiat of power, but as a legal and constitutional obligation. In his first inaugural, he argued that the Union was perpetual by design, that rebellion held no legal standing, and that the presidency required him to preserve the structure he had sworn to uphold. Lincoln remained faithful to the

Constitution while expanding executive authority beyond prior bounds. He suspended habeas corpus to contain rebellion, invoked emergency powers to preserve the Union, and issued the Emancipation Proclamation as a wartime act of necessity. Legal structure was not abandoned. Moral purpose did not override institutional design. Lincoln held both in tension—reconciling constitutional restraint with national survival. The fusion preserved the republic and redefined the presidency. That creative duality stands as a clear case of integrative complexity in action.

The level of integrative complexity depends on two variables: differentiation and integration. "Differentiation" is the ability to see distinct dimensions within an issue. "Integration" is the ability to connect them into a whole (Conway III et al., 2008). As Fig. 1 illustrates, the two-party system differentiates the People's interests into two sides. Then, Congress integrates those interests into political solutions through compromise. Differentiation requires the capacity and willingness to accept that an issue has more than one viewpoint and to acknowledge the legitimacy of those competing perspectives.

Fitzgerald's "opposed ideas" capture differentiation as the ability to move from one viewpoint to the opposite view while holding the resulting complexity together. Differentiation means drawing out the distinct elements of an issue rather than collapsing them into a blur. In politics, this may mean separating questions of state power from questions of individual liberty, or distinguishing economic arguments from cultural ones. In debate, it may mean isolating the strongest claim of an opponent before formulating a counter. In daily life, it may be as simple as weighing the short-term convenience of debt against the long-term burden of

The Art of the Compromise

repayment. Differentiation clarifies the strands so that integration later has material to work with.

The second element, "integration," is the ability to form conceptual links among viewpoints and weave those perspectives into a coherent whole. Differentiation is a prerequisite for integration. Congress is the seat of integration for our political system, and compromise is the primary mechanism for that integration. Today, our parties do well at creating strong differentiation in the first step of Fig. 1, but Congress often fails to integrate those ideas in the second step. Instead, Congress has fallen victim to what Jim Collins calls the "Tyranny of the Or" or what I call the "Tyranny of the Deal." Without sufficient integration, Congress simply selects one party's solution over the other's—whichever party holds the majority—so the Art of the Compromise stops working. The result is that solutions emerging from Congress lack high integrative complexity. They are not as good as they once were.

As Mihaly Csikszentmihalyi, the renowned professor of psychology at the University of Chicago, explains. When we say a system—or a thought—is complex, we mean it is differentiated, having many distinct parts, yet integrated, with those parts working smoothly together (Csikszentmihalyi, 1996). For example, a mechanical watch is a complex system with high differentiation and high integration. Refer to Fig. 31 for an illustration.

Gears, springs, lever arms, and other gadgetry synchronize in harmony to tick off each second of each minute of each hour. The parts work together as an integrated whole. By contrast, a well-differentiated but poorly integrated system is complicated but not truly complex. Such a system is chaotic and confusing. The same watch, disassembled and spread out on a table, is an obvious example of a well-differentiated system that lacks integration.

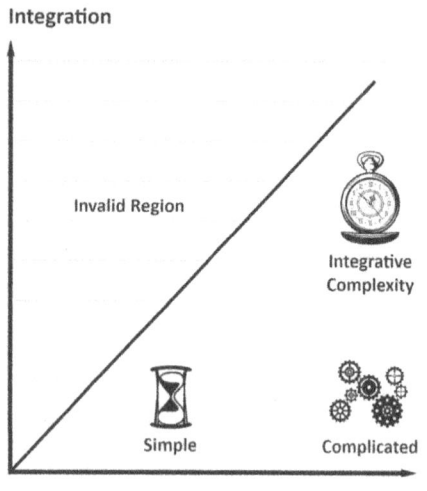

Figure 31. Visualization of integration (vertical axis) and differentiation (horizontal axis) for a timekeeping example. Limited differentiation and low integration lead to simple mechanisms like an hourglass in the lower left. Good differentiation with limited integration creates complicated arrangements, like a jumble of watch gears in the lower right. A well-differentiated and well-integrated system achieves true complexity, like a working watch in the upper right.

This simple example is instructive, as the jumble of parts would appear chaotic and confusing and would not be a functional timepiece. Similarly, a well-integrated system with limited differentiation* is also not complex. A sand-filled hourglass is an example of a simple timepiece with good integration but limited differentiation. The hourglass has a few parts, mainly the glass vessel and the sand, which work well

---

*Differentiation is necessary but not sufficient for integration. A system with no distinct parts has nothing to integrate.

The Art of Compromise

together. This simple solution does keep time up to a certain point, but the solution lacks complexity and is, therefore, rigid and redundant.

The "Invalid Region" of Fig. 31 indicates that differentiation is a prerequisite for integration. A system cannot have integration without some differentiation. For timekeeping, most folks would likely prefer a functioning assembled watch over a jumble of disassembled watch parts and even more over an hourglass to mark time. Differentiation and integration are necessary to achieve complexity, which is as significant in decision-making as in keeping time.

In extreme cases, low differentiation creates black-and-white thinking with little awareness of alternatives or tolerance for ambiguity. Black-and-white thinking, more formally called dichotomous thinking, sorts people, things, and actions into strict binaries—black or white, good or bad, right or wrong, friend or enemy, all or nothing. Such dichotomous thinking has little room for shades of gray. A person, for example, who thinks guns are evil and that gun owners are "bitter" and "cling" to their guns[*] out of desperation holds a cognitively simple viewpoint.

---

[*]In 2008, while running for the Democratic presidential nomination, Barack Obama infamously remarked, "And it's not surprising then they get bitter, they cling to guns or religion or antipathy toward people who aren't like them or anti-immigrant sentiment or anti-trade sentiment as a way to explain their frustrations" (Fowler, 2008). Speaking at a fundraiser in San Francisco, he was clumsily trying to explain why the Democratic Party was losing working-class votes. In doing so, Obama relied on the very dichotomous thinking he was attributing to Republican voters. The pot calling the kettle black?

Such rigidity ignores alternatives. Their viewpoint is rigid and leaves no room for flexibility. They cling to a few ideas and remain predictable in their one-dimensional thinking. The Tyranny of the Deal follows this same dichotomous thinking. The solution of one party must win out over the solution of the other. Republicans must win in Congress, and Democrats must lose, or vice versa.

By contrast, a person with higher differentiation would recognize the legitimacy of other viewpoints—seeing guns as evil but also seeing hunting as a legitimate use for them. Yet this differentiation alone, without linkage between perspectives, is low integration—like watch parts scattered on a table. Without integration, the differentiation has no center, no continuity. This person's opinions shift with the moment. They appear wishy-washy. The contradiction has no anchor. One might wonder if this person is pro-gun or anti-gun? Where do they stand? Such a person is complicated but not complex in their thinking.

Higher levels of integration bridge these separate views. A person with moderate integration might see guns as evil when used for murder, but legitimate for hunting. Their integrated thinking softens contradictions. As differentiation and integration increase together, the person's view grows more complex and less shallow.

On abortion, a person with little differentiation and integration might declare, "There's only one way to look at abortion. Plain and simple. Abortion is murder. No exceptions." The other side might declare, "There's only one way to look at abortion. My body. My choice. No one can tell me otherwise." While some might admire the resolve of such hard-line positions, this kind of thinking offers no workable path for a nation as large and diverse as the United States, where both sides of the abortion issue hold real and significant support.

The Art of the Compromise

A key point of this book is that individual citizens may hold such rigid views, but the nation cannot be governed that way. Congress must move beyond absolutes and pursue integrative complexity, as generations of politicians—including the Founding Fathers—have done.

Like the either-or choice in the Tyranny of the Deal, low differentiation and low integration in political thought create no real choice. Imagine if our modern world of financial transactions, mobile communications, and other time-sensitive systems had to rely on hourglasses for precision time. Complex thinking is necessary for complex problems, including guns, abortion, and other charged issues. Fortunately, the U.S. Constitution and our two-party system still allow this kind of integrative thinking at the national level, but not automatically. Our two parties do a fine job of differentiation. On major issues, we can usually guess where the GOP will stand and where the Democrats will line up. We can even predict the details each side will highlight. Yet too often, Congress fails to take those differentiated positions and weave them into a workable whole. That breakdown brings us back to the branch the Constitution built to do exactly that: integrate. Congress.

Watch Gears of Governance

Congress operates not in isolation, but as the integrating gear within a larger watch—one that keeps time not in seconds, but in decisions. Alexander Hamilton writes of the Legislative Branch in *Federalist No. 70* relative to their integrative capacities. "The differences in opinion, and the jarrings of parties," according to Hamilton, "promote deliberation and circumspection, and serve to check excesses in the majority" (Hamilton et al., 2015).

In Hamilton's language, the Legislative Branch is "best adapted to deliberation and wisdom." This deliberation slows the decision-making speed of Congress but deepens its capacity for differentiation and integration—the core of integrative complexity. Congress must integrate multiple differentiated viewpoints—435 in the House and 100 in the Senate, even though the two parties dominate these positions—to pass a resolution. Because Congress is a plural body, the integrative process demands compromise and consensus. Congress must struggle through debate and deliberation to produce true integration.

The slow nature of compromise is well known, and autocratic regimes like China often point to the plodding pace of democratic decisions as a crippling weakness. Professor Matthew Schousen, writing in *Time Magazine*, notes that gridlock is a baked-in design element of the U.S. Constitution (Schousen, 2018). Legislative decisions move slowly through Congress. As Hamilton writes in *Federalist No. 70*, the speed of decision-making "will generally characterize the proceedings of one man in a much more eminent degree than the proceedings of any greater number" (Hamilton et al., 2015). The 535 members of Congress require time to integrate. Integration takes more time within a group than with one person.

China's President Xi Jinping believes that the inability of the U.S. and other democracies to streamline their integrative decision-making will doom their existence in the next century (Stasavage, 2020). In May 2022, President Joe Biden recalled a conversation with Xi (Wong, 2023):

> *[President Xi] said democracies cannot be sustained in the 21st century; autocracies will run the world. Why? Things are changing so rapidly. Democracies require consensus, and it takes time, and you don't have the time.*

The Art of the Compromise

Xi believes that the integrative thinking, centered on his singular authority in his autocratic China, can help it move faster and make better political decisions than clumsy democracies like the U.S.

While Xi's observations expose the truth of gridlock, his comments lack understanding of the integrative complexity endowed by the U.S. Constitution and our two-party system. Our Executive Branch has the power to move fast within the confines of the Constitutional separation of powers and respond to emergency threats such as war, famine, and pandemics, but the deliberative nature of Congress can slow some decisions, such as taxation, spending, and civil liberties. In a 2020 article, Scholar David Stasavage analyzes the response to the COVID-19 pandemic, including comparing China and the U.S. relative to their respective authoritarian and democratic governments (Stasavage, 2020).

Stasavage's sober conclusions favor neither form of government, as each has advantages and drawbacks. He observes that autocracies can move fast but may conceal problems or silence dissent, while democracies trade speed for openness and responsiveness, accepting slower action as the cost of shared power. Stasavage echoes that autocracies have more integrative power, while democracies produce more differentiation. The Constitution's two-path design creates a tradeoff: the Executive Branch provides a fast path with less deliberation and less differentiation; the Legislative Branch provides a slower path with more deliberation but often less integration.

The tradeoffs between authoritarian and democratic systems of leadership rose to fame in the late 1930s through the experiments and writings of Kurt Lewin and his colleagues (Lewin & Lippitt, 1938; Lewin et al., 1939). Working with Ronald Lippitt and Ralph White, Lewin developed experiments involving ten-year-old boys under three different leadership styles: autocratic, democratic, and laissez-faire. The original purpose of the studies was to observe the resulting patterns of aggressive behavior from the various philosophies of leadership styles guiding the boys' work.

The conclusions on group cohesion, productivity, and creativity have become impactful findings. Lewin and his colleagues found that autocratic leadership, such as in China, generated the most significant productivity gains by the groups but tended to yield lower group satisfaction. On the other hand, democratic leadership, such as in the U.S., had more modest productivity gains but more favorable group satisfaction. Laissez-faire leadership, as one might expect, did poorly in both dimensions. In creativity, a less nuanced answer emerged. Democratic leadership tended to exhibit more creativity in outcomes than autocratic leadership, where the latter depended most on the leader's creative ability.

The Lewin experiments support the mixed style of leadership that the U.S. Constitution has created, with quasi-autocratic leadership in the President, who remains democratically elected, balanced by quasi-democratic leadership in the Congress, where elected representatives have the opportunity to generate solutions with high integrative complexity.

This same tradeoff appears when we map whole governments, not just leadership styles. Like a working watch, a functioning republic must balance high differentiation with high integration to keep time—political time. Figure 32 locates the United States, China, the Soviet Union, and Europe on this same chart. The U.S., when healthy, holds the upper right: many views, woven together. Autocracies like China maximize integration but suppress differentiation. Europe's multi-party systems often scatter widely but struggle to

The Art of the Compromise

weave back into one working mechanism. Put simply, where our political watch lands on this map explains why it still ticks.

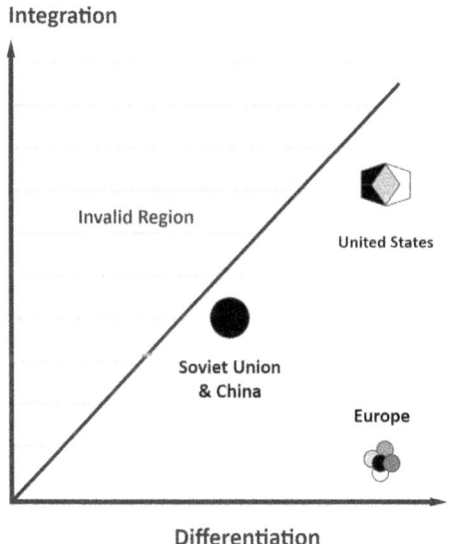

Figure 32. Visualization of integration (vertical axis) and differentiation (horizontal axis) for national systems of governance. The United States aims for high differentiation and high integration, placing it in the upper right: many voices, held together. China and the former Soviet Union sustain high integration but suppress differentiation, locating them in the middle left. Europe's multi-party systems maintain high differentiation but often struggle to integrate fully, placing them toward the lower right. A resilient democracy must be both well-differentiated and well-integrated, like a watch that keeps good time.

That ticking mechanism—the system's ability to hold many voices in tension—rests on a foundational insight from James Madison. Structure was not merely a safeguard but an engine for judgment.

A Comparison Engine

James Madison believed that factions could be weakened by scale. Extend the sphere of the republic—across geography, culture, and interest—and no single faction could dominate. The noise of Many would drown out the ambition of One. *Federalist No. 10* proposed a constitutional solution to a human pattern (Madison, 2016). Factions could not be eliminated, but they could be diluted. The theory required breadth: more voices, more variety, more distance between camps. Consolidation, not disagreement, posed the real threat.

With time, as the American Constitution was being formed, Madison adjusted that view as his theory gave way to practice. As the Constitution shifted from parchment to power, Madison also had to shift from fathering the Constitution to shepherding that document's practical implementation. The first challenge came from Alexander Hamilton. As we will discuss in a later chapter, Hamilton promoted a national bank in response to debates over national versus state debts. Hamilton's proposal would deepen financial centralization of the Union as he advocated policies that Madison feared tilted toward monarchy.

The clash marked more than a policy dispute. It fractured the Federalist vision itself. To check Hamilton's ascent, Madison aligned with Jefferson and helped form the Democratic–Republican Party—not as an endorsement of partisanship, but as a restraint upon it. (Ketcham, 1990). Madison sensed growing partisanship in the early days of the Constitution, and rather than assume a failure of his "extend the sphere" innovation, he succumbed to human nature and embraced the partisanship. He began to couch his politics as those individuals—like Hamilton—who were trying to contort the U.S. into a constitutional monarch, and the true republicans—like

The Art of the Compromise

himself and Thomas Jefferson—who were protectors of the people and the intent of the Constitution (Feldman, 2017).

Noah Feldman, in *The Three Lives of James Madison*, describes the moment as a turning point in Madison's political life (Feldman, 2017). The theorist of broad republican balance became the builder of a party. The scholar of factions became the partisan tactician. Madison did not abandon the principle of moderation, but rather he embraced a method of opposition. As the Federalists under Hamilton gained influence, Madison gathered his own influence. A party would answer a party. Conflict, when structured, could prevent collapse.

That instinct formed the foundation of the American two-party system. Not through labels, but through logic. Hamilton represented one vision for the republic. Madison stood for another. Both men drew from the same constitutional source, but pursued divergent ends. The new republic did not resolve the tension—it framed the tension. Notably, both men embraced the familiar partisan rhetoric known today: the other side is evil and out to destroy the nation. Their side, however? Each man's own political side and party were the true protectors of the "faith" and of the People. The result was contrast.

This contrast is one of the major theses of this book. That partisanship is ugly. Partisanship is dirty. Partisanship is mean-spirited. In an ideal world—the world that led Madison to theorize about constitutional mechanics of extending the sphere and establishing checks and balances—parties would be unnecessary as George Washington famously hoped. Yet, human nature in the real world cannot shrug off partisanship. Human systems inevitably devolve into partisanship—even the self-controlled, well-reasoned, and logic-bound James Madison could not resist the temptress of parties. In the end, human judgment thrives on contrast. Parties are necessary.

Behavioral science confirms the advantage of comparative reasoning through contrast. Daniel Kahneman and Amos Tversky demonstrated through Prospect Theory* that people evaluate outcomes relative to baselines, not absolutes (Kahneman & Tversky, 2013). Gains and losses feel

---

*Prospect Theory, developed by Daniel Kahneman and Amos Tversky in 1979, challenged the core assumptions of classical economic models (Kahneman & Tversky, 2013). Rather than making decisions based on expected utility and absolute outcomes, people evaluate choices relative to a reference point—typically the status quo or, in political terms, the opposing party. Losses loom larger than equivalent gains, creating an asymmetry in judgment known as loss aversion. Prospect Theory explains why individuals deviate from rational models when facing risk, uncertainty, or tradeoffs. The theory became a cornerstone of behavioral economics and laid the groundwork for later research on heuristics, framing effects, and bounded rationality.

A common example involves investment behavior. A person who gains $1,000 may feel modest satisfaction, but a $1,000 loss often provokes much stronger emotional distress. Yet the emotional impact depends on where the loss begins. A $1,000 drop from $1 million to $999,000 may barely register, but a $1,000 loss from $1,000 to zero feels catastrophic. The reference point—what the person thinks they have—matters more than the actual numbers. The comparison is asymmetric, and context defines the perceived loss.

In politics, the same cognitive mechanism helps explain the durability of two-party systems. With two clear reference points—the GOP and the Democrats—voters can anchor their preferences and evaluate change as gain or loss. A proposal from the other party is judged not in isolation, but relative to the voter's anchor, often as a loss. When one party is pro-abortion, the other party seizes the ground and becomes pro-life. That contrast sharpens decision-making. One-party systems, on the other hand, suppress such contrast, and multi-party systems scatter the contrast across too many axes. When choices multiply without a dominant frame of reference, the evaluative process breaks down. The two-party system, for all its flaws, aligns with how the human mind compares, judges, and chooses. Prospect Theory helps explain not only why the system polarizes, but why it persists and why it works better than other single- or multi-party systems.

The Art of the Compromise

larger or smaller depending on the surrounding context—the other party's viewpoint. Judgment lacks precision in isolation but sharpens in juxtaposition. Our two-party system generates these contrasts as each party—Republican and Democrat—sharpens its position relative to the other.

The Decoy Effect* in social science supports the same conclusion. When a third, inferior choice enters the mix, preferences between two better options shift dramatically (Huber et al., 1982). Value emerges through contrast. Even perception bends toward comparison. These arguments also

---

*The *Decoy Effect*, also known as *asymmetric dominance*, describes a shift in preference between two options when a third, less attractive option is introduced. The decoy holds no real appeal on its own—it exists to make one of the original choices appear more reasonable or valuable by comparison. This behavioral pattern contradicts the assumptions of rational choice theory (Kahneman & Tversky, 1986), particularly the principle of invariance, which holds that preferences should not shift when identical choices are presented in different forms (Von Neumann & Morgenstern, 1953). First demonstrated by Joel Huber, John Payne, and Christopher Puto in 1982, the effect reveals how context shapes perceived value and distorts decision-making (Huber et al., 1982).

A familiar example (Ariely, 2008) comes from a pricing strategy once used by *The Economist* magazine. Readers could subscribe to the online edition for $59, the print edition for $125, or both print and online access—also for $125. Almost no one chose the print-only option, yet its presence made the combined offer appear more valuable by contrast. The decoy increased demand for the bundled subscription without lowering prices or adding new content. The shift in preference came not from a change in product, but from a change in framing.

In American politics, minor parties often play a similar role. They rarely command majority appeal, yet their presence reframes the contest between Republicans and Democrats, making one major party appear more aligned with the splintered voters' concerns. In this way, the Decoy Effect helps explain how the two-party system absorbs small third-party movements rather than fracturing.

validate, in a subtle manner, why America's two-party system persists. The emergence of a third party can initiate the Decoy Effect, facilitating a hidden push of the electorate towards a similar dominant party, whether it be the Republican or Democratic Party that aligns with the new third party, acting as a functional decoy. The Republican or Democratic Party readily absorbs the new initiatives from the nascent third party, most similar to either of the two dominant party platforms.

Further support comes from social science research in the work of Antonio Damasio, who added another layer through neuroscience (Damasio, 2006). Emotion helps encode preference through somatic markers—bodily signals that guide decision-making. Reason alone rarely governs choice. Context, memory, and affect shape judgment long before logic arrives. Emotion often outweighs logic in decision-making, and our two-party structure has anticipated—by design or by instinct—the cognitive architecture that later science would confirm.

Two distinct visions—placed side by side—offer the mind a frame for reflection. A single directive, no matter how clear, invites skepticism. A balanced opposition invites deliberation, and three or more, especially more, viewpoints confuse and crowd our ability to compare and decide. Compromise does not begin with agreement. Compromise begins with recognition through contrast. Opposing ideas, when viewed honestly, create the conditions for judgment. Our Republic does not need a unanimous voice. Our Republic needs discernment. Clarity does not follow silence—it follows contrast.

Madison's embrace of partisanship did not mark a retreat from his ideals but rather a practical embrace of human nature. The shift reflected an understanding of how humans choose. Not through perfection. Through difference. A working republic depends on Congress weighing alternatives—

The Art of the Compromise

holding two visions in the public sphere and still functioning. Two minds. Two parties. Two frames. Each offering a different viewpoint. Madison did not demand a single answer. Madison demanded a choice.

Comparison is the engine. Not unanimity. Not purity. Comparison. The human mind is a comparison engine (Blachowicz, 1998). Madison may not have known dopamine from utility theory, but he knew the structure mattered. A single truth imposed from above does not produce consent. Yet two well-argued positions, in tension, allow Congress to weigh, deliberate, and choose. This "two minds" structure is not unity of opinion but unity of process. That insight forms the first step of integrative complexity. Before synthesis comes differentiation. To navigate a republic of factions, the Congress must first recognize opposing ideas—not as enemies, but as instruments of clarity. Contrast builds discernment. Deliberation depends on difference.

Our two-party system is not a failure of Madison's idealism, but a triumph of realism, which Madison himself came to understand. He saw what the human mind could bear. Not unanimity. Not purity. Comparison. Opposition, yes—but structured, visible, and bounded by rules. No compromise can be forged without known alternatives. The capacity to compare—to weigh two sides, to judge between alternatives—anchors the logic of the two-party system. What follows is not a weakness in design, but a test of function.

In Sum

When functioning well, our two-party system produces durable political solutions with high integrative complexity. The two parties differentiate the multitude of political ideas—the

Many—into two opposed sides, in the spirit of Fitzgerald's test of first-rate intelligence.

Where our system struggles today is not in differentiation but in integration. Congress was built to bring the nation's "two minds" together through the Art of the Compromise. Yet this integration cannot mean merely picking one party's idea over the other—the Tyranny of the Deal—nor can it mean simply splitting the difference down the middle. Jim Collins warns in *Built to Last* of the danger in compromises that drift to "the midpoint, fifty-fifty, half and half" (Collins et al., 2005).

History offers a sharper warning still. When King Solomon faced two women, each claiming to be the mother of the same child, he proposed to cut the infant in half and give each woman a share (Yancey & Stafford, 2024b). The one who was not the mother agreed; the true mother recoiled, preferring to lose her claim rather than see the child destroyed. Solomon's test revealed what was real and what was counterfeit. No one wants half a baby. A false compromise can destroy the very thing it seeks to preserve. Likewise, we cannot settle for a mushy midpoint between individual freedom and personal responsibility—an empty no man's land—but must instead build a nation where citizens are both free and responsible.

Meet-in-the-middle is not the goal. When our system works as designed, it finds a way to hold both extremes at once. Instead of choosing **A** *or* **B**, the best solutions embrace **A** *and* **B**: freedom and responsibility, liberty and equality, faith and reason, order and dissent, tradition and progress, security and privacy, individual rights and collective justice. While individual citizens may think in "or" solutions, Congress must think in "and" solutions.

The Constitution's promise—that "all men are created equal"—demands continual synthesis. The "Genius of the

The Art of the Compromise

And" and the Art of the Compromise are not merely political habits, but a national commitment to high integrative complexity. These principles hold the Republic together through seemingly irreconcilable tensions: Republican and Democrat, conservative and liberal, urban and rural, Red States and Blue States, believers and skeptics, immigrants and native-born, elites and populists, hawks and doves—held together, Out of Many, One. A republic made resilient by the "Genius of the And."

Two minds alone, however, are not enough. They must meet, clash, and fuse. Out of difference emerge solutions strong enough to endure—not by halving the distance between sides, but by forging something entirely new. The next chapter explores how real compromise works—not an easy surrender, but an artful collision.

Integrative complexity explains how individuals and institutions can hold conflict without collapse. Yet not every complexity yields a breakthrough. Many compromises aim for balance and stop short of transformation. Political creativity demands more than moderation. Real change begins with the collision of worldviews and ends in a synthesis drawn from opposing truths. That rare kind of resolution marks the next step in the journey. The Art of the Bisociated Compromise.

CHAPTER 4

With Compromise

THE FINAL STEP FROM "Many to One" in the Art of the Compromise fuses our two opposing parties' differentiated viewpoints into sustainable political solutions. In recent decades, however, our political system has faltered in producing compromises that endure beyond a single election cycle. Congress passes legislation one year, only to see that work undone the next when power shifts hands. This Tyranny of the Deal churns out brittle solutions that collapse with each new majority. We have drifted from the path. We must return to an environment where compromise is not only possible but expected—where Congress shapes durable resolutions instead of endless skirmishes.

Half a Loaf

"I have always figured that half a loaf is better than none." This wisdom of Ronald Reagan on the value of compromise came in response to a question in 1983 from Ed Lecius of commercial broadcast WSMN, 1590 kHz on the AM radio dial, out of Nashua, New Hampshire (Reagan, 1983). Early in Reagan's

With Compromise

first term, he struggled to follow through on his promised economic agenda and tax reform.

Lecius keyed into this feeling that Reagan was moving away from the policies and principles that got him elected. Reagan's full response reveals his deeper view of compromise as the practical path to achieve his goals.

> *I'm not retreating an inch from where I was. But I also recognize this: There are some people who would have you so stand on principle that if you don't get all that you've asked for from the legislature, why, you jump off the cliff with the flag flying.*
>
> *I have always figured that a half a loaf is better than none, and I know that in the democratic process you're not going to always get everything you want. So, I think what they've misread is times in which I have compromised—for example, our entire economic program.*

Reagan hardly sounds like the hardline, no-compromise right-winger that cable news outlets portray him to be today. Reagan understood the Art of the Compromise over the Tyranny of the Deal.

In 1981, Reagan took office with a divided government. Republicans controlled the Senate, but Democrats, led by Speaker Thomas "Tip" O'Neill, controlled the House of Representatives. Working with O'Neill in a publicly contentious but privately cordial relationship, Reagan pushed the tax and domestic spending cuts outlined in Reagan's response to Lecius above. The divided government under Reagan and O'Neill also found an uneasy compromise for massive deregulation and increased defense spending within the 97th session of Congress from 1981 to 1983. Beyond that session, Reagan and O'Neill continued to build compromises for landmark tax reform, comprehensive immigration reform, and Social Security reform.

The Art of the Compromise

In public, Reagan and O'Neill were well known to trade barbs as each had profound philosophical disagreements on the role of government. Reagan saw government as the problem; O'Neill saw it as the solution. As Martin Tolchin noted in *The New York Times*, O'Neill found the President "appallingly ignorant of the intricacies of government; indeed, he called him the most ignorant man who had ever occupied the White House" (Tolchin, 1994). As for Reagan, he once compared the Speaker to the then-popular Pac-Man game as "a round thing that gobbles up money" (O'Neill, 2012).

These barbs hardly sound like friends and would fit right in on today's cable news. What is different about the relationship between Reagan and O'Neill is not that they were cordial in private—though such civility likely parlayed into joint political success—but they both hated the inaction of political stalemates. The President and the Speaker differed profoundly on issues, yet they found ways to work together for the country's good.

In a 2012 opinion article entitled "Frenemies: A Love Story," O'Neill's son writes about the unique political relationship between Reagan and his father. He argues that today, rose-colored glasses, with a growing popularity and a sentimental tinge, have tainted a retrospective view of the Reagan–O'Neill relationship. He does not remember his father and Reagan being as cordial as history has portrayed them. He writes, "A misty aura has grown around the O'Neill and Reagan years. That mist obscures some hard truths—and harder words" (O'Neill, 2012).

No love was lost between the two men as their dueling philosophies of government played out throughout the 1980s. The tax and spend compromises of the 97th Congress were "among the most bruising my father and Reagan ever had," writes the younger O'Neill. While many look back at Reagan and O'Neill with nostalgia (including this book and me), the younger O'Neill points out that the two men were no different from the bitter rivalries we see today in politics, except for one trait—the willingness to compromise.

O'Neill's son offers invaluable insight that illuminates the lesson of compromise and the "frenemies" relationship between Reagan and O'Neill. Despite having nearly opposite political views and a willingness to publicly name-call one another, both men had a commitment to America that was more significant than their personal beliefs and party loyalty. The son writes (O'Neill, 2012):

> *What both men deplored more than the other's political philosophy was stalemate, and a country that was so polarized by ideology and party politics that it could not move forward. There were tough words and important disagreements over everything from taxation to Medicare and military spending. But there was yet a stronger commitment to getting things done.*

Country over party. In recent years, we have seen a similar dislike between opposing leaders. We have watched pairs like Obama–Boehner or Trump–Pelosi trade the same jabs Reagan and O'Neill once did, but without the will to get things done. Party has overtaken country. The Tyranny of the Deal has overtaken the Art of the Compromise.

Bisociated Compromise

Reagan's sentiment was to implore the need for compromise, but one must be careful to seek the right compromise. While half of a loaf is better than no loaf, is half of a baby better than no baby? These metaphors highlight the challenge of compromise and why leadership guru Jim Collins argues against framing compromises as merely finding a balance between two

The Art of the Compromise

opposing sides, moving to the midpoint, or cutting in half. A more nuanced approach to compromise is necessary.

Veteran FBI negotiator Chris Voss advises in his book on negotiating to never split the difference (Voss & Raz, 2016).* A couple debating whether to have a child shows why. One spouse wants a baby; the other does not. Half a baby is nonsense—and forcing either outcome risks resentment. A child born into a family where one parent is not fully committed is a bad start. Half a baby does not work. A different solution— say, adopting a dog—might honor both viewpoints. It's not half a baby, nor a forced win for either side, but a new, shared path. This approach is not splitting the difference but finding a third way, and is the essence of what I call a *bisociated compromise*.

The term *bisociated* comes from Arthur Koestler's classic book, *The Act of Creation* (Koestler, 1964). He saw creativity—in science, humor, or politics—as the clash of two frames that do not naturally fit together. With that clash comes something new. Unlike simple "either–or" logic, bisociation works in more than one plane at once, fusing ideas into something

---

*Unfortunately, Voss argues never to compromise. He cites Bill Hoest's 1970s cartoon *The Lockhorns*, where the husband suggests, "Let's compromise...That way we'll both be angry." Yet context matters. Voss built his career in hostage negotiations, not legislative chambers. His real warning is not against compromise itself, but against the lazy reflex to split the difference—a "half-baby" outcome that satisfies neither side and leaves room for exploitation (Voss & Raz, 2016). When one party bargains in good faith and the other does not, compromise becomes capitulation. Neville Chamberlain's 1938 bargain with Hitler stands as the textbook case (Bouverie, 2020). That lesson, however, belongs to life-and-death diplomacy, not to Republican–Democrat debates over healthcare or fiscal policy.

With Compromise

new. Not a watered-down blend but a fusion that reshapes both sides—a pet dog rather than a baby.

This creative blending is what our politics needs. The U.S. Constitution itself rests on a bisociated compromise: the "Great Compromise" that formed our bicameral Congress. Large states wanted representation by population; small states wanted equal representation. The compromise did not simply split the difference—it created two chambers, the House by population and the Senate by equality.

A simple diagram in Fig. 33 illustrates the bisociation concept. On the left, we see two viewpoints, **A** and **B**, that are undifferentiated and lack reference for compromise. We might think of these viewpoints as one person holding an opinion on raising taxes and a second holding an opinion on building a new monument. Little to no differentiation exists. A meet-in-the-middle compromise is point **C'**, which floats unanchored between **A** and **B**. The plane that contains **A**, **B**, and **C'** is arbitrary and satisfies neither party.

In the right-hand pane, we see the two viewpoints fully differentiated. Debates have clarified the issues, tradeoffs, and dimensions that shape each side's acceptable solutions—unlike the arbitrary plane on the left. The shaded planes show this richer context. Within these planes, individuals can now integrate their positions and land on a compromise point, **C**. Unlike the hollow midpoint, the new point **C** is anchored in the shared interests of both **A** and **B**, making the solution acceptable to both parties.

The Art of the Compromise

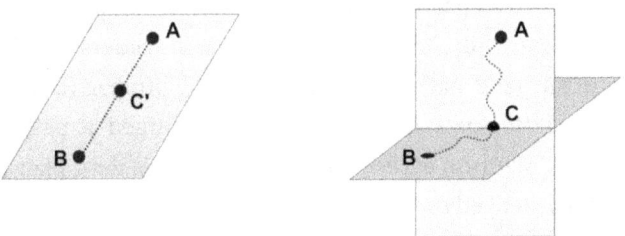

Figure 33. Two different compromise solutions between viewpoints **A** and **B**. On the left, **C'** shows a simple meet-in-the-middle compromise with little differentiation or integration. On the right, **C** illustrates a bisociated compromise, anchored in differentiated planes and integrated paths.

When no integration occurs, the result mirrors the left-hand diagram: a single, arbitrary plane with a superficial intersection point **C'**. That flat surface contains neither party's full solution space. The compromise appears shared, but the structure beneath is hollow. In contrast, the right-hand diagram shows two distinct planes, each representing the full frame of reference for one side. The shared solution point **C** emerges not from erasure, but from overlap. Each plane bends just enough to intersect. In politics, when that intersection fails to form, debate stalls. Lawmakers speak past each other, grounded in differentiated positions but unable—or unwilling—to construct shared coordinates. Bisociated compromise does not emerge from proximity alone. Shared space must become shared structure. Without that, the geometry collapses into gridlock.

The abstract structure just described found real expression in one of the earliest and most enduring political compromises in American history. Charles Cerami, in *Dinner at Mr. Jefferson's* (Cerami, 2008), tells how Jefferson, Hamilton, and Madison struck a landmark deal over dinner in 1790. Hamilton needed Congress to assume state debts to restore public credit (**A**)—a step Southerners like Madison and Jefferson opposed. Meanwhile, Madison and Southern leaders sought to secure the new national capital on the Potomac (**B**). Over wine at Jefferson's quarters, the three forged a path forward (**C**). Madison agreed to back Hamilton's debt plan, and Hamilton pledged to help deliver the Potomac location for the capital. The Compromise of 1790 did not merely split the difference; but rather, Hamilton and Madison fused two separate disputes into one creative resolution.

Historian Joseph Ellis calls the Compromise of 1790 "one of the landmark accommodations in American politics" (Ellis, 2002). The dinner deal showed how the young Constitutional system could differentiate clashing interests and weave them into a workable whole. Such bisociated compromises demand more than simple horse-trading—they are rare but remain the real measure of American democracy's strength.

Bisociated compromise should not be mistaken for concession. Concession ends in subtraction—one side yields ground to avoid conflict. Bisociation produces addition. A new solution enters the frame, forged from tension rather than erasure. Neither party walks away with full victory, but neither returns diminished. The conflict reshapes the possibilities. What seemed incompatible gives rise to something neither side imagined alone. That achievement is the difference between surrender and synthesis.

Franklin Roosevelt, decades later, faced a similar challenge. Could one President forge a compromise strong enough to bind rival factions, outlast the moment, and anchor a divided nation for generations?

The Art of the Compromise

Roosevelt's Bridge

By the summer of 1935, Franklin Roosevelt faced the same fear he had named so plainly at his first inauguration—fear that freezes a nation's will and turns hope inward (Kennedy, 1999). The Great Depression had turned household savings to ash, left state relief coffers barren, and forced Americans to admit that no patchwork of charities or local aid could stand alone against an industrial economy in collapse (Brinkley, 1996). Roosevelt could have rammed a national plan through on sheer party muscle, leaning on his massive Democratic majorities. Yet he understood that paper majorities would not hold if the plan itself could not stand once the celebration faded.

The political risk ran deeper than a divided Congress. Roosevelt's own majorities were not the only obstacle. A deeply conservative Supreme Court was swinging its axe at the New Deal's early experiments—striking down the National Industrial Recovery Act, gutting the Agricultural Adjustment Act, and threatening programs that smelled of federal reach into state powers or local markets. Opposition leaders in the Republican ranks denounced Social Security as a back door to European-style socialism (Leuchtenburg, 1963). Some Southern Democrats, powerful in the committees that could kill most bills, threatened to abandon Roosevelt entirely if the plan reached into farm labor or domestic service—sectors where racial and economic politics made unity fragile (Altman & Kingson, 2015). Roosevelt knew the votes were there if he forced the issue. He could apply the Tyranny of the Deal. He had the votes. He also knew a fragile plan would not outlast its moment.

So he chose a harder path—compromising on structure but holding firm on principle (Kennedy, 1999). Social Security

With Compromise

would not arrive as a direct grant from Washington, nor as a federal charity. Instead, workers would see money deducted from each paycheck. The program rested on Congress's clear power to tax, not on new and untested claims of federal dominion over economic life (Steuerle, 2008). To keep Midwestern conservatives and Southern Democrats at the table, Roosevelt's team carved out agricultural and domestic workers. The exclusions were unjust with racial and gender bias, but they were calculated to preserve fragile support. The resulting compromise, imperfect in moral reach, was designed for political survival against the next court challenge, the next Congress, and the next wave of reaction.

When the final roll call came, the coalition behind Social Security was broad enough to anchor the promise for generations. As shown in Fig. 34, nearly ninety percent of House Democrats voted in favor, joined by eighty percent of Republicans, four-fifths of their caucus. The Senate vote reflected the same durable mix of support. The design worked. Other New Deal programs fell to the Supreme Court's hammer or faded under later majorities hostile to federal intervention (Altman, 2012; Steuerle, 2008). Yet Social Security grew. Congress expanded its reach in 1939, adding survivors' benefits, disability insurance, and, later, Medicare. The pattern shown in Fig. 35 demonstrates this durability in cold numbers. Attempts to dismantle the program rose and fell with changing tides. Even Barry Goldwater's blunt promise to tear it down helped bury his presidential bid in 1964 (Branch, 2007). No serious repeal of Social Security has survived.

The Art of the Compromise

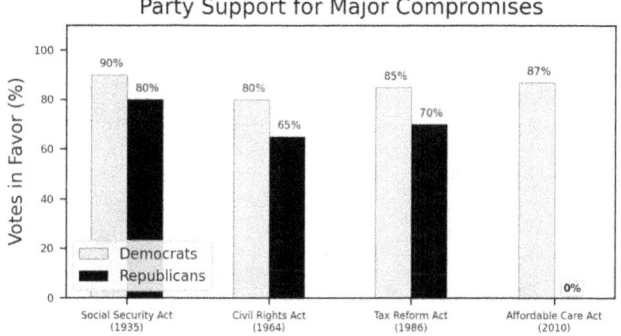

Figure 34. Party support for landmark laws: Social Security Act (1935), Civil Rights Act (1964), Tax Reform Act (1986), Affordable Care Act (2010). The first three laws represent bipartisan support resulting from bisociated compromises—*The Art of the Compromise*. Yet the final law represents a one-sided vote with no compromise—The Tyranny of the Deal. Data compiled from Caro (2002), Murray and Birnbaum (1988), and Obama (2020).

The lesson is written in roll calls and decades. A compromise that merely splits the difference breaks apart when the wind shifts. A true compromise binds the opposition within the promise itself, anchoring the compromise in both camps. Social Security's bridge still holds because both parties poured concrete under its piers. The Art of the Compromise is not just a handshake across an aisle—it is the patient craft of building structures that outlive the builders.

The historical record, born out in the figure plots, makes the pattern unmistakable. When the presidency and Congress stay engaged in the work of bridging factions, compromise endures—anchored by coalitions broad enough to make reversal politically dangerous. When that engagement lapses, fractures appear at once. The Obama years brought the next test. Both executive and legislative ground shifted, and the country was reminded—yet again—that without sustained engagement, even the strongest compromises grow fragile.

With Compromise

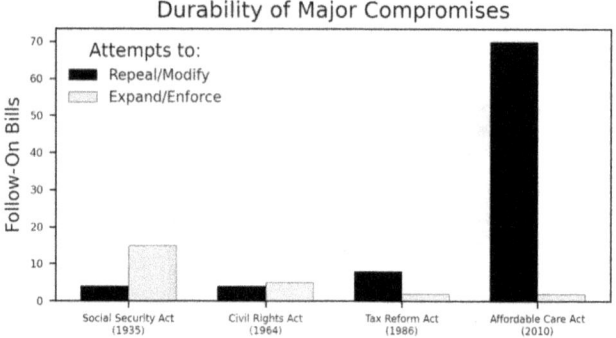

Figure 35. Follow-On Legislative Attempts: Erode vs. Expand Major Compromises. Major repeal or expansion efforts for the same landmark laws over time. Data drawn from Altman (2005), Altman (2012), Branch (2007), Murray and Birnbaum (1988), Steuerle (2004), Steuerle (2008), Klein (2020), and Congressional Budget Office reports.

The Regret of Obama

"What I can say is maybe if I had the genius of an Abraham Lincoln or the charm of FDR," reflected President Barack Obama during *The Ultimate Exit Interview* with historian Doris Kearns Goodwin in *Vanity Fair* (Goodwin, 2016). Despite his rhetorical gifts, Obama rarely forged bisociated compromises, and his record offers a telling lesson. In that interview, Goodwin pressed him on partisanship, polarization, and the narrative that his administration failed to build bridges with Congress.

Obama was candid about the distance between his aspirations and his results. In 2008, on election night, he called on both parties to "resist the temptation to fall back on the same partisanship and pettiness and immaturity that has poisoned our politics for so long" (Obama, 2008). Yet within days of taking office, he undercut that pledge in a closed-door conversation with House Republican Whip Eric Cantor. Obama

The Art of the Compromise

said to Cantor and the Republican caucus, "Elections have consequences, and at the end of the day, I won" (Cantor, 2017). That line revealed a preference for either–or solutions rather than the "Genius of the And." The blunt remark clashed with the moral high road later made famous by Michelle Obama's slogan during the 2020 Democratic National Convention: "When they go low, we go high" (Scipioni, 2020).* The Obamas' self-assurance—and borderline arrogance, especially toward opposing views—remains an open secret in Washington (Goodwin, 2016). Such a tone often undercut the promise of unity that fueled the campaign's early hope.

In his interview with Goodwin, Obama offered partial regret but stopped short of a true admission. He pointed back at proposals, speeches, and invitations as evidence of good faith. "The notion that we weren't engaging Congress, or that we were overly partisan, or we didn't schmooze enough...that whole narrative just isn't true." Goodwin, steeped in presidential history, did not allow that defense to stand untested. "But that narrative took hold, right?" When Obama invoked Lincoln's genius and FDR's charm, Goodwin shot back with a reminder of Lyndon Johnson's approach—a President willing to host lawmakers "every night for dinner." Her jab exposed what the White House often lacked—an iron stomach for the daily grind of forging real political deals.

---

*At one level, I am jealous of this catchphrase for its political cleverness, and perhaps I secretly wish a Republican rather than a Democrat had coined this memorable taunt. Yet at its core, the line remains just that, a taunt that divides rather than unites. The phrase is an 'either-or' expression—either one goes low, or one goes high—rather than one of inclusive 'and' that moves both sides forward together.

With Compromise

To be fair, impartial observers still debate the source of the impasse. Some scholars blame Congress; others fault Obama's reluctance to court rivals behind closed doors. Either way, the record stands—visible in the numbers in Fig. 34 and Fig. 35. Major accomplishments such as the Affordable Care Act and climate measures rested on party-line votes or executive orders—wins without the anchor of shared buy-in. When Republicans regained power, those policies faced immediate attempts at repeal. No durable bisociated compromise held them firm.

No clause in the Constitution outlines how a President and Congress must build bridges between factions. Yet history offers the same verdict, again and again—etched in the vote splits and repeal attempts that fill Fig. 34 and Fig. 35. Lasting achievements demand more than grand speeches. Lincoln, Roosevelt, Johnson—even Reagan and Clinton—proved that compromise is not capitulation but craft.

The craft lies not only in persuasion but in endurance: holding the coalition together through amendments, concessions, and late-night bargaining. Each of these presidents secured victories that outlasted their terms because they stayed engaged with Congress until ink met law. The Affordable Care Act, the Reagan tax reforms, the Civil Rights Act, and Social Security stand as reminders that the presidential podium can inspire, but only legislative compromise can endure. A President without the Art of the Compromise inherits only slogans, not a legacy.

Few Presidents understood that craft better than Lyndon B. Johnson. He wielded the levers of persuasion, procedure, and personal pressure with unmatched force, bending Congress toward landmark legislation. Johnson embodied both the promise and the peril of political mastery.

The Art of the Compromise

The Dirty Secret

"Well, what the hell's the presidency for?" Johnson snapped (Balz, 2014). Four nights before, a crazed lone gunman had shot and killed John F. Kennedy in Dealey Plaza. Thrust into office, LBJ was now prepared for his first address as President. In those late hours, aides pleaded with him to avoid the Civil Rights bill—too risky, too divisive. One advisor warned, "The presidency has only a certain amount of coinage to expend, and you oughtn't to expend it on this" (Caro, 2012).

Johnson ignored the caution. He chose to spend every bit of that coin—and more—on the cause. In that speech, Johnson vowed to honor Kennedy's legacy by pushing civil rights forward. The defiant push worked. He rallied moderate Republicans and Democrats to pass the landmark Civil Rights Act of 1964—anchored in the same bipartisan strength we see in Fig. 34 and confirmed in the decades of expansion in Fig. 35. Johnson approached compromise not as surrender but as power at work. LBJ took a very different approach to compromise than Obama.

Today, columnists such as Dan Balz at *The Washington Post* compare Obama's passage of the Affordable Care Act to LBJ's "what-the-hell" urgency (Balz, 2014). Yet the difference runs deeper than slogans. LBJ secured votes from both parties to hold the bridge firm; Obama forced Obamacare through on party-line votes and framed it as victory enough. Where Johnson built bridges in private, Obama often bypassed the backroom table altogether.

Johnson had spent decades crafting compromises and building coalitions that led to the passage of the 1964 Act, which for him was not a single burst of one-hit legislative success but rather a sustained bipartisan string of hits, going back

With Compromise

to his time as the Senate Majority leader in the 1950s. LBJ was the quintessential bisociated compromiser, while Obama, having served only three years in the U.S. Senate and as a relative newcomer on the federal stage, seemed locked into either–or deal-making. Obama did not have the political network to broker deals like the Civil Rights Act. The Affordable Care Act instead represented Obama's either–or mindset.

LBJ was not one to stuff legislation down the other party's throats; Obama, by contrast, forced the Affordable Care Act to a vote along party lines (recall the zero bar in Fig. 34) with Republicans in the House of Representatives excluded from the process. The narrative that Obama provides to explain his inability to build a coalition is that the Republicans, particularly in the House, were intransigent and unwilling to cooperate. Obama does have a point. The lockstep voting of the Republicans is well-documented. Yet 34 Democrats joined Republicans in the House to vote against the bill (Pear & Herzenhorn, 2010). On the other hand, the dismissive blame by Obama on the Republicans harkens to the quote from Scar[*] in The Lion King, "I'm surrounded by idiots!" or, in Obama's words, "I won."

What Obama failed to realize is that the Republicans also won and were elected by the People to hold their offices, too. Perhaps Scar was not surrounded by idiots; instead, he may have just treated them that way. Obama, as well, was not

---

[*]The villainous voice of Jeremy Irons, who portrayed Scar in the animated movie, is essential to this line because it carries the hubris and power-hungry tone of Mufasa's younger brother, scheming for the Pride Lands.

The Art of the Compromise

surrounded by losers; he just treated the Republicans that way. Such treatment does little to build coalitions and compromises. The dirty little secret of successful American politics is that our leaders, regardless of their political affiliations and public pronouncements, must work towards compromise and collaboration; otherwise, our system of government is doomed.

LBJ mastered that truth. His entire Senate career was a workshop in the Art—documented by Gary Donaldson in *The Secret Coalition* (Donaldson, 2014) and Matt Grossmann in *Artists of the Possible* (Grossmann, 2014). In the White House, Johnson deployed the famous "Johnson Treatment"—leaning on lawmakers, bullying some, flattering others. He instinctively knew the tight tune to play for the Congressman listening, and he never played "I won." Historian Matt Grossmann's research shows that this patient arm-twisting powered the most productive domestic legislative burst in modern American history: the Civil Rights Act of 1964, the Voting Rights Act of 1965, Medicare, the Great Society, and others. Whatever one's politics, the scale of that accomplishment shows what the Art of the Compromise can deliver.

Grossmann's data reinforces the point. Johnson's political ties ran deep—nearly 25 years in Congress built trust, favors owed, and phone numbers ready to ring at midnight. Obama, by comparison, had no such roots and never built a team to close that gap. The core of Grossmann's thesis is simple: durable policy is not just about who wins an election, but who can gather a coalition big enough to hold once the headlines fade. The charts in Figs. 34 and 35 show that pattern in stark relief—where the bridge holds, the policy lasts. Where no bridge stands, repeal attempts come swift and often.

In the end, the Constitution does not guarantee bisociated compromise, just as it does not promise moral leadership. The

With Compromise

framework only creates space. Real leaders—Jefferson, Lincoln, FDR, LBJ—build the bridge themselves. Without such builders, we get the Tyranny of the Deal.

Nowhere has that craft been tested more persistently than in the realm of taxation. Among the hard truths that endure, few bind the Republic tighter than taxes—and the fight to shape them. Benjamin Franklin knew it,[*] and each generation since has tested how to raise revenue, share burdens, and balance conflicting interests without losing the Union's fragile glue. To understand how the Art of the Compromise survives in that arena, we turn to President Reagan and the corridors of Gucci Gulch.

---

[*] "Are you still living?" wrote a worried Benjamin Franklin, in French, to his scientist friend in Paris, Jean–Baptiste Le Roy, on Friday the 13th in November of 1789 (Deis, 2010). The French Revolution's terror was underway, and Franklin—83 years old and watching America's new federal Constitution take root—feared for his friend's safety as he sensed his own end near.

That moment produced one of Franklin's most quoted lines about government and life (Deis, 2010).

> *Notre constitution nouvelle est actuellement établie, tout paraît nous promettre qu'elle sera durable; mais, dans ce monde, il n'y a rien d'assure que la mort et les impôts.*

Or, for the more familiar English translation:

> *Our new Constitution is now established, everything seems to promise it will be durable; but, in this world, nothing is certain except death and taxes.*

The compromises necessary to suspend death belong to theologians and the Devil. Taxes, however, sit squarely in the realm of constitutional politics—and often demand the roughest forms of compromise to hold a large, diverse republic together.

The Art of the Compromise

Gucci Gulch

Steven Levitt and Stephen Dubner, in *Freakonomics* (Levitt, 2005), highlight how taxes twist incentives in unexpected ways. The Boston Tea Party remains the best-known lesson—two pennies in duty pushed a sequestered port into rebellion, and the rebellion sparked a Revolution. As Jefferson put it, "So inscrutable is the arrangement of causes and consequences...a two-penny duty on tea...changes the condition of all its inhabitants" (Levitt, 2005). Taxes are never simple—and tax compromises are never clean.

By the 1980s, America's tax code had become a mountain of contradictions—70,000 pages of tweaks, carve-outs, and hidden loopholes (Grossman, 2014).[*] The code practically begged Americans to bend or break it. The creativity of the American taxpayer far outpaces the government bureaucracy that attempts to tax it. Levitt and Dubner recall an infamous outcome of the 1986 Tax Reform Act, which has come to be known as the Great Disappearing Act of 1987. With the new requirement of a valid Social Security number for each dependent, seven million supposed "children" were wiped—vanished—from the tax forms almost instantly. Some were double-counted kids in custody fights, but millions more were pure tax fictions, erased at midnight when the loophole

---

[*]The 70,000-page count is likely a myth, but helpful in illustrating the complexity of the tax code. In a 2014 article in Slate, Andrew Grossman unrolls this 70,000-page myth and arrives at a more realistic number of 2,600 pages, which is still a large page count (Grossman, 2014). As Grossman notes with a twist of humor, that length is about two and half times the length of Stephen King's novel "It"—except we should replace "scary clown" with "accounting methods."

closed (Kristof, 1990; Liebman, 2000). The fix brought in $2.8 billion in new revenue—proof that even a single line of the code can reshape behavior overnight.

Yet few lawmakers wanted to be remembered as the ones who "killed seven million children," even metaphorically. The tax code's leviathan demanded not just minor edits but sweeping reform—exactly the kind of tangled problem that only a bisociated compromise could solve.

Jeff Birnbaum and Alan Murray's *Showdown at Gucci Gulch* (Murray & Birnbaum, 1988) remains the definitive account of how that improbable deal came together. "Gucci Gulch" was the insiders' nickname for the carpeted hallway outside the tax-writing committees of the House and Senate—haunted by lobbyists in fine suits and finer shoes, paid to defend loopholes tooth and nail.

Lobbyists bet the Gulch would bury real reform, as it had countless times before. Yet 1986 was different. A cast of unexpected characters—President Reagan, Bob Packwood, Dan Rostenkowski, Donald Regan, and James Baker—broke from the usual script. They did not erase the code in public view but instead worked behind closed doors to stitch together a plan that could outlast the Gulch's sniping. They unknowingly followed the classic bisociated formula: different interests, different fears, bound by a design that could hold together under pressure.

Reagan cast tax reform as his second-term moonshot in his 1984 State of the Union. Treasury Secretary Donald Regan drafted the first blueprint, known as Treasury I—technically brilliant, politically radioactive. When James Baker traded posts with Regan, the tone shifted. Baker brought a gift for the backroom compromise that Regan lacked. He understood the social arithmetic of coalition-building: policy anchored in cross-faction roots endures, while policy forced through by

The Art of the Compromise

one side alone collapses. The bars in Figs. 34 and 35 illustrate that lesson with stark clarity.

Baker was key to the story. He understood compromise where it truly lives—in private, not in press lines. Peter Baker (no relation) and Susan Glasser, in *The Man Who Ran Washington*, describe how James Baker mastered a craft few ever learn. He knew when to reveal his cards and when to hold them close (Baker & Glasser, 2021). They write about his gift for behind-the-scenes orchestration—moving insiders, smoothing rivalries, and turning frozen policy into moving parts. Regan, the policy wonk, could design tax reform on paper, but his draft was doomed in isolation. Baker transformed Regan's fragile draft into political reality. Regan was the technician; Baker, the closer.

Packwood and Rostenkowski joined Baker to reshape Treasury I into what they quietly called "Consensus I." The rebrand mattered. Label the bill "Reagan I," and Democrats would bolt.* Wrap it in consensus, and the other side could claim credit too—exactly the point. Baker knew what Regan did not. The nameplate on a compromise can decide whether

---

*President Obama at first embraced the branding, telling a crowd, "I have no problem with folks saying 'Obama cares.' I do care. If the other side wants to be the folks who don't care, that's fine with me" (Cohn, 2011). Yet later, when the political cost mounted, he distanced himself. "They were the ones who named it Obamacare because they want to personalize this and feed on antipathy toward me as an organizing tool, as politics. But I don't have pride of authorship on this thing, if they can come up with something better" (Nelson, 2017). The two quotes juxtaposed reveal Obama's instinctive petulance, arrogance, and defensiveness, and they also show how a single name on policy—without bipartisan claim—can turn a hard-fought reform into a fragile brand.

it lives or dies. They hammered out the bargain in private, just as Jefferson once did over dinner with Hamilton and Madison, and as LBJ did in back rooms with Southern Democrats and Northern Republicans. It is the kind of work today's Congress too often forgets. Consensus and compromise built the bridge, and the name made it crossable.

When the final roll call came, the Tax Reform Act of 1986 passed the Senate 97–3 and cleared the House by a wide bipartisan margin, Fig. 34. The Act has proven remarkably durable ever since, Fig. 35 (Murray & Birnbaum, 1988). *The Washington Post* headline captured the moment: "The Impossible Became the Inevitable" (Russakoff, 1986). That is the mark of true compromise—an outcome dismissed as unthinkable until it became unavoidable. Reagan's reform never bore his name alone; ownership was shared. By contrast, Obama's health care law, branded from the start as "Obamacare," wore its partisanship on its sleeve and never found shelter in shared ownership.

The Art of the Compromise won in Gucci Gulch—an unlikely place for principle to hold, but the perfect crucible for integrative complexity to do its quiet work. The lesson echoes forward. When leaders share the name, the bridge holds. When they stamp only one side's seal upon it, the bridge cracks.

No issue shows that cost more sharply than healthcare.

The failure to secure durable reform did not begin with Obama. Its roots stretch back decades, to another missed handshake—when Nixon and Kennedy nearly struck a grand bargain and let it slip away.

The Art of the Compromise

Healthcare

An illustration of the importance of compromise is when we fail to reach one. The long struggle for bipartisan healthcare reform proves that point and traces back to the 1970s with a deal that almost was. President Richard Nixon and Senator Edward "Teddy" Kennedy nearly forged a bridge that might have delivered universal coverage decades before the Affordable Care Act. Kennedy, the youngest brother of John and Robert, built a storied Senate career that spanned nearly 47 years (Broder, 2009). Over that time, Kennedy introduced more than 2,500 bills, with over 550 enacted into law, a testament to his instinct for coalition and deal-making. Yet his greatest regret was the compromise he did not make—the healthcare compromise left on the table with Nixon (Stockman, 2012).

In 1971, Kennedy put forward his "Health Security Act," a universal single-payer plan funded by taxes. Nixon, wary of Kennedy's growing national stature and eyeing the 1972 election, countered with a private-sector approach. "Government has a great role to play," Nixon argued, "but we must always make sure that our doctors will be working for their patients and not for the federal government" (Stockman, 2012). The lanes of differentiation were clear. Our two-party system was working. Kennedy's single-payer versus Nixon's employer mandate. The ground for integration lay open, exactly the fertile terrain our system depends on.

Then came Watergate. With scandal swirling, Nixon sought to change headlines and tasked Health Education and Welfare Secretary Caspar Weinberger with recapturing momentum. Weinberger's plan proposed mandatory employer coverage alongside federally funded insurance for lower-income Americans. Kennedy publicly attacked it but privately

With Compromise

sent staff to negotiate, again, the American system at work. The outlines of a compromise were ready. Yet Kennedy walked away, calculating that Nixon's fall would yield a stronger position under a possible future Democratic president. Nixon resigned in 1974. Compromise failed. Our system is not perfect, but I would argue that it is the best yet devised. Kennedy, years later, admitted his miscalculation, "That was the best deal we were going to get" (Stockman, 2012). Kennedy knew he had failed.

Strangely, the missed chance came again. With Nixon gone, the White House turned Democratic as Kennedy had hoped, and Kennedy expected a better path under Jimmy Carter. Carter, however, came to Washington as an outsider—decent, honest, but green in the Art of the Compromise. He favored an incremental reform extending private insurance, far from Kennedy's single-payer vision. Kennedy blocked it, betting again on a more sweeping plan in his own time. The gamble failed. Carter, bitter even decades later, told an interviewer in 2010, "We could have had comprehensive healthcare now, had it not been for Ted Kennedy's deliberately blocking the legislation that I proposed" (Miga, 2010). The Miller Center's oral history captures Carter's bitterness. "He [Kennedy] did not want to see me have a major success in that realm of life" (Miga, 2010). The party fracture that followed Kennedy's 1980 presidential challenge weakened Democrats for a generation. The bridge never got built.

The third failure came under the Clintons. By then, Kennedy was the Senate's resident master of health reform. But President Bill Clinton tapped First Lady Hillary Clinton to craft the plan and handed her an army of policy advisors, including Nixon-era veteran Stuart Altman. Yet when asked if the Clintons consulted him, Kennedy bristled. The Clintons' operation "became disjointed, it became uncoordinated," he lamented. The lanes of differentiation were there again, but the Clintons never found the path to integration. "We missed the opportunity," Kennedy said later (Goldstein, 2016). The missed bridge shows again when no bipartisan claim holds the structure in place, repeal attempts come swiftly and often.

The lesson of healthcare is a hard one. Edward Kennedy understood the craft of compromise as well as most modern senators, yet politics, timing, and misjudgment cut each bridge short. From Nixon's employer mandate to Carter's incremental plan to Clinton's sprawling failure, each moment showed the same truth. The Constitution can create fertile ground for compromise, but it does not guarantee it. Someone must stand in the breach and hammer the bridge into place. Without that work, the lanes remain divided and the compromise remains undone. Our system can lead the horse to water—better than any other political system—but it cannot make the horse drink. That restraint is no flaw. In a republic, bipartisan mandates are the only ones built to last.

The record confirms this verdict. The charts in Figs. 34 and 35 echo the same pattern. When legislation lacks a bipartisan anchor, repeal attempts come quickly, and erosion follows.

The cautionary tale of healthcare did not end with Kennedy, Nixon, Carter, or the Clintons. The saga continued with Barack Obama, who pressed ahead on healthcare without bipartisan cover. He forced the issue into law, but without shared ownership, the fragility of the achievement was exposed from the start.

Go It Alone

As discussed, Obama chose a path devoid of bisociated compromise in pursuing what the world now knows as

With Compromise

Obamacare. That bill passed the House 219–212 with no Republican support and 34 House Democrats joining the opposition. The Senate vote ran 60–39, again strictly along party lines (Price & Norbeck, 2021).

That lonely path still fuels the strife and controversy that swirl around healthcare today. A policy born without cross-faction shelter remains exposed to repeal attempts and partisan warfare. Compromise is hard. Gathering consent across divides does not come easy. Obama famously chose a go-it-alone strategy, leaning on executive power and bypassing Congress to notch short-term wins. Yet when the middle is left empty, the foundation cracks.

John Harwood, writing for *The New York Times*, cut to the heart of this failure in 2014. "Unilateral White House action, even if it furthers a president's goals, cannot provide as durable a basis for national policy as law enacted with at least some support from both Republicans and Democrats" (Harwood, 2014). Harwood continued, "That is one reason the president's health care law, passed with only Democratic votes, remains unpopular." Either–or solutions are tempting in the near term but brittle in the long run. The value of compromise lies in joint ownership, where each side shares in the outcome and holds a stake in its care. Ben Franklin knew this well. In his final speech to the Constitutional Convention, he pleaded for unanimity so the Constitution might be "well administered" by all, not wielded by one faction alone. Obama, though trained as a constitutional scholar, seemed never to learn that lesson.

At the 2010 signing ceremony for Obamacare, Vice President Joe Biden leaned in and summed up the moment with characteristic bluntness. "This is a big fucking deal!"—his hot mic slip echoing around the world (R. Adams, 2010). He was right about the stakes. Healthcare consumes nearly 20

The Art of the Compromise

percent of America's gross domestic product—about $14,000 per person in 2020, up from just seven percent in 1970 (McGough et al., 2023). Within two generations, costs relative to GDP have more than tripled. The dollars show what the votes did not, that the scale demanded a bridge that Obama never got built, or was unwilling to build.

With no Republican stake in Obamacare, Republicans were free to hammer the law from the sidelines. No share means no shield—Democrats passed it alone and were left to defend it alone. The party chose total victory, but as General Stanley McChrystal warns from the battlefield, winning alone is often a double-edged sword (McChrystal, 2018). Sustainable victory demands the restraint to negotiate and the patience to compromise. Obama chose an "I won" strategy rather than a "we won" settlement, and thus, healthcare has remained a fragile political football ever since

Franklin would have cringed. Compromise is more than finding a solution that both sides can support today; it is also about building a solution that both sides will invest in together for tomorrow. Our Constitution was formed by a string of compromises that created buy-in from multiple factions: large and small states, slaveholding and free states, coastal merchants and inland farmers, planters and tradesmen, creditors and debtors, Federalists and Anti-Federalists, urban elites and rural settlers. Each faction could point to a clause or concession as proof of its stake—its piece of the bargain, its piece to defend. That shared claim bound them to the whole and forged durability. The go-it-alone strategy offers no such anchor. The result is the Tyranny of the Deal—fragile victories that break at the first hammer strike. Obama sees himself above Trump, but his preference for the Tyranny of the Deal over the Art of the Compromise leaves them riding the same horse.

The lesson is simple. Without the daily grind of persuasion, charm, and the unglamorous labor of trading favors, the lights of self-government flicker.

Turning the Lights On

A president's popularity can launch a campaign, but only the daily, often thankless grind of negotiation keeps a republic running. When Ronald Reagan signed the Tax Reform Act of 1986—the improbable victory of *Gucci Gulch*—he did so not by fiat but by sharing drinks, swapping jokes, and finding the few holdouts who could be convinced to accept half a loaf instead of none (Murray & Birnbaum, 1988). That was the old Washington way—charm, carrots, threats, and a phone call at just the right hour.

In the decades since, our presidents have found wearing both hats harder—the crowd-pleasing performer over the backroom broker. Barack Obama, for all his intellect and rhetorical grace, governed more like a solitary constitutional scholar than a flesh-pressing compromiser. Historians and journalists have noted again and again how little he cared for the retail trade of politics—the glad-handing, the horse-trading, the dinners and small favors that make reluctant legislators feel seen (Edwards, 2012; Fournier, 2013). As we have seen, Doris Kearns Goodwin's final reflections with Obama pull this into sharp relief. In *Leadership: In Turbulent Times*, Goodwin recounts how Obama told her plainly that Congress was simply too broken—a mess of petty fools who could not rise to meet him at his level (Goodwin, 2019). Yet when a leader points at each person in the room and calls them fools, history warns us that the real fool may be the one who believes himself too pure for the compromise.

The Art of the Compromise

The Affordable Care Act was, in truth, less a triumph of bipartisan bridge-building than a test of how far a president could push through a party-line victory before the window slammed shut. When the old tools failed him, Obama turned inward. "I've got a pen and I've got a phone," he said in 2014 (Obama, 2014). He was signaling a turn away from legislative persuasion toward executive action and direct appeals to the nation. Trump is less nuanced, but again, he rides the same horse.

In this compromise-be-damned approach, Obama was not so different from Donald Trump, though the contrast in style blinds many to the similarity in substance. Trump is the overt demagogue, a populist by design and a factionalist by instinct. He learned quickly how to command crowds and punish defectors, but he never learned how to shape a compromise that could last longer than a headline. His great wall foundered on appropriations and lawsuits (Fandos, 2019). His promise to repeal and replace Obamacare crumbled with a single thumbs-down from Senator McCain, a stage gesture that reminded the nation that even a president with a partisan majority must still persuade (Pear, 2017). His biggest legislative trophies—the 2017 and subsequent 2025 tax cuts[*]—were driven more by

---

[*]Trump famously sold the 2025 tax-and-spending package as his "Big Beautiful Bill," echoing the same phrase he floated for a border wall, immigration reform, and infrastructure before Congress shut him down in 2017 (Hubbard et al., 2025). This time, the GOP delivered the win, not because Trump mastered the Art of the Compromise, but because he mastered the art of bending a party to his brand. If he still shows little patience for the legislative grind, he has grown sharper at claiming credit for the final product when his faction does the work for him (Erikson et al., 2025).

Republican leadership than by a master plan from the Oval Office (Erikson et al., 2025).

Both men—the aloof professor and the noisy demagogue—found ways to reach over Congress when patience failed them. One used moral lectures, the other grievance rallies. Both trusted the direct line to the people more than the slow, humiliating work of bringing adversaries along. Each, in his own way, showed how the Art of the Compromise has atrophied at the very top of our government. One may find that Trump and Obama, operating by fiat and a preference for executive orders, are different sides of the coin.

The Founders never dreamed that faction would disappear. Madison knew better, even if George Washington did not. Yet they did believe that ambition would check ambition, and that leaders would stay at the table long enough to strike bargains no one liked but most could live with. When presidents abandon that table—whether out of cold disdain or hot contempt—the heavy machinery of democracy begins to seize. We live with a politics rich in performance but poor in trade, led by men who speak beautifully or thunder furiously, but too rarely do the mundane, honest labor that makes republican government possible.

Popularity can hand one the keys to the house, but only compromise keeps the lights on. We need fewer Obamas and Trumps, and we need more LBJs and Reagans.

Failure to Integrate

The failure to reach compromise solutions on healthcare does not necessarily translate into a catastrophic healthcare failure. The two-party political system, since the introduction of employer-sponsored healthcare insurance in the 1920s (Thomasson, 2002), has worked to differentiate the

The Art of the Compromise

elements of the healthcare debate. While our healthcare system seems monolithic and daunting, the United States, interestingly, has a unique hodgepodge healthcare system that is, in many ways, a combination of the multitude of systems found worldwide.

America's healthcare is well differentiated but poorly integrated and therefore complicated. T.R. Reid, in *The Healing of America*, explains this best. What Americans think of as our healthcare system is really a mash-up of German Bismarck insurance, British Beveridge public hospitals, Canadian single-payer Medicare, and, tragically, the out-of-pocket chaos of the developing world (Reid, 2010). For most working people, coverage looks like Germany's—employer-backed, multi-payer. For veterans, the Veterans Administration follows the British model—government-owned clinics funded by taxpayers. Senior citizens rely on Medicare, a single-payer system closer to Canada's design. Then for the uninsured millions, the system too often defaults to charity clinics or emergency rooms—if you can pay.

This chaotic structure emerged because integration failed where it might have succeeded. Nixon nearly forged that bridge in the 1970s with Kennedy—the employer mandate paired with government coverage for the poor. When scandal intervened, Kennedy held back, hoping for a sweeter deal under Carter. Instead, Carter's more incremental plan died on Kennedy's opposition. The Clintons tried again, but without Kennedy's experienced hand to unify the factions, the proposal unraveled. By the time Obama entered the fray with the Affordable Care Act, the go-it-alone path he chose had hardened into habit. No Republican stake meant no bipartisan shield, and so repeal attempts keep coming, as the data in Fig. 35 makes painfully clear.

With Compromise

Yet the framework remains within reach. The healthcare fragments we have could be integrated. Nixon's moment shows how surprising the champions can be. His cabinet was stunned when he ordered Weinberger to deliver a plan for universal coverage. Nixon did not fit the ideological boxes: sometimes conservative, sometimes liberal, often just fiercely practical—a transitional figure in the pivot from mid-century liberalism to the conservative realignment. Grossmann's data (2014) shows Nixon ranks just behind LBJ for major policy enactments—a reminder that big, durable changes require leaders willing to cross lines and gather unlikely coalitions. Nixon's environmental revolution, his Great Society expansions, his unfinished bid for healthcare reform—each piece shows how a leader's push can create openings for the Art of the Compromise.

The system we have today is not optimal, but it is not broken beyond repair. Our American healthcare system remains functional because each fragment works well enough alone. Yet a bisociated compromise—a bridge across the split factions—could stitch these working parts into a system both sides own. If that bridge stands, the next repeal attempt finds no easy target—just as Social Security has weathered storms for generations. Whether in a burst of bundled compromise, as in 1787, or a slower stitching over years, either path works, but only when the real work of integration resumes.

The fragments, as Reid reminds us, already exist—scattered but waiting. The Art of the Compromise does not conjure something from nothing; it binds what stands apart into a durable whole. If America can do for healthcare what LBJ did for civil rights, what FDR secured for pensions, what Reagan's unlikely trio forged for taxes, then this patchwork might yet become the envy of the world. The American system of government does not promise the perfect compromise

The Art of the Compromise

at the perfect moment, but it does bend us toward progress—progress over perfection.

The same pattern threads through each chapter of our story—divides waiting for steady hands to stitch them together. Compromise does not erase differences; it tempers them into something stronger. The fragments remain, but so does the task: to bring them together behind closed doors, to forge a handshake that holds in the open air, to build a bridge strong enough to carry disagreement across the years.

In Sum

The private dinner Jefferson hosted—linking Hamilton's debt plan to Madison's capital site—stands as more than a historical footnote. That quiet meal shows how American democracy grows not by changing minds but by *bisociating* them. The best compromises in our story do not split the difference—they fuse opposing aims into something sturdier than either side could claim alone.

A bisociated compromise is never just halfway. The Founders did not turn large states into small ones. They carved out a new shape: a Senate and House that stitched the Union together. FDR did not bribe conservatives to love the welfare state—he made Social Security more like earned insurance, so the opposition stayed under its roof. LBJ did not lecture segregationists into saints—he welded moderate Republicans to his coalition and set civil rights law in bipartisan stone. Reagan's team did not brand tax reform *Reagan I*—they named it *Consensus I*, so both sides could stand on its deck when the lobbyists came for blood.

The data on modern compromises reminds us (Figs. 34 and 35) what happens when that bridge holds—and what follows when no bridge stands firm. Nixon and Kennedy nearly met at the health care bridge but never crossed. Carter's and Clinton's missed shots scattered the parts again. Obama's solo push revealed that when one side tries to claim the whole loaf alone, the other side sharpens knives before the ink even dries. The real art lies in building something new across that trench—designing the unexpected plank wide enough for both factions to stand on without surrendering their old ground.

The Constitution cannot guarantee that this labor will be done. The document provides the stage; the building belongs to real leaders—those willing to host the private dinner, swallow their pride, and find the seam where difference locks into difference. That seam is the bisociated compromise, the rough edge where a fractured republic binds itself into a durable whole.

Yet structure alone cannot hold. Compromise lives not only in chambers, but in choices—habits practiced beyond marble halls. The next one waits not just for the next builder, but for those willing to stay in the ring and move beyond the Deal.

CHAPTER 5

Beyond the Deal

BENJAMIN FRANKLIN STEPPED into the Philadelphia street on September 17, 1787, after a summer that tested the fragile promise of self-government. The Constitutional Convention had kept its debates sealed behind closed doors, away from the rumors drifting through taverns and street corners. Within the Philadelphia chamber, delegates wrangled through weeks of discussions, debates, doubt, silence, and at last, agreement was hammered into compromise. The thirteen colonies had fought together but distrusted one another. European monarchs waited in the shadows for signs of collapse. A single charter of parchment stood between unity and unraveling—the rough shape of self-government stood in the breach.

A question met Franklin at the door of the convention hall. An unnamed woman asked the elder delegate whether the gathering had delivered a king or something more daring. Franklin answered without ceremony, "A republic, if you can keep it." Those words carried more unease than triumph. Franklin understood the restless energy of factions better than most Founders. Revolutions sparked easily; durable constitutions demanded discipline long after musket shots faded.

Throughout that tense summer in Philadelphia, Franklin's gaze, while he sat and listened to his colleagues, had often drifted to the high-backed mahogany chair behind George Washington's shoulders. The chair's crest rail held a half-sunburst carved into the wood—rays pressed outward, direction uncertain. The sun's position was ambiguous—not yet rising, not yet setting. Franklin remarked:

> I have...often in the course of the session...looked at that [chair] behind the President without being able to tell whether it was rising or setting. But now at length I have the happiness to know that it is a rising and not a setting sun.

Franklin wondered whether that sun marked dawn or dusk for the fledgling Republic assembled in Philadelphia.* By the final signatures, Franklin chose to trust that the light rose rather than fell. The carving's answer depended not on the

---

*This puzzle of a rising or setting sun is one that painters have often exploited to their advantage. The English painter Joseph Mallord William Turner painted the same puzzle. In *The Fighting Temeraire* (1838), Turner set a once-mighty warship against a smeared sky—sails stripped, masts bare, a steam tug dragging the hull toward a breaker's yard. Behind that ghost of Trafalgar, Turner left a sun tangled in the haze, light drifting into night or edging toward dawn, depending on one's interpretation. Historians have debated the scene ever since (Esterson, 2020). Some see final ruin for the empire's old fleet. Others see the promise of a new age driven by iron and steam. Turner offered no answer on canvas. The burden fell, as always, on those watching from the shore. Franklin pondered a similar puzzle in Independence Hall that summer on the back of Washington's chair. America has a long history of seeming to be a setting sun only to rise again the next day—stronger and more durable than before.

The Art of the Compromise

artist's chisel but on citizens willing to hammer disagreement into unity without surrendering principle.

The Republic holds the same question. Some stand before Franklin's sun, convinced only darkness waits beyond the horizon. Others fix their eyes on a new dawn—messy, unfinished, stubbornly alive. The chairback carving offered no final verdict. The choice passes to each generation that claims the title of American citizen. Is our sun setting? Or is it rising? This final chapter brings our discussion down to scale, down to the citizen, down to us. What does political compromise mean to us? The final measure belongs not to parchment, but to the individuals of the Many—*We, the People*—who keep the Republic alive. The test now shifts from marble halls to our everyday lives.

Madison understood where that answer must take shape. Passion alone never holds the line. No single voice shouts a republic into existence. Factions brawl and scatter—yet somewhere the hammer must strike order from noise.

The Many, the One

America's durability has never rested on unanimity. In Chapter 1, we discussed the noise—factions, riots, Whitman yawps—and found Madison's faith in the Many. He trusted that a republic stretched across a broad sphere would scatter conspiracies and blunt the fury of mobs. Extend the sphere and diffuse extremism.* No single passion could smother the Many when contradiction filled the air.

---

*The Madisonian muting of extremism may not seem obvious in light of the January 6 riot, but the distinction between Shays's

Yet sprawl alone cannot forge coherence. A common Soul is necessary to move a nation forward. Chapter 2 reminded us that unity demands more than boundaries on a map to hold a nation together. Lincoln bore the cost when unity failed—cannon smoke at Antietam, brothers torn apart at Shiloh, the slaughter of Gettysburg. Faction unchecked* spirals and fractures. A house divided cannot stand. Thus, the lesson remains. Congress cannot abdicate when political sides split into insurmountable divides. Our representatives cannot ignore problems—slavery, tariffs, or other wounds—and importantly, a political faction cannot simply flee—take their ball and leave—when the votes fall against them. To govern is to remain in the ring. A democratic republic will never succeed if a faction can simply walk away at will when it finds itself in a minority position.

Rebellion and later riots is instructive to Madison's point. Shays's insurrection was a homogeneous uprising of indebted farmers against tax collectors, unified in grievance and narrow in scope. By contrast, the January 6, 2021, Capitol riot, as well as other riots such as the 1968 Chicago protests, were heterogeneous in composition and motivation. Participants brought conflicting aims, ideologies, and grievances under one roof—or one street—making unity fragile and incoherence inevitable. Recall Ben Hamilton's January 6 description as a disjointed episode of *Monty Python*, or Abbie Hoffman's admonition that the 1968 rioters could hardly agree on lunch. At first glance, these episodes may appear parallel as eruptions of mob energy, but the differences reveal Madison's point. The extended sphere dilutes single-issue mobs, producing disorder, but not the kind of consolidated conspiracy that can topple a republic.

*The verb *unchecked* is not used casually. The ultimate check on factions rests with the federal government's capacity—if necessary—to use force against violence. Shays's Rebellion was decisive in this regard, helping to spur the Constitutional Convention of 1787 by demonstrating the need for a national government strong enough to respond to such unchecked factions.

The Art of the Compromise

Equally, a republic cannot survive on the untamed voices from the Many that form a democratic, yet unchanneled, cacophony. As Madison observed, parties inevitably form to channel the democratic chaos into a representative republic. Chapter 3 traced how our two-party system takes on this role to sharpen arguments through contrast and to discipline the passions of the Many into policy. To this end, two minds—not three or four or worse one party—can spar without rupture. The GOP and the Democratic Party work to sift and differentiate the views of the Many into two distinct sides. Yet, differentiation is only half the work; integration must follow, or discord frays the frame.

So then, where does compromise find a home in our Republic? If the Many remain loud and unruly, and our national unity is worth the struggle despite our disunity of thought, the burden then of compromise falls to Congress. Chapter 4 carried the lesson forward. Compromise—true, bisociated compromise—binds what no single faction can hold alone. Compromise that seeks *and* rather than *or* solutions yields resilience. Such agreements do more than bridge parties; they bind the nation itself, forging solutions meant not merely to pass legislation for near-term gains, but to last generations for long-term progress.

Yet the power and strength of Congress drift when it is not nurtured. War powers abdicated to the Executive. Moral puzzles punted to the Supreme Court. Congress is drifting from a coequal branch to a minor supporting role where real bargaining yields to speeches staged for cameras. The Many scatter into tribes, locked in permanent campaigns. The One withers into staged performance and partisan theatrics. The hammer softens; the sun begins to dip behind Washington's chair.

Headlines today tell this story in sharper tones. Donald Trump personifies the Deal more than the Compromise. No other leader embodies the "Tyranny of the Or" with such bravado. Trump's first presidential term battered institutions with transaction after transaction, brash and chaotic. Trump's second term—astonishing in his return—reveals a more capable negotiator working Congress's levers. Trump has learned important lessons from his first term. Some applaud his newfound skill. Others flinch when his political victories are framed more as conquest for greatness than progress for goodness. Trump drifts toward spectacle, not stewardship. A republic cannot stand on spectacle alone.

To return America to better days, this final chapter offers a discussion that moves us as individuals towards the Art of the Compromise and away from the Tyranny of the Deal. We begin with the trend of criminalizing politics, where spectacle tempts rivals into trading debate for indictment. Today, when persuasion fails, factions turn to prosecutors to settle disputes. Arguments belong in Congress. Trials belong in court. Confusing the two endangers both.

Decriminalizing Politics

A dark impulse threatens the space where compromise breathes—the temptation to criminalize politics itself. Lavrentiy Beria, Joseph Stalin's henchman in the former Soviet Union, once bragged: "Show me the man and I'll find the crime." Beria's words seem to come to life in American politics today. Dictators strengthen control by converting disagreement into guilt. A self-governing republic stumbles toward the same trap when failed politics becomes a court case, when the Deal divides political negotiators into courtroom enemies. No bisociated compromise can emerge in an atmosphere where political risk carries prosecutorial threat.

The Art of the Compromise

The Trump era does not mark the creation of political criminalization. That shift began long before and will continue unless the underlying instincts are reversed. Trump and his fiercest opponents represent the culmination of a longer drift—a national habit of transforming political opposition into prosecutorial spectacle. American politics has shifted from electoral contests to courtroom battles (Morgan & Reynolds, 1997).

Richard Nixon is perhaps patient zero. Nixon fell under the weight of Watergate's tapes. Ronald Reagan's second term staggered beneath the shadow of Iran–Contra. Bill Clinton faced impeachment proceedings rooted in personal misconduct. Dick Cheney drew sustained scrutiny over ties to Halliburton during the Iraq War. Barack Obama endured relentless conspiracy claims about his citizenship. Hillary Clinton's email server triggered years of classified-document inquiries. Hunter Biden's business dealings now fuel ongoing investigations and political theater. Finally, the criminalization of Trump—whether justified or not—appears to have consolidated primary support and galvanized small-donor fundraising, a dynamic that plausibly aided his return to the Executive office.* In an ironic twist of history, the criminalization of politics may have dethroned Nixon but may have elevated Trump.

---

*After Trump's first indictment in March 2023, his lead in the GOP primary widened substantially (FiveThirtyEight, 2023). His campaign also reported record fundraising, including more than $52 million within 24 hours of his May 30, 2024, conviction (Ingram & Rosen, 2024).

Beyond the Deal

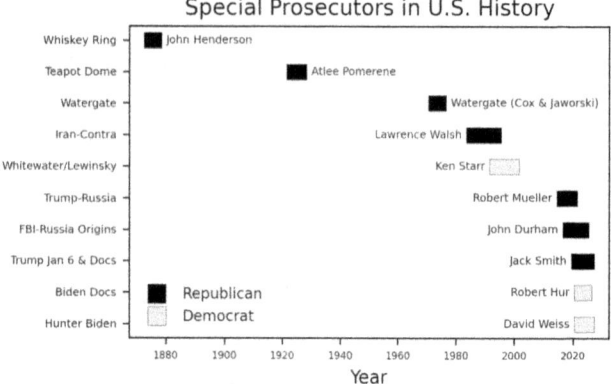

Figure 36. Special prosecutors and independent counsels in U.S. history (1875–2025). The timeline traces the duration and frequency of federal special prosecutors tasked with investigating political actors. Data compiled from publicly available records, including the U.S. Department of Justice, the National Archives, and major news organizations. Analysis informed by Mann and Ornstein (2006) and Morgan and Reynolds (1997).

Each episode sharpens the instinct to punish rivals through legal means, turning contests of policy into trials of character. Disagreement once marked a difference of opinion; now it too often implies criminal guilt. In that climate, persuasion yields to prosecution. The historical record makes the shift visible. Since the 1970s, special prosecutors* have appeared with increasing frequency and have remained in office

---

*The office of special prosecutor was first invoked in 1875 when President Ulysses S. Grant appointed former Missouri senator John Henderson to investigate the Whiskey Ring, a vast network of tax evasion implicating Grant's administration. Henderson's appointment came during the turbulent Reconstruction period, when federal authority faced sustained regional resistance and corruption scandals threatened public confidence (Kutler, 1992).

for longer stretches. What began as a rare recourse has become a recurring stage for political theater. The trend grows markedly after Watergate, reflecting the increasing use of legal processes to adjudicate political conflict. The chart in Fig. 36 traces that rise, a steady drift from persuasion in Congress toward prosecution in court.

The Constitution anticipates the danger of using legal mechanisms to suppress political action, even if only minor ones. Article I, Section 6 grants members of Congress limited immunity from arrest while attending legislative sessions, except in cases of treason, felony, or breach of the peace. The clause was not intended to shield corruption. The purpose was to protect public deliberation from the kind of harassment once wielded by English kings against Parliament.

In England, arrests for debt or trumped-up charges were used to intimidate members whose speech challenged the Crown. The Framers, well read in that history, sought to guard Congress from the same royal abuse (Lock, 1989; Madison, 2022). The safeguard reflects a deeper principle. Legal authority should not become a tool of political retaliation, yet genuine misconduct must answer to the rule of law.

Twelve Jurors

Today, the line between criminality and dissent grows dangerously thin. As former prosecutor Harvey Silverglate observed, the average citizen unknowingly commits multiple federal offenses each day (Silverglate, 2017). These "offenses" lay dormant—unprosecuted like a lion in the bush waiting to pounce—until the government needs a pretext to shake down an unsuspecting citizen (Stuntz, 2013). The problem lies not in sudden moral collapse, but in the sprawling expansion of law, so dense and ambiguous that missteps of judgment or procedure may be recast as crimes. In this environment, politics cannot thrive. No statesman will risk a handshake if prosecution hovers over the next headline. No bridge crosses a factional divide if the toll is legal ruin. How many Washingtons, Lincolns, Roosevelts, and Eisenhowers have stood on the political sidelines today, calculating the political criminalization cost to be too high (Lawless & Fox, 2010)?

Madison understood the remedy. He did not trust crowns or tribunals to judge public failure of political offices. He placed that trust in the voter. He wrote in *Federalist No. 51*, "A dependence on the people is, no doubt, the primary control on the government" (Hamilton et al., 2015). Courts may police the process, but they must never replace popular control.

As John Hart Ely argues in *Democracy and Distrust* (1981), the legitimacy of government depends on preserving a system in which electoral choice remains primary, with judicial review as a guard, not a substitute. Robert Dahl (1956) likewise insists that democracy's foundation lies in institutions that make elected officials answerable to voters, not in legal or judicial mechanisms for ejecting them. Finally, Adam Przeworski's *Why Bother with Elections?* (2018) pushes the point further. He argues that in functioning democracies, the losers must accept the results of elections, not seek re-resolution in courts or through indictments. When the Judicial Branch holds the power to dismiss members of the Legislative or Executive Branch, the imbalance of power tilts, and corruption finds a doorway to enter.

Madison likewise is arguing that if government officials act poorly, the remedy is not indictment but accountability at the ballot box. The true republican safeguard is a citizenry empowered to judge misconduct through elections. Criminal

The Art of the Compromise

proceedings, by contrast, risk inverting our Republic—substituting twelve jurors or a panel of judges over the will of millions of voters. Where Madison saw elections as the cure for bad behavior, today's partisans see the courtroom as the cure for bad elections. That reversal must be undone.*

After the Watergate scandal of the 1970s, Congress scrambled to close perceived loopholes that may have shielded Nixon's secret dealings and hush-money schemes (Morgan & Reynolds, 1997). The impulse for tighter oversight made sense as no president should hold the power to bury criminal acts in silence. Yet the response to Watergate planted the seeds for a permanent ethics bureaucracy (Mann & Ornstein, 2006)—one built not just to uncover crimes, but to hunt the mere appearance of impropriety—Stalin–Beria style tyranny. In that climate, whispers of suspicion can dismantle a political career more deeply than proof of guilt.

Over time, the post-Nixon bureaucracy expanded far beyond its original purpose. Allegations have become political weapons, and few leaders now leave public life without complaints aimed less at correcting misconduct than at staining

---

*Even local officials now face ethics complaints not for betrayal, but for delivering on the promises voters approved. When prosecution replaces persuasion, the Republic trades argument for accusation, and democracy begins to decay. Glenn Reynolds warns of *Ham Sandwich Nation*—a system so overcriminalized that, as the saying goes, "a vaguely competent prosecutor can get an indictment on a ham sandwich" (Reynolds, 2013). In such a climate, the courtroom becomes a substitute for the ballot box, and local politics shift from policy disagreement to legal warfare—not a republic Madison had designed but perhaps Stalin would approve. The charge itself becomes the punishment, and the people lose their voice to procedural theater.

Beyond the Deal

reputation. Even honest negotiations leave a paper trail that rivals can twist into scandal. The line between corruption and compromise has grown dangerously thin. As accusations multiply, citizens learn to see politics less as deliberation than as corruption on parade—and trust in government erodes with every hearing, every courtroom drama, and every unethical allegation (Morgan & Reynolds, 1997).

The erosion of trust in elected officials is an often-overlooked cost when lost elections give way to retaliation through the courts. If winners are cast as righteous and losers as criminals, such labels corrode faith in governance. Who can trust a leader branded as a criminal? And when power shifts in the next cycle, the same weapon is turned the other way. The result is a metastasizing distrust—an electorate trained to see politics not as a contest but as a crime. Under such criminalized dichotomies, why would citizens ever build trust?

Alexander Hamilton, in *Federalist No. 65*, argued that impeachment—not prosecution—was the constitutional tool for removing officials who betray the public trust. Elected leaders were never meant to answer each disagreement with a defense attorney. Yet over time, we have, often with noble intentions, built an ethics façade—a brittle partition between the branches of government, fragile enough to collapse under pressure yet rigid enough to obstruct the will of the electorate. Hamilton's logic still speaks. The ultimate judgment belongs not to juries or judges, but to *We, the People*, who alone should possess the authority to choose and to remove our leaders.

The Trump era has revealed the cost of this Faustian deal, where ethics no longer serve as standards but as weapons. Alan Dershowitz, the longtime Harvard law professor and defense attorney, stands as no ally of Trump's behavior, yet he

The Art of the Compromise

warns that flawed opinions—loud, sloppy, or petty—should remain shielded by the First Amendment (Dershowitz, 2017, 2023). Dershowitz argues that the courtroom must never become a shortcut for factions too impatient to win the public's vote. A republic tolerates mistakes and half-truths because open disagreement guards freedom better than prosecutions do.* A system that punishes each political bargain as betrayal guarantees no bargains worth striking.

Politics must be decided in the ballot box, not in the jury box. A republic that chooses purity over compromise invites Franklin's sun to set forever, never to rise again. The struggle between the Deal and Compromise is nothing less than a struggle over whether the sun will rise or fade.

The Trouble with the Deal

The Deal promises speed. The Compromise requires patience. That contrast lies at the heart of this book—between the Tyranny of the Deal and the Art of the Compromise. Deals come fast and bright, packaged for headlines and reelection. Yet what wins the political news cycle rarely survives the next one. Government is not a business, and never should be. The

---

*Supreme Court Justice Neil Gorsuch has warned that the expansion of federal criminal law—now filling more than 60,000 pages—has imposed an enormous burden on ordinary citizens, much less politicians (Gorsuch & Nitze, 2024). As previously noted, civil liberties attorney Harvey Silverglate estimates that the average American professional unknowingly violates three or more federal statutes each day (Silverglate, 2017). As Silverglate argues, the sheer volume of law creates an environment where prosecution becomes discretionary and selective—conditions that make political retaliation increasingly difficult to distinguish from legitimate enforcement. Beria is likely smiling.

Beyond the Deal

American Soul does not measure success in quarterly gains. The Republic seeks continuity—life, liberty, and the pursuit of happiness—not profit.

The American system was built to slow political deliberation, not to hurry it. That's why the Compromise—not the Deal—anchors our Republic. Yet moments arise when politics demands speed.* Madison himself warned in *Federalist No. 62* of the dangers of "impetuous counsels" and laws "hastily passed," defending the Senate as a brake against sudden passions.

Hamilton, in *Federalist No. 70,* supplied the counterpoint. The Republic also required an "energetic executive" who could act with "decision, activity, secrecy, and dispatch." Crisis favors velocity; storms do not wait for compromise. The Executive Branch was designed for such moments—for military strikes, flash floods, or late-night phone calls with foreign capitals. History draws out the point. In 1933, Franklin Roosevelt's bank holiday closed the nation's banks on a single morning, arresting a financial panic before Congress could even assemble (Leuchtenburg, 1963). In 1962, John F. Kennedy acted within hours to impose a naval quarantine during the Cuban Missile Crisis, averting escalation while Congress

---

*China's President Xi Jinping has repeatedly argued that democracies are too slow and unwieldy to compete in the modern world. His model of streamlined, autocratic decision-making presents speed as a superiority—a challenge to the very premise of constitutional delay (Stasavage, 2020; Wong, 2023). Xi sees the singular authority of China's system as better suited for speed. Yet America's constitutional design prizes durability over haste. The same friction that slows action also tempers error, invites revision, expands creativity, and—if held with care—still offers the surest path to freedom that lasts.

The Art of the Compromise

still debated its role (Allison & Zelikow, 1971). In 1999, Bill Clinton ordered airstrikes in Kosovo to halt ethnic cleansing, moving with dispatch while legislators disputed constitutional authority (Daalder & O'Hanlon, 2004). A single deal can rescue markets before morning or restrain missiles before they launch. The Executive Branch allows speed, but the greatest branch*—the Legislative—is for compromise.

Political instincts reward simplicity. So do human instincts. Binary thinking—friend or foe, win or lose—activates faster than complexity. Minds evolved to gauge threats, not grade them (Kahneman, 2011). In public life, the same cognitive shortcut reduces governance to spectacle: one vote, one hero, one villain. This mindset produces a style of rule obsessed with singular victories—transactional, theatrical, and fragile, and thus the problem extends beyond speed. A deeper tension lies in the misplaced belief that government should behave like a business.

We perceive the business deal as superior to the political compromise. Businesses pursue efficiency to serve customers and reward shareholders. Governments serve citizens and safeguard rights. Those missions conflict more than they align. The American Republic was not designed for efficiency but for constraint. The Constitution reflects a profound mistrust of concentrated power. As Max Weber observed, government alone holds the monopoly over violence—a power

---

*Madison and the Framers often described the Legislative Branch as the most powerful branch. In *Federalist No. 51*, Madison teaches that "In republican government, the legislative authority necessarily predominates." The whole reason for bicameralism, House plus Senate, was to divide and check that "greatest" branch.

Beyond the Deal

no business commands, nor should it (Max & Gerth, 1946). Such power demands limits, not acceleration. No corporate business model requires staggered terms, bicameral legislatures, or checks among three branches. The federal structure was not designed to be streamlined. It was designed to restrain—and rightly so. Authoritarian systems may mimic a business and grant leaders CEO-like speed—as in Xi Jinping's China—but the American path, tested by time and compromise, requires the consent of the governed.

The temptation to chase efficiency never disappears. In recent years, calls to run government "like a business" have resurfaced with renewed force. The creation of a Department of Government Efficiency, DOGE, directed by figures such as Elon Musk and Vivek Ramaswamy, rests on a fundamental confusion (Dunbar, 2025).* A nation does not consist of customers. A democracy cannot operate on quarterly returns.

---

*As a conservative, I am sympathetic to the goals behind DOGE, despite my limited support for Trump. The federal government has grown not only in scale but also in scope—expanding into domains once managed by local communities, markets, and families. Antonio Gramsci described how ideology can seep into civil society through norms, language, and institutions, ultimately shaping what appears neutral or natural (Hoare & Smith, 1971). The result is "Gramsci-creep"—a slow, cultural takeover not by decree but by drift. DEI (Diversity, Equity, Inclusion), ESG (Environmental, Social, Governance), and other modern institutional movements often stem from these same impulses. While rooted in moral ideals and good intentions, they risk becoming hegemonic projects—replacing old orthodoxies with new ones. In this light, DOGE's attempt to prune back the overgrowth should not be seen as anti-government but as the long-overdue weeding of an untended national garden. Yet Congress must act to bless or deny these DOGE activities through compromise legislation, as this book has argued. Otherwise, the work becomes a political football to be undone with the next administration.

The Art of the Compromise

Voluntary market exchanges reward speed and innovation. Public governance requires durability and consent—an often slower process.

No durable public structure emerges without friction. The only viable path for a diverse, self-governing republic lies in managing conflict, not eliminating it, to echo Madison. That argument lies at the center of the bisociated compromise. Lasting governance demands integrative complexity—the mental discipline to hold competing values in the public sphere and forge a structure neither side would reach alone. Bipartisan coalitions produce legislation that remains stable across decades.

Recall the data in Figs. 34 and 35, which reveals the pattern clearly. Policies forged through cross-party alliances endure longer, face fewer legal challenges, and invite broader public trust. By contrast, majorities acting alone—even with numerical strength—often craft policies that collapse under partisan weight. The historical record bears this out. The most durable reforms in American governance—FDR, LBJ, Reagan—followed the logic of integrative compromise, not ideological purity. Without cross-party ballast, landmark achievements drift in contested waters.

Franklin Roosevelt built the New Deal not as a progressive manifesto—though his instincts leaned in that direction—but as a coalition platform, crafted with an astute eye for the political realities of the moment. Social Security passed with substantial Republican support. So did banking reform and public utility regulations. These reforms endured not because of ideological purity, but because of bipartisan resilience. Roosevelt invited disagreement without surrendering coherence. He and his cabinet learned to work both sides of the political aisle for bisociated compromises. The New Deal adapted, absorbed, and lasted.

Beyond the Deal

Lyndon Johnson understood the same bisociated calculus. The Civil Rights Act of 1964 was passed only after months of private conversations, procedural maneuvers, and cross-party bargaining. Johnson spent political capital as though the nation's Soul depended on the outcome—because it did. The final votes crossed sectional, ideological, and partisan lines. The law has survived because the coalition behind it was broad enough to resist collapse.

Reagan's team followed a similar path in 1986. His initial tax reform proposal collapsed under the weight of theoretical purity, but James Baker, Bob Packwood, and Dan Rostenkowski revived the effort through legislative craftsmanship. They stitched together a bisociated compromise built not on shared philosophy but on mutual necessity. Lobbyists flooded the hallway outside the Senate Finance Committee—dubbed "Gucci Gulch"—where tax reform had previously gone to die. This time, the coalition held. The Tax Reform Act of 1986 was passed with strong support from both parties.

And then came Obamacare.

Barack Obama secured passage of the Affordable Care Act without bipartisan support. The law has survived, but remains one of the most litigated and politically divisive measures in modern history. Obama pursued a go-it-alone strategy that deliberately excluded Republican cooperation. He justified the move with a declaration that elections have consequences—I won. That phrase signaled not collaboration, but command. The data in Figs. 34 and 35 make the aberration clear. The Affordable Care Act stands apart from the legislative patterns established by Roosevelt, Johnson, and Reagan—each of whom built durable reforms through cross-party coalitions. The result stands as a vivid example of what follows when bisociated compromise yields to partisan control.

The Art of the Compromise

Without compromise, the law carried the force of statute but never the ballast of agreement.

No single party or ideology holds the secret to durability. The common thread across these moments lies in bisociated statesmanship. Legislative compromise demands slow hands, clear thinking, and a willingness to trade applause for stability—doing the hard work of integrating differentiated political solutions. Few enduring laws have passed without internal contradiction. The Civil Rights Act of 1964 outlawed segregation but carried exemptions and amendments that reflected the price of passage (Caro, 2002). The Social Security Act of 1935 built a pension system, but excluded millions of agricultural and domestic workers to secure Southern votes (Leuchtenburg, 1963). Coherence arrives not through partisan purity but through bisociated refinement over time. Representative government was not built to perform. It was built to deliberate.

Deals win elections. Compromises build republics. Durable governance depends not only on what happens inside the halls of Congress, but also on what surrounds those halls—habits of trust, civic connection, and the capacity of ordinary citizens to support compromise, not just demand outcomes. The work of politics does not end with votes tallied or bills passed; it continues in the spaces where citizens meet, talk, and share life together.

Break Bread

No constitution can rescue a nation where neighbors refuse to break bread with one another. The roots of the Republic do not rest in parchment but in practice. The most durable compromise in American history—the Compromise of 1790—did not begin on the House floor. That compromise began at dinner. Recall our discussion about how Jefferson hosted Hamilton and Madison at his rented home in New York. They dined on politics and philosophy. They drank French wine and likely savored dishes influenced by Jefferson's years in Paris. No press. No statements. No spin. By the end of the evening, the nation's capital would move south, and Hamilton's financial plan would move forward. That meal secured more than a compromise. The evening fed a republic.

Democratic soil still depends on dinners—like Jefferson's in 1790—that bind rivals into partners. The strength of Congress rises from the strength of community. Robert Putnam has charted the slow decay of American community in his landmark book *Bowling Alone* (2000). Our old networks—church basements, union halls, bowling leagues, bridge clubs—once taught Americans how to disagree without retreating. Civic trust grew in places without microphones and smartphones. Those places now sit dark, quiet, or for sale. Digital networks now span the globe with unmatched reach, and the human networks that once sustained the Republic have now frayed in silence, replaced by digital noise. This massively connected digital world has made us more alone than ever—bowling or otherwise.

Each shuttered hall leaves a vacancy in the public square. Each solitary dinner narrows the imagination. Each glance downward, fixed on a smartphone screen, pulls us further from the room we are in. We are no longer connecting. We are shouting. Putnam grounded his book in hard numbers. *Bowling Alone* did not simply mourn a loss of community spirit. The book measured that loss with data, declining membership charts, falling participation rates, and statistical curves tracing the slow erosion of civic trust. The metaphors were moving, but the case rested on math. The evidence

The Art of the Compromise

pointed to a simple truth. Without strong social ties, democracy frays.

Alexis de Tocqueville recognized that fragility long before Putnam's charts gave the idea shape. In his 1835 volume of *Democracy in America* (Mansfield & Winthrop, 2000), Tocqueville saw the Republic's vitality not in government offices but in the gathering habits of free people, nearly 200 years ago. Associations—not laws—form the ligaments of self-rule. A republic breathes not through orders but through cooperation and community. Not just liberty, but fraternity. Will Rogers captured the same spirit in a single line: "I never met a man I did not like" (Rogers, 2012). That line was more than sentiment; it was strategy. Friendship does not require agreement. Curiosity comes before conversion. Without the habit of grace, fellowship shrivels and compromise collapses. We have traded dinners with neighbors for digital duels with online strangers—Twitter wars fought in ALL CAPS.

Each of us, as citizens, has a Tocquevillian duty to join in Putnam's bowling leagues, to stitch back the associations that once held us together. We must once again break bread together. The Art of the Compromise does not rest only in Congress—it belongs to us. Invite the neighbor whose yard sign triggers suspicion. Share a table with the retired union boss whose bumper sticker still stings. Sit down with the friend who voted the other way. The goal is not persuasion but presence. Be present. Each meal shared across disagreement echoes Jefferson's table, which moved a capital and secured a financial system. Be Hamilton. Be Madison. Write the letter to the elected official who dares to compromise. Be Jefferson. Applaud the courage. Resist the scorn. Be Washington.

Compromise is not about finding agreement but finding a path forward together. The Art of the Compromise at the individual level is not meant to extinguish our passion but to temper our anger. Will Rogers was right: enemies are hard to find up close. Social science has confirmed his intuition. Proximity breeds empathy. Neighbors, coworkers, and fellow congregants who see one another face to face are far less likely to treat one another as foes. Studies of "contact theory" in political psychology show that sustained, cooperative interaction reduces hostility and builds trust, even across partisan and racial divides (Allport, 1954; Pettigrew & Tropp, 2006). To share a table with someone whose views clash with our own is healthy. To let disagreement curdle into hate is not.

The habit of disagreement—cultivated in basements and bridge clubs—teaches the mental agility that sustains two minds within one republic. Recall F. Scott Fitzgerald's test of a first-rate intelligence is the ability to hold two opposing ideas at once. That duality may strain the individual mind, yet the Republic depends on that tension to govern wisely. No republic endures on ideology alone. The true test of a first-rate government is the ability to hold opposing views in the public sphere and still retain the capacity to govern. Compromise in marble halls begins with manners at the dinner table.

The ability of two citizens to hold deep disagreement and still break bread together—or share a supreme pizza—is a mark of a first-rate democracy. Self-government does not shout—it listens. The table invites, but does not compel. Compromise waits for the first seat to be taken in good faith. Madison and Hamilton sat once. Who will sit today?

From Shame to Weaponization

Our dinner tables on January 6 looked very different. What bread did Michael Sparks and other rioters share before crawling through the Capitol windows on January 6? The record is not clear, but what is clear is that within hours, families,

The Art of the Compromise

friends, and social networks began to light up the smartphones of the rioters as history teacher Ben Hamilton documented in his first-hand account (Hamilton, 2022).

Hamilton gathered with the rioters at Union Station, as I noted in Chapter 1 where spouse texts, family group chats, and coworker messages began to circulate the same footage among the rioters. These folks knew their names and faces and shared dinners with them. One can imagine the incredulous conversations, likely starting with a common phrase, "What are you doing?" This early counter feedback cracked the performative spell and likely led to the early end of the riot. Hamilton recalled the dramatic shift from a celebratory mood just four hours earlier to a sullen atmosphere thick at Union Station.

The effect was not abstract. The crowd that stormed the Capitol skewed older and employed—business owners, veterans, churchgoers, and managers, Tocquevillian citizens. They had reputations to protect, children to face, pastors to answer, and jobs to report to the next morning. Those bonds, usually reservoirs of trust, became sudden channels of shame. Social capital turned back on itself, binding the riot tighter than a police line could achieve.

While social media is often credited with radicalizing the Trump crowd and inciting the violence that day, we often overlook the effect that social media had on shaming the crowd. Hamilton retells the scene as he walked away from the Capitol with the mob. The rioters were "starting to get feedback from their friends and family all around the country. I think that feedback influenced the way these people perceived their own actions." Hamilton went on to note, "Gone were the smiling, open faces rehearsing how they'd tell their grandkids this story. Now the faces were confused and defensive."

In the days that followed, the circle widened beyond kin and coworkers. Strangers joined the chorus. What began as shame from family and friends soon became vengeance from the other side of the political spectrum. A loose collective calling themselves "Sedition Hunters" scoured the Internet and livestreams, tagging faces, geolocating scenes, and posting identification threads (Tenorio, 2023). News outlets amplified those efforts, printing galleries of the "most wanted." A meme or selfie that once promised heroism now served as a court exhibit.

The state soon codified that shift. The Department of Justice charged hundreds, often using side-by-side comparisons of selfies and surveillance footage. Congressional hearings replayed the worst moments on national television, recasting neighbors and coworkers as insurrectionists. Political opponents seized the imagery to paint entire movements as existential threats to the Republic. The same networked flows that subdued the riot before sundown supplied the evidence for months of prosecution and years of political weaponization.

To be clear, the actions of January 6 were criminal, violent, and indefensible. Yet the political narrative elevated the chaos of that afternoon into the language of a coup d'état. Legal scholars, historians, and political leaders diverge over whether the riot rose to the level of insurrection or not. What is beyond dispute is that partisan framing transformed an episode of mob lawlessness into a touchstone for national identity, a rhetorical cudgel wielded on both sides of the aisle. I am also not arguing that a few dinner casseroles and homemade desserts would have avoided this catastrophe and the resulting political tug of war over January 6, but the reminder that many rioters were embedded in households, congregations, and workplaces helps explain why the frenzy burned itself out in hours rather than days. Unlike Shays's Rebellion,

The Art of the Compromise

shame played a major role, more so than government suppression, on January 6.

Networks of kinship and reputation did not prevent the riot from beginning, yet they imposed limits on its duration. The same people who stormed the Capitol had to face families that evening, employers the next morning, and congregations the following Sunday. That tether pulled harder than ideology—a lesson important to the Art of the Compromise. The paradox is that these bonds—once they turned from permissive to restraining—shortened the violence even as they later fueled cycles of shame, prosecution, and political weaponization.

The Civil War marked the tragic counterexample to January 6. Where the Trump riot flared for four hours before kinship ties pulled rioters back home, the rupture of 1861 lasted four years because those same bonds failed to restrain and instead split along sectional lines. Four hours versus four years—the measure of how fragile bonds can either contain conflict or magnify it. The argument that might have remained inside Congress burst instead into secession and cannon fire. Lincoln then faced the ultimate test of compromise: yield the Union to dissolution, or stand against rebellion.

Two Roads Not Taken

A peaceful green light for secession would have set a precedent for fracture on demand, which Lincoln warned exactly against in his First Inaugural. Once a minority can exit the Union when they no longer agree with the majority, future minorities will do the same, leaving behind "anarchy." To acquiesce would not have produced stability but rather a Balkanized continent—serial break-offs, commercial rivalries, and foreign entanglements—than one durable Union. Later, in

Texas v. White (1869), the Supreme Court confirmed that the Union is "indissoluble," giving constitutional gloss to the wisdom Lincoln voiced in March 1861. Allowing secession would have meant not one nation, but many.

The other counterfactual is what if the South had accepted electoral loss and remained in the Union? Conflict would have remained bitter, perhaps poisonous, yet it would have been bound inside the frame of ballots, laws, and courts rather than muskets. The Art of the Compromise—as traced across this book—does not dissolve disagreement but channels it into forms that move forward. In this alternate road, the Union survives, the argument continues, and progress—halting and uneven—remains possible.

The pre-war Republican policy aimed first at containment. Slavery was barred from new territories while free-state populations surged. That arithmetic promised a slow but decisive tilt inside Congress and the Electoral College (Ransom, 1998). Recall the charts and graphs in Chapter 2. Southern leaders would have resisted, but the machinery of the Union would have forced their resistance into statute and amendment rather than rebellion. Lincoln's own tools were designed for such a setting. He argued for compensated emancipation (Gunderson, 1974), gradual timelines, and constitutional guarantees to soothe pride (Fogel & Engerman, 1995). He introduced federal buyouts, piloted the idea in Washington, and even drafted a constitutional amendment to finance abolition through bonds (Goodwin, 2009). These measures would have embodied compromise—not harmony, but progress.

Would slavery have ended peacefully under such a path? Scholars are divided on the issue (Fogel & Engerman, 1995; Stampp, 1978; Wright, 2006). Some argue that profitability could have prolonged bondage absent the shock of war (Fogel & Engerman, 1995), pointing to the Corwin Amendment as

The Art of the Compromise

evidence of potential entrenchment. Others note how the cotton boom had already peaked by 1860 (Wright, 2006), leaving slavery vulnerable to economic erosion. Either way, the Union would have forced conflict to grind through debate rather than secession, making space for compromise to work slowly upon a hardened institution. Economists even calculate that a nationwide buyout would have cost no more than the war itself (Hummel, 2013).

The question then turns forward. Would a peaceful Union have spared America the long shadow of Jim Crow? Probably not (Woodward, 2001). Unfortunately, racial hierarchy does not vanish with law alone. A South that lost in argument rather than war may have yielded less violent backlash, but prejudice would likely have entrenched itself through statute rather than bayonet. Segregation may have emerged more legally, less chaotically—but still endured. The compromises that preserved the Union would have been the same compromises that slowed racial justice—a shameful but perhaps inevitable expression of human tribal instincts (Sapolsky, 2017; Tajfel et al., 2001).

Counterfactuals are slippery ground (Pearl & Mackenzie, 2018). No one can know the alternate history with certainty. What matters is that choices existed. Southern leaders could have accepted loss and remained within the argument, however bitter. Instead, they chose war. They turned from compromises toward cannons. Lincoln pleaded in his First Inaugural for the "mystic chords of memory" to bind the nation back together (Lincoln, 1953). The South refused. In rejecting compromise, they rejected the very architecture that made republican government possible.

Lincoln asked for a nation willing to bend rather than break, but his call went unanswered. To endure self-government requires more than obstinacy and more than surrender.

It requires a stance that can yield without collapsing, a posture of strength disguised as humility.

The Willing Knee

The phrase *"on bended knee"* conjures images of supplication—an act of reverence, surrender, or plea. Yet another kind of kneeling exists. One not born of desperation, but of purpose. A posture not of collapse, but of preparation to rise differently. That kind of movement—measured, intentional, principled—is what James Madison practiced throughout his public life, and one that we as citizens should observe with care. If Madison, the father of our Constitution, could bend a knee to seek progress over purity, then so too must we be willing to follow his lead.

As Noah Feldman argues in *The Three Lives of James Madison*, Madison lived not one political life but three: constitutionalist, partisan, and statesman (Feldman, 2017). Each required not only a shift in strategy but a transformation of the man himself. He began as a theorist—a brilliant architect who believed that careful design and logic could neutralize faction and secure liberty. With time, he adapted—not by retreating, but by redirecting his energy toward a Bill of Rights, a concession he once deemed unnecessary but now saw as essential to national unity.

He did not stop there. When Hamilton pushed for greater national power through the Treasury and central banking, Madison pushed back. In reaction to his once friend and now foe, Madison helped found the first political party—a move he once feared would tear the republic apart—to counter the growing power of Hamilton and his Federalist entourage. Later, as President, Madison governed a divided nation through war, defending institutions he had once criticized.

The Art of the Compromise

His trajectory was not a retreat from principle, but a deepening of principle, forged in the crucible of conflict.

Madison did not change with the winds, but he did change as a practical matter as he gained experience in the realities of politics. He would often bend a willing knee. He began his political life as perhaps America's first political scientist, but as time progressed, Madison became one of our nation's most pragmatic statesmen. His transformation was not one of submission but the steps of a man growing into his role—learning to govern a living republic, not a theoretical one.

To kneel willingly is not to yield for its own sake, but to adapt for the sake of something larger. Madison had seen enough to know that a structure too rigid will crack under pressure—whether made of stone or of law. Flexibility preserves form. He wrote, "The choice must always be made, if not of the lesser evil, at least of the GREATER good" (Madison, 2016). The willingness to change—to rethink, reframe, reposition—is not weakness. Such movement preserves what still matters.

In our own time, politicians are praised for standing firm, even when the ground beneath them shifts. Yet the Founders were not fixed monuments. They moved. They negotiated. They bent their knees—sometimes on principle, sometimes in pain, but always with the intent to rise again, stronger and more aligned with the moment. Progress over perfection. Pragmatism over purity.

Madison's journey—from abstract theorist to practical politician—was not a fall from grace, but a rise toward stewardship. A republic is not kept by those who never move, but by those who know when and how to bend without breaking, how to adapt without surrendering conviction. The Art of the Compromise lives in such moments. We, the People, must learn from Madison's example. Compromise requires a willing knee, on occasion, to find a path forward.

Yet no public posture of compromise endures unless it is rooted first in the inner life of the citizen. The capacity to bend without breaking begins in the singular citizen's mind before it can guide a nation's hands.

Internal Tension

The pragmatism of the Art of the Compromise begins in our private thoughts, the small, silent voice in our heads. Before compromise can shape a nation, it must first shape a citizen. The willingness to bend in public grows out of the discipline to weigh, test, and restrain in private. The habits of judgment do not emerge fully formed, but they rest on a deeper structure. Understanding that structure can help us to differentiate our own political viewpoints and—with experience—the viewpoints of others in a more consistent manner. Such understanding cultivates and enables integration towards better political solutions and judgments.

Beneath our mental deliberation lies moral foundations: the innate, universal psychological mechanisms that guide human morality. If we can understand human decisions through the lens of morality in a structured manner, we can engage our political world in a more rational way. The argument of this book is not only about governance but about discernment—how our nation formulates political judgments and creates bisociated compromises. Each chapter has traced a method for seeing beyond faction, for joining the Many into the One, for holding two minds in tension. Here, the lens turns inward into how we and our fellow citizens make political decisions.

The Art of the Compromise

At the center of such decisions is Moral Foundations Theory. This theory, developed by Jonathan Haidt, the Thomas Cooley Professor of Ethical Leadership at the New York University Stern School of Business, identifies six moral dimensions—care, fairness, loyalty, authority, sanctity, and liberty (Haidt, 2012). See Fig. 37. The theory is much like the better-known theory of human personality traits, popularized through the Myers–Briggs Type Indicator test (Myers & Myers, 2010) and grounded in the empirically-derived Big Five personality traits (McCrae & Costa, 2003). If one is familiar with these personality tools, one is also familiar with how useful they are in the corporate world. Myers Briggs and the Big Five yield personality insights that help business leaders, managers, and other decision makers navigate relationships, careers, and personal growth by revealing one's inherent preferences and behaviors. Similarly, insights from Moral Foundations Theory can enable better self-awareness, more effective deliberation, and more bisociated framing for political thought.

Through the framework of Moral Foundations Theory, we can recognize that each citizen organizes their moral thought along the six different mental lines. These dimensions do not operate in abstraction. They form a scaffold of intuition—a moral compass—through which conviction takes shape. That scaffolding structures the inner voice that tests ideas before they reach the public square. Political belief matures through internal friction. Ideas are not simply adopted wholesale; they are wrestled with—pulled, stretched, weighed, and refined. Real issues sharpen along these moral axes. The deep dive that Haidt's *The Righteous Mind: Why Good People Are Divided by Politics and Religion* provides into Moral Foundations Theory, and the insights the 2012 book provides for understanding political viewpoints, is worth a serious read.

Beyond the Deal

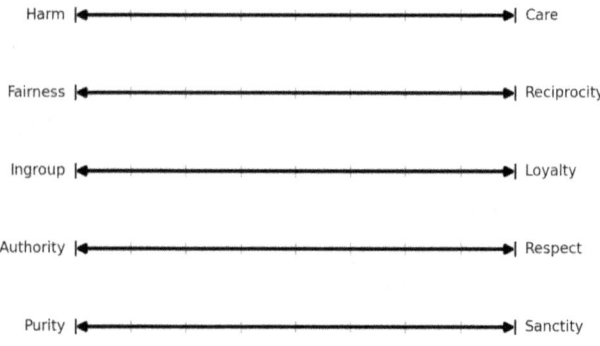

Figure 37. Moral Foundations Theory. Five Core Dimensions of Moral Intuition. Each horizontal axis represents one of the five foundations identified by Jonathan Haidt (2012). The diagram serves as a neutral template for introspection, political analysis, and understanding divergent value systems.

Consider abortion as a political issue. One citizen may feel instinctive compassion for a pregnant teenager—the care dimension. Conviction in that same citizen may rise to protect an unborn fetus—sanctity. A third impulse may defend an individual's autonomy—liberty. A fourth may trust longstanding Biblical teachings or inherited roles—authority and loyalty. No single value resolves the dilemma. One's position often emerges not from alignment of the dimensions, but from wrestling with each one—an imperfect synthesis forged in moral tension. The answer matters, but so does the citizen's struggle to reach that answer. The citizen slides their thoughts along the axes in Fig. 37, testing how each moral foundation shapes one's individual stance on abortion and other political issues.

As another example, consider immigration. A refugee family fleeing violence may evoke care and fairness in the citizen's mind, but concern for law and national cohesion may

The Art of the Compromise

activate authority. On the other hand, loyalty to country, cultural identity, or workforce protection may conflict with impulses toward openness. Religious tradition may elevate hospitality. Cultural fear may demand caution. Each dimension tugs our inner voice in a different direction. A citizen who stays with the struggle long enough to explore the tension of each dimension may arrive at a view that balances enforcement with empathy or some other bisociated solution that represents an internal mental compromise. That view may remain uneasy, but it is earned. If we understand these six dimensions and how each individual may dial their viewpoint along each line, then we can begin to understand through introspection where disagreement rests and where possible compromise may also reside.

To be clear, I am not advocating moral relativism. Quite the opposite. Individuals may—and should—retain moral absolutes if conscience demands it. Yet if we collectively agree as a nation that the rule of law must prevail—*render unto Caesar*—then our federal Constitution embodies that law. Imperfect as it may be—for men are not angels—it defines a process for channeling conflict into compromise and has proven robust for longer than any other modern republic.

As a result, this inner wrestling differs in the public arena. In private, the axes emerge from intuition. In public institutions, party platforms, media filters, and precedent are the tools that structure the boundaries. The public sphere becomes less nuanced than our internal thoughts as the two-party system does its job to differentiate the issues. Thus, the abortion issue polarizes into pro-life and pro-choice with little territory in between. Immigration reduces to closed or open borders with a vast no-man's land in between. Complexity flattens. Nuance vanishes. The axes narrow. We must recognize this polarization in action and not be alarmed.

This tension between our internal moral foundations on issues and the polarized differentiation of our two-party system leads to an interesting phenomenon in American politics. The health of the Republic depends not only on outcomes but on the depth of struggle required to reach them. A citizen who resists shortcuts—who listens, wrestles, reflects—helps create the conditions where compromise becomes possible. Without that internal tension, no external structure will hold.

The practice begins within. One mind burns with outrage, urgency, and moral clarity. The other steadies with judgment, caution, and reflection. Like a blacksmith at the forge, self-governance depends on the tension between these two minds. Fire alone leaves metal too soft. Cold alone leaves the blade unfinished. Enduring law is tempered in the blacksmith's rhythm—heated, struck, tested, and made strong—forging the Art of the Compromise over the Tyranny of the Deal.

Governing over Winning

That inner forge is only the beginning. To govern requires more than private conviction; it demands a framework for understanding where concessions can be made and bridges built. Moral Foundations Theory provides such a framework. It clarifies our own internal wrestling and helps us glimpse the moral logic of others. With that understanding, we can move beyond winning arguments toward governing through compromise. To frame this more precisely, we return to the work of Lepora (2012) and Spang (2023).* Lepora first categorized

---

*I must confess that I wished I had read Lepora (2012) and Spang (2023) sooner, but the reality is that I read their work after writing

The Art of the Compromise

types of political compromise with a novel insight: the nature of concessions shapes the agreement reached. Spang, building on Lepora, refines this into three distinct forms. See Table 1.

Table 1. Types of Compromises and Examples.

Type	Definition	Constitution	Congress
Intersection	Use only shared ground.	Bill of Rights	Social Security Act (1935)
Conjunction	Fuse both sides.	Great Compromise	Civil Rights Act (1964)
Substitution	Invent a new frame.	Electoral College	Tax Reform Act (1986)

The first form is an *intersection compromise*, which arises when agreement rests only on overlapping ground. Each side advances only what both already accept. Such bargains are thin, but durable. Conversely, a *conjunction compromise* accepts elements from both sides, including those once opposed, so that each party must live with something it dislikes alongside something it values. These bargains sting, but they bind. Finally, a *substitution compromise* moves further still, abandoning both original demands to create a new principle altogether, one not envisioned by either side at the outset. These bargains surprise, but they can also transform.

These categories illuminate the compromise patterns of the Constitutional Convention and the political maneuvering

---

the hardback edition. As a result, I have had to bolt their concepts onto this paperback edition without weaving their concepts into the broader narrative. To do so would have essentially required a full rewrite of the book, rather than a mere revision and expansion.

through the Bill of Rights to gain passage for the adoption of the Constitution. The Bill of Rights, for example, was an intersection compromise. The Federalists and Anti-Federalists alike agreed on protecting basic liberties, even if they disagreed about the Constitution itself. Liberty served as an intersection for compromise. Alternatively, the Great Compromise, blending proportional representation in the House with equal representation in the Senate, was a conjunction compromise, fusing irreconcilable demands into one governing structure. The magic of Jim Collins' "and" approach. Finally, the Electoral College exemplified a substitution compromise. The two sides—direct election and legislative appointment—formed and differentiated at the Convention for the selection of the Executive. Neither side prevailed; instead, a novel mechanism was invented, one that no side had originally imagined—the Electoral College.

The same patterns recur throughout our history in Congressional legislation, as Chapter 4 traced. For example, the Social Security Act of 1935 rested on shared ground, a recognition across party lines that old-age poverty demanded protection—an intersection compromise. The Civil Rights Act of 1964 represented a conjunction compromise, where both advocates of equality and defenders of stability accepted provisions they had once resisted. Finally, the Tax Reform Act of 1986 was a substitution compromise. Both sides abandoned original tax philosophies to create a new, simplified framework that satisfied neither party completely, yet endured as landmark legislation. The Constitutional examples remind us that compromise structured the Republic from the beginning, and the Congressional examples show how the same methods have carried forward—sometimes by finding overlap, sometimes by fusing opposites, and sometimes by creating what neither side first envisioned.

The Art of the Compromise

The lesson does not belong to Congress alone. We as citizens, too, must practice this same art. Moral Foundations Theory shows why we differ—care, fairness, loyalty, authority, sanctity, liberty—and why disagreement runs deep. We may never build consensus, and we may need to yawp from time to time, but by learning to recognize these differences and by choosing the appropriate type of compromise, we can move beyond the hunger to win arguments. Our charge is not to silence rivals but to build solutions. The Republic depends on leaders who dare to govern through compromise, and it depends just as much on citizens—We, the People—willing to support them when they do.

Such habits are not new demands, but the very conditions that made the Republic possible. From Franklin's chair in 1787 to our own divided Congress today, the question remains the same. Can Americans sustain the discipline of compromise long enough to keep the Union whole?

Entering the Arena

The answer to that question resides within each of us. The Art of the Compromise lives at the human scale—in habit, judgment, and daily restraint. The Republic survives not because of the occasional hero, but because ordinary citizens carry those habits into the ring. The discipline that sustains compromise begins not with the state, but with the self.

Louis Brandeis once said, "The most important political office is that of the private citizen" (Mason, 2019). That role is not honorary but demands vigilance. Before he joined the Supreme Court in 1916, Brandeis earned his reputation as the "people's lawyer"—a defender of workers, a critic of monopolies, and an advocate for the public good. Once on the Court, he brought moral seriousness to the First Amendment and the emerging right to privacy. In *Whitney v. California* (1927), he warned that "the greatest menace to freedom is an inert people," and urged that the antidote to bad ideas is not repression, but "more speech" (Blasi, 1987). We must not fall victim to apathy.

Brandeis's influence ran deeper than doctrine. He saw democratic life as a moral calling. Habits of listening, restraint, and participation—quiet choices repeated over time—form the muscle memory of a free people. Without them, law becomes brittle and public life drifts toward spectacle. A republic, in Brandeis's view, is sustained not by grand gestures but by citizens who take responsibility for their silence, their speech, and their share of the common good.

Self-government should not reward the loudest voice, the sharpest insult, or the most viral contempt. Enduring compromise grows from the quiet discipline to hear before reacting, to stay at the table after disagreement, to seek understanding when outrage would feel more satisfying. The Republic depends not on volume, but on listening—a skill both rare and essential in the Art of the Compromise.

Theodore Roosevelt once praised the citizen "who strives valiantly; who errs, who comes short again and again, because there is no effort without error and shortcoming; but who does actually strive to do the deeds" (Roosevelt, 1910). The credit, he said, belongs not to the critic but to the one "who is actually in the arena, whose face is marred by dust and sweat and blood." The compromises required by a self-governing people are forged in that same ring—not from purity or ease, but from the courage to stay, possibly fail, and try again. The instinct to leave the table at the first note of discord must be replaced with discipline. Pause. Listen. Take a sip of water. Lean in.

The Art of the Compromise

Stepping into the arena, as Roosevelt described, does not require grandeur. The work begins with habit. Discipline, not drama, sustains a republic. The following habits strengthen that posture:

Listen without pre-loading a rebuttal.

Ask a second question instead of repeating a position.

Share a meal with someone from another camp.

Decline to pass along a half-true meme.

Support candidates who favor outcomes over applause.

Praise a leader who dares to cross the aisle.

Resist the impulse to shame those who change their mind—grace withheld today may be needed tomorrow.

Small habits build the discipline that keeps self-government alive.

Some disagreements will not end in harmony. Some proposals demand rejection. Some divisions resist resolution. On occasion, parting ways honors principle. Yet the standard should not be perfection. Progress should weigh more than purity. The hard work of the Republic, as Roosevelt implores, is persistence. Endure long enough in the tension to build a better tomorrow—a more perfect Union.

Yet even persistence has limits. Habit must yield, at times, to humility. Some moments require not just endurance, but transformation. Discipline steadies the hand; wisdom knows when to let go. Compromise is not the end of disagreement but the beginning of progress.

Beyond the Deal

In Totum

As at the start of this chapter, so at the close, we return to the sun behind Washington's chair. The rays stretched outward, direction uncertain. Was the Republic rising—or already falling? The wood offered no answer. Franklin's gaze returned often to that emblem across the long, heated summer of 1787. Only at the end did he find resolution. The national sun was rising. I hope that this book's chapters have also inspired a rising, rather than a setting, sun.

Outside the Philadelphia Hall, his words struck harder. When the woman asked, "What have we got?" Franklin did not offer comfort. He delivered a challenge. Those words still echo, less as prophecy, more as instruction. A republic endures not by design alone, but through the discipline and responsibility* of those who claim its promise.

No singular collapse brings down a republic. No wave of banners or flash of bayonets. Decline arrives more quietly—through casual scorn, tribal spite, and the gradual erosion of civic trust until, eventually, no one cares, as in the Soviet twilight. The riot on January 6 did not, by itself, begin a crisis. The event was a spark in the combustible atmosphere

---

*As to responsibility, Viktor Frankl, in *Man's Search for Meaning* (1985), proposed a Statue of Responsibility for the West Coast to complement the Statue of Liberty on the East—a symbolic counterweight reminding citizens that freedom demands stewardship. Efforts to realize the monument have surfaced in recent decades, though momentum has varied. Frankl's challenge remains timely: liberty requires discipline. As Lawrence Lessig argues in *America, Compromised* (2018), responsibility in a self-governing republic begins when citizens hold themselves accountable—not only by voting, but by seeking out trustworthy information and engaging with the public square in good faith.

The Art of the Compromise

Madison warned against—a nation thick with factions, ready to ignite on resentment. The riot did not stand alone; the backlash followed—calls to silence dissent, prosecute rivals, and mistake pluralism for decay. Protests may not rise to nobility; backlashes may not reflect patriotism. Yet both must be endured. The Constitution was designed not to suppress these factions but to channel them, to contain discord without extinguishing it.

Factions do not live in the margins. The instinct begins in the homeowners' association, the school board meeting, the comment thread, the church committee, and the family table. The failure to govern disagreement in these small rooms foreshadows the collapse of governance on the national stage. A republic that cannot tolerate friction at the dinner table will never withstand the pressures of the world stage. President Xi's critique of American-style democracy thus finds its mark unless we prove him wrong. When Lincoln spoke at Gettysburg on the why that government of the people, by the people, and for the people shall not perish from the earth, he addressed not only a divided Union but the monarchs of Europe who doubted popular government could endure. His words should still resonate with today's autocrats such as Xi. Republics are not built in marble. The habits that sustain self-government are practiced at a human scale. The Art of the Compromise does not originate in Congress. The craft begins within each citizen—*We, the People*.

No singular figure will redeem the Republic. The burden rests within ourselves, as Brandeisian citizens. Personal belief need not be abandoned. We must preserve our zeal. Universal agreement is not necessary and should not be our goal. No one should expect a national chorus of *Kumbaya, my Lord* to sweep across the land. Harmony is not the precondition of democracy. What matters is choice—the choice to remain in Teddy

Roosevelt's arena long enough to govern together, to find compromise towards progress.

The Constitution emerged from such a process with the collective in Philadelphia during the summer of 1787. Argument gave way to structure, not unanimity, but coherence. The final product came from sealed debate, from collision and reconciliation. The Constitution lives not as a record of consensus, but as a record of disciplined compromise.

A republic, if you can keep it.

Keep it—by compromising.

Compromise ain't easy, and it ain't for the weak.

—

Stay strong.

Acknowledgments

BEFORE I BEGIN WITH acknowledgments, let me say a few words about self-publishing this book—both the softcover and the hardcover editions. First, I do not enjoy writing, nor do I enjoy reading. Both experiences are painful for me. However, much like physical exercise, I may not enjoy the process—the blood, the sweat, the tears—but I do enjoy the results. I enjoy the clarifying and focusing that writing brings to my ideas and the expansion and engagement that reading brings to my thoughts. Self-publishing is much the same. The process is painful, including writing, editing, formatting, proofing, indexing,[*] and the steps necessary to lay out and publish a book. These tasks are daunting. Yet I am profoundly satisfied with the results.

I should also confess—as with the hardcover edition—that this book's readers are the first to review it. I have again not used an editor. Perhaps I should have. For good or for bad, this copy is a lone effort—my effort. My apologies to the reader. I had a tight budget. While I did not use AI tools such

---

[*] I have come to learn that book indexing remains one of the few endeavors that continues to be elusive to computer automation. Automated programs are on the market, but really good indexes are still in the realm of skilled humans and not AI bots, at least not yet.

Acknowledgments

as ChatGPT for the hardcover edition, I did make use of AI in preparing this expanded paperback edition—to clarify structure, harmonize themes, and refine key arguments, with a careful eye toward preserving my own voice and intent. ChatGPT also served as a research partner, helping compile data, develop Python code, and generate the many new figures found throughout this edition. AI has become an indispensable tool in my research efforts, like having a cadre of graduate students—tireless, fast, and occasionally insightful—on call at all hours.

Now, on to the thank you notes. First and foremost, I must thank my wife, Lisa, and daughter, Grace, for allowing me to pursue this hobby. This project started during the COVID-19 pandemic, specifically in December 2021. For the next two years, they gave me time and space to read and write on weekends and over vacations, and they also had to put up with my ramblings and digressions over meals and movies about some random *The Art of the Compromise* topic that I was deep-diving at that particular moment. They are a blessing in my life.

The next person that I must acknowledge is Chris Austin. Chris is an invisible hand that has unknowingly encouraged me to publish my political thoughts and ideas. My intellectual journey with Chris began in 2008 when I joined his first-Friday-of-the-month poker game. This card game became a gathering of nerds, entrepreneurs, geeks, thinkers, and plotters that enriched my thinking on a variety of topics from local politics to college football to Star Wars to John Galt to John Wayne to Def Leppard to black holes to the three-body problem and all things in between. In the fall of 2023, Chris also led a book club centered on Julia Cameron's *The Artist's Way*, and that discussion group inspired me to take a serious look at converting my COVID-19 writings into a self-published book—much thanks to Chris.

The Art of the Compromise

In January of 2024, I completed the essence of this book, which stood at about 150,000 words. At this point, I stared at a jumbled mass of words with zero knowledge about self-publishing. Lisa and Grace, again, had to endure a new round of ramblings as I dove deep into the world of self-publishing. I have a couple of folks to thank here. Heather Nuchols, a longtime friend from college, helped point the way. Heather has a couple of self-published fiction books under her belt, and she gave me some invaluable insights that kick-started my journey. Shout out to Heather.

I also must thank Barry Fox. I have never met Barry in person, but he was kind enough to spend a few hours on phone calls with me to discuss the self-publishing business. Barry helped me realize that no one would want to read 150,000 words from a no-name author like me. He encouraged me to trim the work to a more digestible 55,000 words for my first book. That process was like squishing Jell-O to form a sculpture—quite difficult. Barry also offered other insightful tips that nudged me further toward publication. I cannot thank him enough.

For this paperback edition, I should also acknowledge the *Donuts for Democracy* discussion group. These Saturday morning gatherings became a proving ground for many of the ideas in this revised and updated edition. Thanks to Andy Andrew, Brian Walker, Martin Ammons, and—once again—Chris Austin for showing up with curiosity, challenge, and good humor.

Clint Jones is a close friend who has unknowingly contributed to this book. I must thank him for his indirect contributions. Former Senator Phil Gramm of Texas used to have the "Dickey Flatt Test" to help him decide whether a federal government program should be funded or not. Dickey Flatt was Gramm's constituent, living in Mexia, Texas. The test

Acknowledgments

consisted of asking Dickey whether a given government expenditure improves his life or not. If a program was good for Dickey Flatt, it must be suitable for America, went Gramm's reasoning. Clint is my Dickey Flatt. He is a hard-working guy who deserves "life, liberty, and the pursuit of happiness" as much as anyone, if not more. When faced with a political conundrum, I ask myself, "Is it helpful to Clint?"

Finally, I must thank my family. Their love and support over the years have helped me understand our responsibility as citizens to remain active and engaged in political life in much the way Alexis de Tocqueville described over two centuries ago. Thank you to my brother Dan and his family, my late father and mother Bobby and Shirley Page, my late uncles Lon and Bill Boyd, my late aunt Betty Hensley, and my late uncle Laddie Harwood. My family has spanned both sides of the political spectrum, from Democrat to Republican, and I have witnessed *The Art of the Compromise* lived out in their daily choices.

Further Reading

WHILE MANY BOOKS HAVE inspired the thoughts and ideas in this book, the titles below extend the ideas explored here—from bisociated compromise to political identity, from the roots of reason to the resilience of the Republic. These works appear in the Works Cited section but deserve repeating here, both for emphasis and for readers ready to continue the journey.

Bisociated Compromise

The Man Who Ran Washington and *Showdown at Gucci Gulch* are case studies in bisociated compromise: the creative overlap of opposing worldviews forged into practical law. Baker mastered the deal not for its own sake, but to govern.

Baker, P., & Glasser, S. (2021). *The Man Who Ran Washington: The Life and Times of James A. Baker III.* Anchor.

Murray, A. S., & Birnbaum, J. H. (1988). *Showdown at Gucci Gulch.* Vintage.

Decriminalize Politics

Many may not like Donald Trump, but the legal pursuit to jail Trump and other political actors has escalated to dangerous levels. These two books examine how shifting politics from the ballot box to the jury box threatens democratic legitimacy and invites retribution in place of persuasion.

Dershowitz, A. M. (2017). *Trumped Up: How Criminalization of Political Differences Endangers Democracy*. Bombardier Books.

Morgan, P. W., & Reynolds, G. H. (1997). *The Appearance of Impropriety: How the Ethics Wars Have Undermined American Government, Business, and Society*. The Free Press.

Revitalize Congress

For those seeking a path back to a functional, deliberative Congress—one that rewards compromise over grandstanding—these books offer both diagnosis and roadmap.

Mann, T. E., & Ornstein, N. J. (2006). *The Broken Branch: How Congress is failing America and how to get it back on track*. Oxford University Press.

Mason, L. (2018). *Uncivil agreement: How politics became our identity*. University of Chicago Press.

Reason and Rhetoric

These works are essential reading for anyone who seeks to practice integrative complexity. They help us understand the limits of our own reasoning before we seek to correct the reasoning of others—a critical step toward political humility.

Heinrichs, J. (2017). *Thank you for arguing: What Aristotle, Lincoln, and Homer Simpson can teach us about the art of persuasion*. Crown.

Lakoff, G. (2014). *Don't Think of an Elephant!* Chelsea Green.

Mercier, H., & Sperber, D. (2017). *The Enigma of Reason.* Harvard University Press.

Community Engagement

As discussed earlier, Tocqueville recognized that American democracy grows from the ground up—in habits of association, not decrees from above. Putnam's *Bowling Alone* diagnoses what happens when those habits fade, and civic ties unravel.

Putnam, R. D. (2000). *Bowling Alone: The Collapse and Revival of American Community.* Simon and Schuster.

Electoral College

These books clarify how the Electoral College, far from being a relic, functions as an engine of compromise—preserving geographic balance, party stability, and peaceful transfer of power through structured political conflict.

Alexander, R. M. (2019). *Representation and the Electoral College.* Oxford University Press.

Rosenblum, N. L. (2010). *On the Side of the Angels: An Appreciation of Parties and Partisanship.* Princeton University Press.

Ross, T. (2019). *Why We Need the Electoral College.* Gateway Editions.

Further Reading

The Authoritarian Challenge

As China advances under a unified political system, America must rely not on unity of party but unity of purpose. These books highlight the stakes—and the need for bipartisan resolve forged through difficult compromise.

Mahbubani, K. (2020). *Has China Won? The Chinese Challenge to American Primacy*. Hachette UK.

Ringen, S. (2016). *The Perfect Dictatorship: China in the 21st Century*. Hong Kong University Press.

Wong, C. H. (2023). *Party of One: The Rise of Xi Jinping and China's Superpower Future*. Simon and Schuster.

Founding Fathers

These authors show that the Founders were not gods or saints, but masters of managed disagreement. Their legacy lies not in unanimity, but in the strength to argue, differ, and still unite.

Ketcham, R. L. (1990). *James Madison: A Biography*. University of Virginia Press.

Ricks, T. E. (2020). *First Principles: What America's Founders Learned from the Greeks and Romans and How That Shaped Our Country*. Harper Perennial.

Wood, G. S. (2017). *Friends Divided: John Adams and Thomas Jefferson*. Penguin.

The Art of the Compromise

Riot and Rebellion

The American Republic was born in a riot. From the Boston Tea Party to Shays's Rebellion, from Watts to January 6, disorder has never been far from democracy. Riots test the boundaries of the First Amendment and the patience of a republic built on consent. They are not just eruptions of lawlessness—they are often signals that lawful systems have failed to absorb dissent. These books explore the uneasy relationship between protest and politics, and how rebellion, when properly understood, can warn, rupture, or renew. A nation that tolerates factions must also contend with their more volatile expressions.

Gilje, P. A. (1999). *Rioting in America*. Indiana University Press.

Snyder, T. (2017). *On Tyranny: Twenty Lessons from the Twentieth Century*. Ten Speed Press.

Graeber, D. (2013). *The Democracy Project*. Spiegel & Grau.

Work Cited

Adams, A. (2010). Abigail Smith Adams. In D. Schneider & C. J. Schneider (Eds.), *First Ladies: A Biographical Dictionary*. Infobase Publishing.

Adams, R. (2010). Joe Biden: 'This is a big fucking deal'. The Guardian. https://www.theguardian.com/world/richard-adams-blog/2010/mar/23/joe-biden-obama-big-fucking-deal-overheard

Alesina, A., Devleeschauwer, A., Easterly, W., Kurlat, S., & Wacziarg, R. (2003). Fractionalization. Journal of Economic Growth. 8(2), 155–194. https://doi.org/10.1023/A:1024471506938

Alexander, R. M. (2019). *Representation and the Electoral College*. Oxford University Press.

Allison, G. T., & Zelikow, P. (1971). *Essence of decision: Explaining the Cuban missile crisis* (Vol. 327). Little, Brown Boston.

Allport, G. W. (1954). The nature of prejudice. *Reading/Addison-Wesley*.

Alter, A. (2016). A Fraud? Jonah Lehrer Says His Remorse Is Real. The New York Times. https://www.nytimes.com/2016/07/12/books/a-fraud-jonah-lehrer-says-his-remorse-is-real.html

Altman, N., & Kingson, E. (2015). *Social Security Works!: Why Social Security Isn't Going Broke and How Expanding It Will Help Us All*. The New Press.

Altman, N. J. (2012). *The battle for Social Security: From FDR's vision to Bush's gamble*. John Wiley & Sons.

Amar, A. R. (1998). *The bill of rights: Creation and reconstruction*. Yale University Press.

Ariely, D. (2008). *Predictably irrational: the hidden forces that shape our decisions*. HarperCollins Publishers.

Work Cited

Baker, P., & Glasser, S. (2021). *The Man Who Ran Washington: The Life and Times of James A. Baker III*. Anchor.

Balz, D. (2014). *Obama and LBJ: Measuring the current president against the past one's legacy*. The Washington Post. https://www.washingtonpost.com/politics/obama-and-lbj-measuring-the-current-president-against-the-past-ones-legacy/2014/04/12/672718fe-c258-11e3-bcec-b71ee10e9bc3_story.html

Barsanti, C. (2020). *The Ballot Box: 10 Presidential Elections that Changed American History*. Fall River Press.

Bartanen, M., & Littlefield, R. (2013). *Forensics in America: A history*. Rowman & Littlefield.

Beck, P. A. (2003). A tale of two electorates: The changing American party coalitions, 1952-2000. *The state of the parties: The changing role of contemporary American Parties*, 38-53.

Best, J. A. (2004). Presidential selection: Complex problems and simple solutions. *Political Science Quarterly, 119*(1), 39-59.

Bierman, N. (2016). *'Senator, you're no Jack Kennedy' almost didn't happen. How it became the biggest VP debate moment in history*. Los Angeles Times. https://www.latimes.com/politics/la-na-pol-debate-quayle-bentsen-20161004-snap-story.html

Blachowicz, J. (1998). *Of Two Minds: The Nature of Inquiry*. SUNY Press.

Black, D. (2018). *The Revolution Against the Revolution*. City Journal. https://www.city-journal.org/article/the-revolution-against-the-revolution/

Black, E., Black, M., & Black, E. (2009). *The rise of southern Republicans*. Harvard University Press.

Blasi, V. (1987). The First Amendment and the ideal of civic courage: The Brandeis opinion in Whitney v. California. *Wm. & Mary L. Rev., 29*, 653.

Bogage, J. (2020). *Trump drags LSU football team into impeachment fervor during White House visit*. The Washington Post. https://www.washingtonpost.com/sports/2020/01/17/lsu-visits-white-house-celebrate-college-football-national-championship-with-trump/

Bolleyer, N. (2013). *New parties in old party systems: Persistence and decline in seventeen democracies.* Oxford University Press.

Bouverie, T. (2020). *Appeasement: Chamberlain, Hitler, Churchill, and the Road to War.* Crown.

Branch, T. (2007). *Parting the waters: America in the King years 1954-63.* Simon and Schuster.

Brecke, P. (1999). Violent conflicts 1400 AD to the present in different regions of the world. 1999 Meeting of the Peace Science Society,

Brenan, M. (2020). *61% of Americans Support Abolishing Electoral College.* Gallup. https://news.gallup.com/poll/320744/americans-support-abolishing-electoral-college.aspx

Brinkley, A (1996). *The end of reform: New Deal liberalism in recession and war.* Vintage.

Briscoe, T., & Olumhense, E. (2020). *Rage, Riots, Ruin.* Chicago Tribune. http://graphics.chicagotribune.com/riots-chicago-1968-mlk/index.html

Broder, J. M. (2009). *Despite Successes, Kennedy Left Unfinished Business.* The New York Times. https://www.nytimes.com/2009/08/28/us/politics/28record.html

Brown, C. (2016). *The Whole World Was Watching: Public Opinion in 1968.* Roper Center for Public Opinion Research. https://ropercenter.cornell.edu/blog/whole-world-was-watching-public-opinion-1968

Brumback, K. (2019). *Court rules against cop-killing militant formerly known as H. Rap Brown.* Montgomery Advertiser. https://www.montgomeryadvertiser.com/story/news/crime/2019/07/31/court-rules-against-militant-formerly-known-h-rap-brown-jamil-abdullah-al-amin/1876817001/

Bugh, G. (2016). *Electoral college reform: Challenges and possibilities.* Routledge.

Burger, W. E. (1995). *It is so ordered: A constitution unfolds.* William Morrow & Company.

Burnham, W. D. (1970). *Critical elections and the mainsprings of American politics.* Norton.

Cameron, C. (2022). *These Are the People Who Died in Connection With the Capitol Riot.* The New York Times.

Work Cited

https://www.nytimes.com/2022/01/05/us/politics/jan-6-capitol-deaths.html

Cantor, E. (2017). *Eric Cantor: What the Obama Presidency Looked Like to the Opposition.* The New York Times. https://www.nytimes.com/2017/01/14/opinion/sunday/eric-cantor-what-the-obama-presidency-looked-like-to-the-opposition.html

Caramani, D. (2017). *Comparative politics.* Oxford University Press.

Caro, R. A. (2002). *Master of the Senate: The Years of Lyndon Johnson III* (Vol. 3). Knopf.

Caro, R. A. (2012). *The years of Lyndon Johnson: The passage of power* (Vol. 4). Random House.

Carp, B. L. (2010). *Defiance of the patriots: The Boston Tea Party and the making of America.* Yale University Press.

Cerami, C. A. (2008). *Dinner at Mr. Jefferson's: Three Men, Five Great Wines, and the Evening that Changed America.* Wiley.

Christmas, B. S. (2017). *Washington's Nightmare: A Brief History of American Political Parties.* Self-published, CreateSpace.

Clinton, H. R. (2017). *What happened.* Simon and Schuster.

Clodfelter, M. (2017). *Warfare and armed conflicts: a statistical encyclopedia of casualty and other figures, 1492-2015.* McFarland.

Coelho, C. (2013). *Timothy Matlack, Scribe of the Declaration of Independence.* McFarland.

Cohen, E. D. (2020). *The Soul of a Nation.* Psychology Today. https://www.psychologytoday.com/us/blog/what-would-aristotle-do/202011/the-soul-nation

Cohn, J. (2011). *Obama Embraces 'Obamacare'.* The New Republic. https://newrepublic.com/article/93744/obama-embraces-obamacare

Collins, E. (2019). *Did Perot Spoil 1992 Election for Bush? It's Complicated.* The Wall Street Journal. https://www.wsj.com/articles/did-perot-spoil-1992-election-for-bush-its-complicated-11562714375

Collins, J. (2001). *Good to Great.* Random House.

Collins, J. C., Porras, J. I., Porras, J., & Collins, J. (2005). *Built to last: Successful habits of visionary companies.* Random House.

Conway III, L. G., Thoemmes, F., Allison, A. M., Towgood, K. H., Wagner, M. J., Davey, K., Salcido, A., Stovall, A. N., Dodds, D. P., & Bongard, K. (2008). Two ways to be complex and why they matter: Implications for attitude strength and lying. *Journal of personality and social psychology, 95*(5), 1029.

Coppedge, M., Gerring, J., Knutsen, C. H., Lindberg, S. I., Teorell, J., Marquardt, K. L., Medzihorsky, J., Pemstein, D., Fox, L., & Gastaldi, L. (2024). V-Dem Methodology v14. *V-dem working paper forthcoming.*

Csikszentmihalyi, M. (1996). *Creativity: The Psychology of Discovery and Invention.* Harper Perennial Modern Classics.

Current, R. N. (1963). *Lincoln and the first shot.* Lippincott Williams & Wilkins.

Curtis, M. K. (1986). *No state shall abridge: The Fourteenth Amendment and the Bill of Rights.* Duke University Press.

Cyr, A. I. (2020). *Electoral College designed to protect against uncompromised concentration of power.* Chicago Tribune. https://www.chicagotribune.com/2020/11/11/column-electoral-college-designed-to-protect-against-uncompromised-concentration-of-power/

Daalder, I. H., & O'Hanlon, M. E. (2004). *Winning ugly: NATO's war to save Kosovo.* Rowman & Littlefield.

Dahl, R. A. (1956). *A preface to democratic theory* (Vol. 115). University of Chicago Press.

Damasio, A. R. (2006). *Descartes' Error: Emotion, Reason, and the Human Brain.* Random House.

Davis, A. (2022). *Rabbi Who Participated in Jan. 6 Capitol Riot Gets Home Confinement.* Newsweek. https://www.newsweek.com/rabbi-who-sought-50-fine-participating-jan-6-capitol-riot-gets-home-confinement-1671405

Davis, B. (1957). *Gray Fox: Robert E. Lee and the Civil War.* Burford Books.

De Becker, G., & Stechschulte, T. (1997). *The Gift of Fear.* Dell Publishing.

De Vries, C. E. (2020). *Why the EU struggles to agree on anything.* Politico. https://www.politico.eu/article/why-the-eu-cant-agree-on-anything-coronavirus-budget-mff-recovery-fund/

Deis, R. (2010). *"Nothing is certain except death and taxes.".* This Day in Quotes.

https://www.thisdayinquotes.com/2010/11/nothing-is-certain-except-death-and-taxes/

Dershowitz, A. M. (2017). *Trumped Up: How Criminalization of Political Differences Endangers Democracy*. Bombardier Books.

Dershowitz, A. M. (2023). *Being wrong doesn't make Trump a criminal*. The Telegraph. https://www.telegraph.co.uk/news/2023/08/03/being-wrong-doesnt-make-donald-trump-a-criminal/

DeSilver, D. (2016). *Trump's victory another example of how Electoral College wins are bigger than popular vote ones*. Pew Research Center. https://www.pewresearch.org/short-reads/2016/12/20/why-electoral-college-landslides-are-easier-to-win-than-popular-vote-ones/

Deutsch, M. E. (1923). E pluribus unum. *the classical Journal*, *18*(7), 387-407.

Diamond, L. (2020). *Ill winds: Saving democracy from Russian rage, Chinese ambition, and American complacency*. Penguin.

DiLorenzo, T. J. (2020). *The Problem with Lincoln*. Simon and Schuster.

Donaldson, G. A. (2014). *The Secret Coalition: Ike, LBJ, and the Search for a Middle Way in the 1950s*. Skyhorse.

Drutman, L. (2018). *Why America's 2-party system is on a collision course with our constitutional democracy*. Vox. https://www.vox.com/polyarchy/2018/3/26/17163960/america-two-party-system-constitutional-democracy

Dunbar, M. (2025). Trump empowers Musk by ordering agencies to cooperate with Doge. Retrieved 2025-02-11, from https://www.theguardian.com/us-news/2025/feb/11/trump-doge-executive-order-musk

Edwards, G. C. (2012). *Overreach: Leadership in the Obama presidency*. Princeton University Press.

Ellis, J. J. (1997). *American sphinx: the character of Thomas Jefferson*. Knopf.

Ellis, J. J. (2002). *Founding Brothers: The Revolutionary Generation*. Vintage.

Ely, J. H. (1981). *Democracy and distrust: A theory of judicial review*. Harvard University Press.

Erikson, B., Cowan, R., Morgan, D., & Sullivan, A. (2025). Republicans muscle Trump's sweeping tax-cut and spending bill through Congress. *Reuters*. Retrieved 2025-

07-03, from https://www.reuters.com/legal/government/us-house-republicans-head-toward-final-vote-trumps-sweeping-tax-cut-bill-2025-07-03/

Esterson, H. (2020). *The Fighting Temeraire: The true story behind William Turner's most beloved painting*. Hero Magazine. https://hero-magazine.com/article/179436/the-fighting-temeraire-william-turner-tate

Fandos, N. S., S. G.; Baker, P. (2019). Trump Signs Bill Reopening Government for 3 Weeks in Surprise Retreat From Wall. *The New York Times*. https://www.nytimes.com/2019/01/25/us/politics/trump-shutdown-deal.html

Farrow, R. (2021). *An Air Force Combat Veteran Breached the Senate*. The New Yorker. https://www.newyorker.com/news/news-desk/an-air-force-combat-veteran-breached-the-senate

Fearon, J. D. (2003). Ethnic and cultural diversity by country. *Journal of Economic Growth*, 8(2), 195-222.

Feldman, N. (2017). *The Three Lives of James Madison: Genius, Partisan, President*. Random House.

Fernyhough, C. (2016). *The voices within: The history and science of how we talk to ourselves*. Basic Books.

Feuer, A. (2021). *A Capitol Police lieutenant won't face charges in the Jan. 6 shooting death of a rioter*. The New York Times. https://www.nytimes.com/2021/04/14/us/capitol-police-ashli-babbitt-riot.html

Feuerherd, B. (2021). *Feds charge NYC sanitation worker in Capitol riot after Post story*. New York Post. https://nypost.com/2021/01/21/feds-charge-nyc-sanitation-worker-in-capitol-riot-after-post-story/

Fisher, D. R., Andrews, K. T., Caren, N., Chenoweth, E., Heaney, M. T., Leung, T., Perkins, L. N., & Pressman, J. (2019). The science of contemporary street protest: New efforts in the United States. *Science advances*, 5(10), eaaw5461.

Fitzgerald, F. S. (2009). *The Crack-Up*. New Directions Publishing.

FiveThirtyEight. (2023). *Polling and Primary Support Data on Donald Trump*. [.]. https://fivethirtyeight.com/politics/

Work Cited

Fogel, R. W., & Engerman, S. L. (1995). *Time on the cross: The economics of American Negro slavery* (Vol. 1). WW Norton & Company.

Foner, E. (2019). *The second founding: How the Civil War and Reconstruction remade the Constitution*. WW Norton & Company.

Fournier, R. (2013). This Is the End of the Presidency. *The Atlantic*. Retrieved 2013-12-17, from https://www.theatlantic.com/politics/archive/2013/12/this-is-the-end-of-the-presidency/461133/

Fowler, M. (2008). *Obama: No Surprise That Hard-Pressed Pennsylvanians Turn Bitter*. HuffPost. https://www.huffpost.com/entry/obama-no-surprise-that-ha_b_96188

Frankl, V. E. (1985). *Man's search for meaning*. Simon and Schuster.

Franks, M. A. (2019). *The cult of the constitution: Our deadly devotion to guns and free speech*. Stanford University Press.

Freehling, W. W. (1992). *Prelude to Civil War: the nullification controversy in South Carolina, 1816-1836*. Oxford University Press.

Friedman, V. (2021). *Why Rioters Wear Costumes*. The New York Times. https://www.nytimes.com/2021/01/07/style/capitol-riot-tactics.html

Galbraith, A. (2022). *Sanford firefighter who took part in Jan. 6 riots sentenced to probation*. Orlando Weekly. https://www.orlandoweekly.com/news/sanford-firefighter-who-took-part-in-jan-6-riots-to-be-sentenced-today-30985170

Gallman, R. E. (1960). Commodity Output, 1839-1899. *Trends in the American economy in the nineteenth century*, 13-72.

Gamm, G., & Kousser, T. (2010). Broad bills or particularistic policy? Historical patterns in American state legislatures. *American Political Science Review, 104*(1), 151-170.

George, J. (1990). The World Will Little Note? The Philadelphia Press and the Gettysburg Address. *The Pennsylvania Magazine of History and Biography, 114*(3), 385-398.

Gilbert, M. (2014). *The second world war: a complete history*. Rosetta Books.

Gilje, P. A. (1999). *Rioting in America*. Indiana University Press.

Ginsberg, B., Lowi, T. J., & Weir, M. (2019). *We the people: An introduction to American politics*. WW Norton & Company, Inc.

Gleditsch, N. P., Wallensteen, P., Eriksson, M., Sollenberg, M., & Strand, H. (2002). Armed conflict 1946-2001: A new dataset. *Journal of peace research, 39*(5), 615-637.

Goldstein, A. (2016). *How the demise of her health-care plan led to the politician Clinton is today*. The Washington Post. https://www.washingtonpost.com/politics/after-health-care-missteps-a-chastened-hillary-clinton-emerged/2016/08/25/2d200cb4-64b4-11e6-be4e-23fc4d4d12b4_story.html

Goodwin, D. K. (2009). *Team of Rivals: The Political Genius of Abraham Lincoln*. Penguin UK.

Goodwin, D. K. (2016). *Barack Obama and Doris Kearns Goodwin: The Ultimate Exit Interview*. Vanity Fair. https://www.vanityfair.com/news/2016/09/barack-obama-doris-kearns-goodwin-interview

Goodwin, D. K. (2019). *Leadership: In turbulent times*. Simon & Schuster.

Gorbachev, M. (1991). *End of the Soviet Union; Text of Gorbachev's Farewell Address*. The New York Times. https://www.nytimes.com/1991/12/26/world/end-of-the-soviet-union-text-of-gorbachev-s-farewell-address.html

Gordon, J. S. (2010). *Hamilton's Blessing*. Bloomsbury Publishing USA.

Gorsuch, N. M., & Nitze, J. (2024). Over ruled: The human toll of too much law. *(No Title)*.

Graeber, D. (2013). *The democracy project: A history, a crisis, a movement*. Random House.

Grammarist. (2019). Two's company, three's a crowd. Retrieved 2019-11-17, from https://grammarist.com/proverb/twos-company-threes-a-crowd/

Grossman, A. L. (2014). *Is the Tax Code Really 70,000 Pages Long? No, Not Even Close*. Slate. https://slate.com/news-and-politics/2014/04/how-long-is-the-tax-code-it-is-far-shorter-than-70000-pages.html

Work Cited

Grossmann, M. (2014). *Artists of the possible: Governing networks and American policy change since 1945*. Oxford University Press.

Gunderson, G. (1974). The origin of the American civil war. *The Journal of Economic History, 34*(4), 915-950.

Haidt, J. (2012). *The righteous mind: Why good people are divided by politics and religion*. Vintage.

Hamilton, A., Madison, J., & Jay, J. (2015). *The Federalist Papers: A Collection of Essays Written in Favour of the New Constitution*. Coventry House Publishing.

Hamilton, B. (2022). *"Sorry Guys, We Stormed the Capitol": Eye-Witness Accounts of January 6th*. The Chasing History Project.

Harvin, D. (2023). *Here's the Intelligence Assessment of Donald Trump that the Government Can't Write*. Politico. https://www.politico.com/news/magazine/2023/08/05/donald-trump-homeland-security-threat-00109928

Harwood, J. (2014). *For Obama, a Go-It-Alone Push Fits the Times*. The New York Times. https://www.nytimes.com/2014/12/08/us/politics/for-obama-a-go-it-alone-push-fits-the-times.html

Heinrichs, J. (2017). *Thank you for arguing: What Aristotle, Lincoln, and Homer Simpson can teach us about the art of persuasion*. Crown.

Hendershot, H. (2018). *How 'Fake News' Was Born at the 1968 DNC*. Politico. https://politi.co/2wv3K3J

Hershey, M. R. (2017). *Party Politics in America*. Routledge.

Himanen, P. (2010). *The hacker ethic: A radical approach to the philosophy of business*. Random House.

History.com. (2018). *1968 Democratic Convention - Protests, Yippies, Witnesses*. https://www.history.com/topics/1960s/1968-democratic-convention

Hoare, Q., & Smith, G. N. (1971). The Intellectuals. Introduction. *Selections from the Prison Notebooks of Antonio Gramsci. New York: International Publishers, 4*.

Holzer, H. (2009). *The Lincoln anthology: Great writers on his life and legacy from 1860 to now* (Vol. 3). Library of America.

Hosenball, M. (2021). *FBI finds scant evidence U.S. Capitol attack was coordinated*. Reuters. https://www.reuters.com/world/us/exclusive-fbi-

finds-scant-evidence-us-capitol-attack-was-coordinated-sources-2021-08-20/
Hsu, S. S., Weiner, R., & Jackman, T. (2023). *Proud Boys led Jan. 6 riot to keep Trump in office, U.S. says at trial.* The Washington Post. https://www.washingtonpost.com/dc-md-va/2023/01/12/proud-boys-trial-openings/
Hubbard, K., Kim, E., & Yilek, C. (2025). House passes "big, beautiful bill," sending it to Trump's desk in 218-214 vote. *CBS News.* https://www.cbsnews.com/news/house-vote-big-beautiful-bill-rules-committee/
Huber, J., Payne, J. W., & Puto, C. (1982). Adding asymmetrically dominated alternatives: Violations of regularity and the similarity hypothesis. *Journal of consumer research, 9*(1), 90-98.
Hummel, J. (2013). *Emancipating slaves, enslaving free men: a history of the American Civil War.* Open Court.
Ingram, J., & Rosen, J. (2024). Trump campaign says it raised $52.8 million after guilty verdict in fundraising blitz. *CBS News.* https://www.cbsnews.com/news/trump-fundraising-guilty-verdict-new-york-conviction/
Irwin, D. A. (2017). *Clashing over commerce: A history of US trade policy.* University of Chicago Press.
Jacobs, H. E. (1919). *Lincoln's Gettysburg World-Message.* United Lutheran Publication House.
Jefferson, T. (1816). Proposals to Revise the Virginia Constitution: I. Thomas Jefferson to 'Henry Tompkinson'(Samuel Kercheval). *Founders Online.*
Jefferson, T., & Madison, J. (1995). *The republic of letters: The correspondence between Thomas Jefferson and James Madison, 1776-1826.* WW Norton & Company.
Johnson, L. H. (1960). Fort Sumter and Confederate Diplomacy. *The Journal of Southern History, 26*(4), 441-477.
Jones, A. (2010). *Justice Scalia's Thoughts on State Secession: Penned to One Man.* The Wall Street Journal. https://www.wsj.com/articles/BL-LB-24975
Jones, C. B., & Connelly, S. (2012). *Behind the dream: The making of the speech that transformed a nation.* Macmillan.
Jones, K. T. (1994). Cerebral Gymnastics 101: Why Do Debaters Debate? In *Cross Examination Debate*

Association Yearbook (Vol. 15, pp. 66-75). George Fox University. http://cedadebate.org

Kahneman, D. (2011). *Thinking, Fast and Slow*. Macmillan.

Kahneman, D., & Tversky, A. (1986). Rational choice and the framing of decisions. *Journal of business, 59*(4), 251-278.

Kahneman, D., & Tversky, A. (2013). Prospect theory: An analysis of decision under risk. In *Handbook of the Fundamentals of Financial Decision Making: Part I* (pp. 99-127). World Scientific.

Kalb, D. (2015). *Guide to US elections*. CQ Press.

Kazin, M. (1998). *The populist persuasion: An American history*. Cornell University Press.

Kengor, P. (2021). *Christmas 1991: The birth of freedom in the death of the evil empire*. Acton Institute. https://rlo.acton.org/archives/122754-christmas-1991-the-birth-of-freedom-in-the-death-of-the-evil-empire.html

Kennedy, D. M. (1999). *Freedom from fear: The American people in depression and war, 1929-1945*. Oxford University Press.

Kennedy, J. F. (1956). *Congressional Record*.

Ketcham, R. L. (1990). *James Madison: A Biography*. University of Virginia Press.

Key, V. O. (1955). A Theory of Critical Elections. *The journal of politics, 17*(1), 3-18.

Klarman, M. J. (2004). *From Jim Crow to civil rights: The Supreme Court and the struggle for racial equality*. Oxford University Press.

Klein, C. (2016, 2019-02-22). *The Soviet Union's Final Hours*. History.com. https://www.history.com/news/the-soviet-unions-final-hours

Klein, E. (2015). *Unlikeable: The Problem with Hillary*. Simon and Schuster.

Klein, E. (2019). *Bernie Sanders is challenging two cherished theories of electability*. Vox. https://www.vox.com/2019/5/20/18630453/bernie-sanders-2020-electability-polls

Klein, E. (2020). *Why we're polarized*. Simon and Schuster.

Koestler, A. (1964). *The act of creation*. Last Century Media.

Kriner, M., & Lewis, J. (2021). Pride & prejudice: The violent evolution of the proud boys. *CTC sentinel, 14*(6), 26-38.

Kristof, K. M. (1990). *7 Million 'Dependents' Have Vanished After Rule Revised*. Los Angeles Times. https://www.latimes.com/archives/la-xpm-1990-12-18-fi-6842-story.html

Kurland, P. B., & Lerner, R. (Eds.). (1977). *Equality: James Madison, Parties* (Vol. 1). University of Chicago Press. https://press-pubs.uchicago.edu/founders/documents/v1ch15s50.html

Kurlansky, M. (2016). *Paging through history*. WW Norton & Company.

Kutler, S. I. (1992). *The wars of Watergate: The last crisis of Richard Nixon*. WW Norton & Company.

Lakoff, G. (2014). *The all new don't think of an elephant!: Know your values and frame the debate*. Chelsea Green Publishing.

Lawless, J. L., & Fox, R. L. (2010). *It still takes a candidate: Why women don't run for office*. Cambridge University Press.

Leatherby, L., Ray, A., Singhvi, A., Triebert, C., Watkins, D., & Willis, H. (2021). *How a Presidential Rally Turned Into a Capitol Rampage*. The New York Times. https://www.nytimes.com/interactive/2021/01/12/us/capitol-mob-timeline.html

Lehrer, J. (2010). *How We Decide*. Houghton Mifflin Harcourt.

Leip, D. (2025). *Dave Leip's Atlas of U.S. Presidential Elections*. https://uselectionatlas.org/

Lepora, C. (2012). On Compromise and Being Compromised. *Journal of Political Philosophy, 20*(1).

Lessig, L. (2018). *America, compromised*. University of Chicago Press.

Leubsdorf, B., Marchsteiner, K. E., & Wilson, C. (2023). Admission of States to the Union: A Historical Reference Guide. *Congressional Research Service (CRS) Reports and Issue Briefs*, NA-NA.

Leuchtenburg, W. E. (1963). *Franklin D. Roosevelt and the new deal, 1932-1940* (Vol. 3025). HarperCollins Publishers.

Leung, T., & Perkins, L. N. (2021). Counting protests in news articles: A dataset and semi-automated data collection pipeline. *arXiv preprint arXiv:2102.00917*.

Levitt, S. D. D., Stephen J. (2005). *Freakonomics: A Rogue Economist Explores the Hidden Side of Everything.* HarperCollins Publishers.

Lewin, K., & Lippitt, R. (1938). An experimental approach to the study of autocracy and democracy: A preliminary note. *Sociometry, 1*(3/4), 292-300.

Lewin, K., Lippitt, R., & White, R. K. (1939). Patterns of aggressive behavior in experimentally created "social climates". *The Journal of social psychology, 10*(2), 269-299.

Liebman, J. B. (2000). Who are the ineligible EITC recipients? *National Tax Journal, 53*(4), 1165-1185.

Liebman, L. (2020). How Bad Was The Trial of the Chicago 7's Judge Julius Hoffman, Really? *Vulture.* Retrieved 2020-10-19, from https://www.vulture.com/2020/10/who-was-judge-hoffman-the-real-story-of-the-chicago-7-judge.html

Lijphart, A. (1999). *Patterns of democracy: Government forms and performance in thirty-six countries.* Yale University Press.

Lincoln, A. (1953). *Collected Works of Abraham Lincoln Vol. 1.* Rutgers University Press.

Little, D. (1996). *1968: Hippies, Yippies, and the First Mayor Daley.* Chicago Tribune. https://www.chicagotribune.com/1996/07/26/1968-hippies-yippies-and-the-first-mayor-daley/

Lock, G. (1989). The 1689 bill of rights. *Political Studies, 37*(4), 540-561.

Madison, J. (2016). The Federalist Papers. In *Democracy: A Reader* (pp. 52-57). Columbia University Press.

Madison, J. (2022). *Notes of Debates in the Federal Convention of 1787.* Ohio University Press.

Mahbubani, K. (2020). *Has China Won? The Chinese Challenge to American Primacy.* Hachette UK.

Mair, P. (1990). *The west European party system.* Oxford University Press, USA.

Mann, T. E., & Ornstein, N. J. (2006). *The Broken Branch: How Congress is failing America and how to get it back on track.* Oxford University Press.

Mansfield, H. C., & Winthrop, D. (2000). *Democracy in America, Alexis de Tocqueville.* University of Chicago Press.

Marshall, M. G., & Gurr, T. R. (2020). Polity5: Political regime characteristics and transitions, 1800-2018. *Center for Systemic Peace, 2.*

Martis, K. C., & Rowles, R. A. (1989). The historical atlas of political parties in the United States Congress, 1789-1989.

Mason, A. T. (2019). *Brandeis: a free man's life.* Plunkett Lake Press.

Mason, L. (2018). *Uncivil agreement: How politics became our identity.* University of Chicago Press.

Max, W., & Gerth, H. (1946). Politics as a Vocation. *From Max Weber: Essays in Sociology, 77.*

McChrystal, S. (2018). *Why a 'Strong, Charismatic' Leader Is Not the Solution to America's Tumultuous Times.* Time. https://time.com/5434629/win-at-all-costs-politics-stanley-mcchrystal/

McCrae, R. R., & Costa, P. T. (2003). *Personality in adulthood: A five-factor theory perspective.* Guilford Press.

McCulloch, H. (1864). *Report of the Secretary of the Treasury on the State of the Finances for the Year 1864.* US Government Printing Office.

McGee, S. (2020). *How Billionaire Ross Perot Brought Populism Back to Presidential Politics.* History.com. https://www.history.com/news/ross-perot-populist-1992-election-changed-politics

McGough, M., Winger, A., Rakshit, S., & Amin, K. (2023). *How has U.S. spending on healthcare changed over time?* https://www.healthsystemtracker.org/chart-collection/u-s-spending-healthcare-changed-time/

McPherson, J. M. (2003). *Battle cry of freedom: The Civil War era.* Oxford University Press.

Meacham, J. (2019). *The soul of America: The battle for our better angels.* Random House Trade Paperbacks.

Mead, W. R. (2013). *Special providence: American foreign policy and how it changed the world.* Routledge.

Mercier, H., & Sperber, D. (2017). *The Enigma of Reason.* Harvard University Press.

Merica, D. (2017). *Clinton: Abolish the Electoral College.* CNN. https://www.cnn.com/2017/09/13/politics/hillary-clinton-anderson-cooper-electoral-college-cnntv/index.html

Work Cited

Miga, A. (2010). *Carter says Kennedy delayed health care years ago*. NBCNews.com. https://www.nbcnews.com/id/wbna39219869

Mitchell, B. L. (1961). *Edmund Ruffin: A Biography*. Indiana University Press.

Mitter, R., & Johnson, E. (2021). *What the West Gets Wrong About China*. Harvard Business Review. https://hbr.org/2021/05/what-the-west-gets-wrong-about-china

Morgan, P. W., & Reynolds, G. H. (1997). *The Appearance of Impropriety: How the Ethics Wars Have Undermined American Government, Business, and Society*. The Free Press.

Mullin, M. (2023). *The Nullification Crisis*. The Hermitage. https://thehermitage.com/andrew-jackson-the-nullification-crisis

Murray, A. S., & Birnbaum, J. H. (1988). *Showdown at Gucci Gulch*. Vintage.

Musielak, Z. E., & Quarles, B. (2014). The three-body problem. *Reports on Progress in Physics, 77*(6), 065901.

Myers, I. B., & Myers, P. B. (2010). *Gifts differing: Understanding personality type*. Nicholas Brealey.

National Archives and Records Administration. (2023). *Electoral College Votes* https://www.archives.gov/electoral-college

Nelson, L. (2017). *Obama just inadvertently revealed one of his biggest blunders with Obamacare*. Vox. https://www.vox.com/obamacare/2017/1/6/14191784/obama-obamacare-name

Nelson, S. (2022). *Trump supporters were armed for battle on Jan. 6, panel report says*. New York Post. https://nypost.com/2022/12/23/capitol-riot-report-details-weapons-toted-by-28k-strong-trump-mob/

O'Neill, P. H. (2017). *Essentials of comparative politics*. WW Norton & Company.

O'Neill, T. P. (2012). *Frenemies: A Love Story*. The New York Times. https://archive.nytimes.com/campaignstops.blogs.nytimes.com/2012/10/05/frenemies-a-love-story/

Obama, B. (2008). *Transcript Of Barack Obama's Victory Speech*. NPR. https://www.npr.org/2008/11/05/96624326/transcript-of-barack-obamas-victory-speech

Obama, B. (2014). Remarks by the President Before Cabinet Meeting. Retrieved 2014-01-14, from https://obamawhitehouse.archives.gov/the-press-office/2014/01/14/remarks-president-cabinet-meeting

Obama, B. (2020). *A Promised Land: The powerful political memoir from the former US President.* Penguin UK.

Pasquino, G. (2014). Italy: The Triumph of Personalist Parties. *Politics & Policy, 42*(4), 548-566.

Paterson, T. G., Clifford, J. G., & Hagan, K. J. (1995). American foreign relations: a history.

Pear, R., & Herzenhorn, D. M. (2010). Obama Hails Vote on Health Care as Answering 'the Call of History'. The New York Times. https://www.nytimes.com/2010/03/22/health/policy/22health.html

Pear, R. K., T.; Haberman, M. (2017). Senate Rejects Slimmed-Down Obamacare Repeal as McCain Votes No. *The New York Times.* https://www.nytimes.com/2017/07/28/us/politics/obamacare-repeal-senate.html

Pearl, J., & Mackenzie, D. (2018). *The Book of Why: The New Science of Cause and Effect.* Basic Books.

Penzenstadler, N. (2021). *Ready for battle: Rioters in tactical gear push popular brands to take a stand.* USA Today. https://www.usatoday.com/story/news/investigations/2021/03/17/violence-protesters-tactical-gear-market-answer-extremists/4671071001/

Perry, M. J. (2001). *We the People: The Fourteenth Amendment and the Supreme Court.* Oxford University Press.

Petersburg Express. (1865). *The Suicide of Ruffin; The Man who Fired the First Gun on Fort Sumter Blows His Brains Out He Prefers Death to Living Under the Government of the United States.* The New York Times. https://www.nytimes.com/1865/06/22/archives/the-suicide-of-ruffin-the-man-who-fired-the-first-gun-on-fort.html

Pettersson, T., & Öberg, M. (2020). Organized violence, 1989–2019. *Journal of peace research, 57*(4), 597-613.

Pettigrew, T. F., & Tropp, L. R. (2006). A meta-analytic test of intergroup contact theory. *Journal of personality and social psychology, 90*(5), 751.

Pierce, C. P., & Warren, M. (2012). *Bill Clinton: The Cover Story*. Esquire. https://www.esquire.com/news-politics/politics/a12383/bill-clinton-interview-2012-0212/

Pilkington, E. (2022). *'US democracy will not survive for long': How January 6 hearings plot a roadmap to autocracy*. The Guardian. https://www.theguardian.com/us-news/2022/jul/23/january-6-hearings-us-democracy-roadmap-autocracy

Plato. (2007). *The Republic* (2nd ed.). Penguin.

Posner, G. (2013a). *Case closed: Lee Harvey Oswald and the assassination of JFK*. Open Road Media.

Posner, G. (2013b). *Killing the Dream: James Earl Ray and the Assassination of Martin Luther King, Jr*. Open Road Media.

Pretzer, W. S. (2002). *Working at inventing: Thomas A. Edison and the Menlo Park experience*. JHU Press.

Price, G., MD, & Norbeck, T. (2021). *A Look Back At How The President Was Able To Sign Obamacare Into Law Four Years Ago*. Forbes. https://www.forbes.com/sites/physiciansfoundation/2014/03/26/a-look-back-at-how-the-president-was-able-to-sign-obamacare-into-law-four-years-ago/

Prokop, A. (2016). *Trump belatedly decides to defend the Electoral College, tweeting that it's "actually genius"*. Vox. https://www.vox.com/policy-and-politics/2016/11/14/13623946/trump-electoral-college-votes

Prosser, M. H. (1963). Communication problems in the United Nations. *Southern Journal of Communication, 29*(2), 125-132.

Przeworski, A. (2018). *Why bother with elections?* John Wiley & Sons.

Putnam, R. D. (2000). *Bowling Alone: The Collapse and Revival of American Community*. Simon and Schuster.

Raby, J. (2023). *Ex-lawmaker who served time for Jan. 6 riot seeks House seat*. Associated Press. https://apnews.com/article/politics-united-states-government-west-virginia-state-riots-9f62fe064158d9641fbe40100bd15300

Rakove, J. N. (1998). Original Meanings: Politics and Ideas in the Making of the Constitution. *JOURNAL OF AMERICAN STUDIES, 32*, 137-138.

Ransom, R. L. (1998). The economic consequences of the American Civil War. In *The Political Economy of War and Peace* (pp. 49-74). Springer.

Rasmussen, D. C. (2021). *Fears of a Setting Sun: The Disillusionment of America's Founders*. Princeton University Press.

Ray, J. (1678). *Digested into a Convenient Method for the Speedy Finding Any One Upon Occasion*. John Hayes, Printer to the University. https://quod.lib.umich.edu/e/eebo/A58161.0001.001?view=toc

Reagan, R. (1983). "Evil Empire," Speech. Voices of Democracy. https://voicesofdemocracy.umd.edu/reagan-evil-empire-speech-text/

Reid, T. R. (2010). *The Healing of America. A Global Quest for Better, Cheaper, and Fairer Health Care*. Penguin.

Reilly, R. J. (2022). *FBI arrests pastor who wore his company jacket on Jan. 6 and pushed into police line*. NBC. https://www.nbcnews.com/politics/justice-department/fbi-arrests-pastor-wore-company-jacket-jan-6-pushed-police-line-rcna50898

Reynolds, G. H. (2013). Ham Sandwich nation: due process when everything is a crime. *Colum. L. Rev. Sidebar, 113*, 102.

Richards, L. L. (2014). *Shays's rebellion: The American revolution's final battle*. University of Pennsylvania Press.

Ricks, T. E. (2020). *First Principles: What America's Founders Learned from the Greeks and Romans and How That Shaped Our Country*. Harper Perennial.

Ringen, S. (2016). *The perfect dictatorship: China in the 21st century* (Vol. 1). Hong Kong University Press.

Rogers, W. (2012). The Autobiography of Will Rogers. In *A Route 66 Companion* (pp. 58-60). University of Texas Press.

Roosevelt, F. D. (1933). *Franklin D. Roosevelt Speeches: Inaugural Address*. Pepperdine School of Public Policy. https://publicpolicy.pepperdine.edu/academics/research/faculty-research/new-deal/roosevelt-speeches/fr030433.htm

Roosevelt, T. (1910). *Citizenship in a Republic*.

Work Cited

Rosenblatt, R. (1987). Words On Pieces of Paper. *Time.* https://content.time.com/time/magazine/article/0,917 1,964937,00.html

Rosenblum, N. L. (2010). *On the side of the angels: an appreciation of parties and partisanship.*

Ross, T. (2004). *Enlightened democracy: The case for the Electoral College.* World Ahead Publishing.

Ross, T. (2019). *Why We Need the Electoral College.* Gateway Editions.

Ruffin, E. (1977). *The Diary of Edmund Ruffin: The Years of Hope, April, 1861–June, 1863.* LSU Press.

Russakoff, D. (1986). *In Taxer, the Impossible Became the Inevitable.* The Washington Post. https://www.washingtonpost.com/archive/politics/198 6/06/29/in-taxer-the-impossible-became-the-inevitable/ff419dfd-8d1e-4260-b60b-e940b1b41902/

Sapolsky, R. M. (2017). *Behave: The biology of humans at our best and worst.* Penguin.

Saric, I. (2022). *The times Trump has advocated for violence.* Axios. https://www.axios.com/2022/05/02/trump-call-violence-presidency

Sartori, G. (1997). *Comparative constitutional engineering: an inquiry into structures, incentives, and outcomes.* NYU Press.

Schattschneider, E. (1942). *Party government: American government in action.* Transaction Publishers.

Schousen, M. (2018). *Yes, Congress Faces Obstruction and Gridlock. That's What the Constitution's Framers Intended.* Time. https://time.com/5360344/congress-democracy-madison/

Scipioni, J. (2020). *Michelle Obama: Why going 'high' when faced with a challenge is so important to her.* CNBC. https://www.cnbc.com/2020/02/12/michelle-obama-on-famous-catchphrase-when-they-go-low-we-go-high.html

Scott, E. (2015). *Trump says Bible is his favorite book, but declines to share favorite verse.* CNN. https://www.cnn.com/2015/08/27/politics/donald-trump-favorite-bible-verses/index.html

Scott, W. (2018). *Marmion: A Tale of Flodden Field.* Edinburgh University Press.

Shays, D. (2013). *The Convulsed Commonwealth.* Massachusetts Historical Society.

https://www.masshist.org/object-of-the-month/may-2013

Sheinin, D. (2023). *Olympic swimmer Klete Keller avoids prison time for role in Jan. 6 riot.* The Washington Post. https://www.washingtonpost.com/sports/olympics/2023/12/01/klete-keller-sentencing-jan-6-capitol/

Siegelbaum, L. (2015). *Baltic Independence. Seventeen Moments in Soviet History.* https://soviethistory.msu.edu/1991-2/baltic-independence/

Silverglate, H. (2017). *Three felonies a day: How the feds target the innocent.* The Notable Trials Library.

Simon, J. F. (2006). *Lincoln and Chief Justice Taney: slavery, secession, and the president's war powers.* Simon and Schuster.

Sinek, S. (2011). *Start with why: How great leaders inspire everyone to take action.* Penguin.

Singer, J. D., & Small, M. (1994). Correlates of war project: International and civil war data, 1816-1992.

Skowronek, S. (1982). *Building a new American state: The expansion of national administrative capacities, 1877-1920.* Cambridge University Press.

Smith, J. D. (2014). *On Democracy's Doorstep: The Inside Story of how the Supreme Court Brought" One Person, One Vote" to the United States.* Hill and Wang.

Snyder, T. (2017). On tyranny: Twenty lessons from the twentieth century. In: Tim Duggan Books: New York.

Sonderegger, P. (2018). *Forget the Turing Test—give AI the F. Scott Fitzgerald Test instead.* Quartz. https://qz.com/1247378/forget-the-turing-test-give-ai-the-f-scott-fitzgerald-test-instead

Spang, F. (2023). Compromise in political theory. *Political Studies Review, 21*(3), 594-607.

Springfield Technical Community College. (2023). *Shays' Rebellion - Person: Daniel Shays.* Springfield Technical Community College. https://shaysrebellion.stcc.edu/shaysapp/person.do?shortName=daniel_shays

Stampp, K. M. (1978). The Concept of a Perpetual Union. *The Journal of American History, 65*(1), 5-33.

Stasavage, D. (2020). Democracy, autocracy, and emergency threats: Lessons for COVID-19 from the last thousand years. *International organization, 74*(S1), E1-E17.

Work Cited

Steuerle, C. E. (2008). *Contemporary US tax policy*. Rowman & Littlefield.

Stockman, F. (2012). *Recalling the Nixon-Kennedy health plan*. The Boston Globe. https://www.bostonglobe.com/opinion/2012/06/22/stockman/bvg57mguQxOVpZMmB1Mg2N/story.html

Stokes, S. C. (1999). Political Parties and Democracy. *Annual review of political science*, 2(1), 243-267.

Stuntz, W. J. (2013). *The collapse of American criminal justice*. Harvard University Press.

Suedfeld, P., & Tetlock, P. E. (2014). Integrative complexity at forty: Steps toward resolving the scoring dilemma. *Political Psychology*, 35(5), 597-601.

Sundberg, R., & Melander, E. (2013). Introducing the UCDP georeferenced event dataset. *Journal of peace research*, 50(4), 523-532.

Sundquist, J. L. (2011). *Dynamics of the party system: Alignment and realignment of political parties in the United States*. Brookings Institution Press.

Tajfel, H., Turner, J., Austin, W. G., & Worchel, S. (2001). An integrative theory of intergroup conflict. *Intergroup relations: Essential readings*, 94-109.

Tenorio, R. (2023). Sedition Hunters: how ordinary Americans helped track down the Capitol rioters. *The Guardian*. Retrieved 2023-10-28, from https://www.theguardian.com/books/2023/oct/28/sedition-hunters-book-jan-6-rioters-fbi-trump

Thomasson, M. A. (2002). From sickness to health: The twentieth-century development of US health insurance. *Explorations in Economic History*, 39(3), 233-253.

Thompson, H. (2018). *Broken Europe: Why the EU is Stuck in Perpetual Crisis*. Foreign Affairs. https://www.foreignaffairs.com/articles/europe/2018-12-10/broken-europe

Tichenor, D. J. (2002). *Dividing lines: The politics of immigration control in America*. Princeton University Press.

Tolchin, M. (1994). *Thomas P. O'Neill Jr., a Democratic Power in the House for Decades, Dies at 81*. The New York Times. https://archive.nytimes.com/www.nytimes.com/books/01/03/11/specials/oneill-obit.html

Trump, D., & Schwartz, T. (1987). *The Art of the Deal*. Random House.
Turner, J. M. W. (1838). *The Fighting Temeraire*. The National Gallery, London.
U.S. Bureau of the Census. (1976). *Historical statistics of the United States, colonial times to 1970*. U.S. Bureau of the Census,.
U.S. Department of Justice. (2021). *One Year Since the Jan. 6 Attack on the Capitol*. U.S. Department of Justice,. https://www.justice.gov/usao-dc/one-year-jan-6-attack-capitol
U.S. Department of Veterans Affairs. (2022). *America's Wars*. Retrieved from https://www.va.gov/opa/publications/factsheets/fs_americas_wars.pdf
U.S. Senate. (2002). *Party Division in the Senate, 1789-present. US Senate Historical Offfice*. Washington, DC: US Government Printing Office.
Uppsala Conflict Data Program. (2017). UCDP conflict encyclopedia. In: Uppsala Conflict Data Program, Uppsala University Uppsala.
Urofsky, M. (1994). *The Supreme Court Justices: A Biographical Dictionary*. Routledge.
Varon, E. R. (2008). *Disunion!: The Coming of the American Civil War, 1789-1859*. University of North Carolina Press.
Varshney, A. (2003). *Ethnic conflict and civic life: Hindus and Muslims in India*. Yale University Press.
Von Neumann, J., & Morgenstern, O. (1953). *Theory of Games and Economic Behavior*. Princeton University Press.
Voss, C., & Raz, T. (2016). *Never split the difference: Negotiating as if your life depended on it*. Random House.
Vysotsky, S. (2020). *American antifa: The tactics, culture, and practice of militant antifascism*. Routledge.
Wang, A. B. (2016). Trump in 2012: 'The electoral college is a disaster for a democracy'. *The Washington Post*. https://www.washingtonpost.com/politics/2016/live-updates/general-election/real-time-updates-on-the-2016-election-voting-and-race-results/trump-in-2012-the-electoral-college-is-a-disaster-for-a-democracy/
Waxman, O. B. (2018). 'Violence Was Inevitable': How 7 Key Players Remember the Chaos of 1968's Democratic

Work Cited

National Convention Protests. Time. https://time.com/5377386/1968-democratic-national-convention-protesters/

Weiner, R. (2022). *Ex-Va. police officer gets more than 7 years for role in Jan. 6 riot*. The Washington Post. https://www.washingtonpost.com/dc-md-va/2022/08/11/robertson-jan6-sentence-rocky-mount-police/

Westphal, M. (2017). Compromise as a Normative Ideal for Pluralistic Politics 1. In *Compromise and Disagreement in Contemporary Political Theory* (pp. 79-94). Routledge.

Wiener, J. (2006). *Conspiracy in the Streets: The Extraordinary Trial of the Chicago Eight*. The New Press.

Wilcox, E. W. (1916). *World Voices*. Hearst's International Library Company.

Wilstein, M. (2021). *Ex-SNL Star: Trump Loved My Racist 'Drunk Uncle' Character*. The Daily Beast. https://www.thedailybeast.com/snls-bobby-moynihan-says-trump-loved-his-racist-drunk-uncle-character

Wong, C. H. (2023). *Party of One: The Rise of Xi Jinping and China's Superpower Future*. Simon and Schuster.

Wood, G. S. (2017). *Friends Divided: John Adams and Thomas Jefferson*. Penguin.

Woodard, J. R. (2011). Lost Rights: The Misadventures of a Stolen American Relic. *The Journal of Southern History*, *77*(4), 1071.

Woodward, C. V. (2001). *The Strange Career of Jim Crow: A Commemorative Edition with a new Afterword by William S. McFeely*. Oxford University Press.

Woolley, J. T., & Peters, G. (1999). The American presidency project. *Santa Barbara, CA. Available from World Wide Web: http://www. presidency. ucsb. edu/ws*.

World Bank. (2023). *Worldwide Governance Indicators: Government Effectiveness* World Bank,. https://info.worldbank.org/governance/wgi/

Wright, G. (2006). *Slavery and American economic development*. LSU Press.

Wu, G. (2016). *The Art of the Deal Is Not the Art of War*. The University of Chicago, Booth School of Business. https://www.chicagobooth.edu/review/art-deal-not-art-war

Yancey, P., & Stafford, T. (2024a). 1 Corinthians 13:1. In *NIV, Student Bible*. Zondervan.

Yancey, P., & Stafford, T. (2024b). 1 Kings 3:16–28. In *NIV, Student Bible*. Zondervan.

Yancey, P., & Stafford, T. (2024c). Mark 5:9. In *NIV, Student Bible*. Zondervan.

Zelizer, J. E. (2018). *How Conservatives Won the Battle Over the Courts*. The Atlantic. https://www.theatlantic.com/ideas/archive/2018/07/how-conservatives-won-the-battle-over-the-courts/564533/

Zug, C. U. (2021). Creating a Demagogue: The Political Origins of Daniel Shays's Erroneous Legacy in American Political History. *American Political Thought, 10*(4), 601-628.

Index

A

abortion, 146, 147, 226, 227
Adams, Abigail, 43, 44
Adams, John, 21, 43
   Boston Tea Party, 34
   cousin, 34
   E Pluribus Unum, 21
   son, 115
   wife, 43
Adams, John Q., 115, 123
Adams, Samuel, 32, 34, 35
Affordable Care Act, 171, 172, 174, 175, 176, 183, 189, 191, 212
all men are created equal, 2, 62, 64, 66, 61–68, 71, 103, 104, 158
Altman, Stuart, 184
amendment, 100
   Civil War, 98
   Corwin, 220
   doctrine of incorporation, 100
   Electoral College, 116
   First, 27, 99, 101, 207
   Fourteenth, 100, 97–101, 104
   lame duck, 3
   Twentieth, 3
America, beginning of the end, 44
American Independence, 31, 90
Anderson, Robert, 92, 93, 95, 96
Anthony, Susan B., 67
Antifa, 32, 39
apportionment, Congressional, 79, 82, 83
Art of the Compromise, the, 7, 9, 10, 17, 19, 20, 21, 23, 57, 94, 114, 128, 140, 143, 158, 159, 161, 162, 164, 171, 174, 177, 178, 182, 184, 190, 192, 207, 215, 220, 223, 231, 232, 235
Art of the Consensus, the, 5
Art of the Deal, the, 9, 20, 207
Articles of Association, 90
Articles of Confederation, 2, 44, 54, 87, 90, 94
authority, 94

B

Babbit, Ashli, 40
baby, half, 158, 164, 165
Baker v. Carr, 118
Baker, James, 180, 181, 212
Balkanized continent, 219
Bankson, Benjamin, 75
Beauregard, Pierre, 95
Bentsen, Lloyd, 117, 118
Beria, Lavrentiy, 200, 205, 207
Berlin Wall, 25
Biden, Hunter, 201
Biden, Joseph, 30, 41, 148, 186
Big Beautiful Bill, 189
Bill of Rights, 74, 75, 99, 100, 101, 229, 230

Index

bipartisanship, 171, 175, 183, 185, 193, 211
bisociated, 165, 180, 213
bisociated compromise, 8, 9, 11, 18, 159, 165, 166, 167, 164–68, 171, 172, 174, 177, 180, 185, 192, 193, 194, 200, 211
Bliss, Alexander, 70
Boaz, David, 30
Boehner, John, 164
Booth, John Wilkes, 97
Boston Tea Party, 31, 30–33, 34, 37, 38, 41, 46, 52, 179
  Adams, Abigail, 44
  Castle Island, 33
  costumes, 32
  damage, 33
  Griffin's Warf, 31
  harbor, 31
  Jefferson, Thomas, 41
  myth, 33–36
  prank, 31
  ships, 31
  Sons of Liberty, 32, 34
  Washington, George, 34
bowling, 214, 215
Brandeis, Louis, 231–32
breaking bread, 167, 173, 193, 213–16
Brexit, 57, 74, 76
British
  healthcare, 191
  independence from, 31, 35
  parties, 133, 138
  property, 34
  reprisals, 35
  rule, 45
  taxes, 31
Brown v. Board, 100, 118
Brown, H. Rap, 58
Buchanan, James, 91
business, 3, 128, 134, 207, 209, 210, 207–11

C

cable news, 30, 35, 162, 163
Calhoun, John C., 98
Canada
  healthcare, 191
  move to, 1, 73
Capitol, 58
  architect, 33
  building, 36, 37
  damage, 33
  Lincoln Address, 87, 89
  police, 40
  riot, 31, 34, 36–41, 49, 56, 59, 217, 219
  Shaman, 37
  window, 36, 67, 216
  zip cuffs, 39
Carp, Jonathan, 33
Carter, Jimmy, 184, 185, 191, 194
Cato Institute, 30
Chamberlain, Neville, 57, 165
Charleston, 93, 94, 95
Charlottesville, 66
Chase, Samuel, 85
Chicago
  1968, 49, 56, 198
  Battle of Michigan Avenue, 48
  Eight, 46, 49
  Manual of Style, 43
  riot, 49, 56, 198
  University of, 9, 143
children, vanished, 179
China
  armed conflict, 55
  authoritarian, 51, 58, 112, 149, 150
  integrative complexity, 150, 151
  Jinping, Xi, 148, 208, 210
  moves fast, 148, 149, 208
  riot density, 29
  single party, 12, 15, 18, 108, 111, 208
Civil Rights, 175, 212

leaders, 67
Civil Rights Act, 52, 100,
  171, 172, 175, 176, 177,
  212, 229, 230
Civil War
  amendments, 97–101
  Anderson, Robert, 92, 93,
    95, 96
  Appomattox, 97
  beginning, 92–96
  casualties, 61
  complexity, integrative,
    141–42
  counterfactuals, 219–21
  delusional echo chamber,
    95
  Electoral College, 220
  electoral realignment, 128
  ending, 95, 97
  Fort Sumter, 92, 95, 96
  January 6, 219
  last battle, 97
  Lincoln provoked, 95
  Lost Cause, 85
  perpetual union, 73–77
  Ruffin, Edmund, 91, 95
  Scalia, Antonin, 73
  Scott, Winfield, 92
  slavery, 67, 68, 77–79, 85,
    86, 103, 104
  why they fought, 68–73
Clinton, Bill
  compromise, 174
  Electoral College, 121,
    123, 127
  ethics, 201
  Governor, 124
  healthcare, 184–85, 194
  impeachment, 201
  Kennedy, Edward, 184
  of two minds, 112
  popular vote, 121
  super plurality, 123
Clinton, Hillary
  classified documents, 201
  Electoral College, 113,
    118, 123, 126, 127
  healthcare, 184–85

irony, 123, 127
plurality, 127
popular vote, 115, 122,
  123, 126
unlikable, 113
votes against, 126
vulgar, 113
coalitions
  after elections, 13
  before elections, 13
  multi-party, 13
  Sartori–Lijphart, 16
  two party, 13
Collins, Jim, 6, 9, 141, 143,
  158, 164, 230
colonies, American, 21, 195
Comey, James, 113
communism, 138, 139
complexity, integrative, 140,
  147
  abortion, 146–47
  bisociated compromise, 7,
    166, 167
  Civil War, 141–42
  complex, 143
  complicated, 143
  Congress, 7, 142, 147, 166
  definition of, 140–41
  deliberation, 148
  differentiation, 142, 145,
    146, 151
  Fitzgerald, F. Scott, 143,
    216
  healthcare (lack of), 185–
    87
  integration, 142, 143, 145,
    146, 151
  Jinping, Xi, 149
  lasting governance, 211
  Lincoln, Abraham, 141–42
  political systems, 151
  simple, 144
  taxes, 182
  Tetlock, Philip, 141
  timepiece examples, 143,
    144
  two party, 142

Index

compromise, 23, 57, 59, 94, 137, 141, 170, 171, 181, 183, 188, 194
  bisociated, 8, 9, 11, 18, 159, 165, 166, 167, 164–68, 171, 172, 174, 176, 177, 180, 185, 192, 193, 194, 200, 211
  conditions for, 228
  conjunction type, 229
  consensus, comparison, 4–6, 14
  craft, 185
  definition of, 4
  factions, 13, 168, 192
  Gorbachev, Mikhail, 25
  healthcare, 183–85
  integrative complexity, 7, 166
  intersection type, 229
  major ones, 171, 172
  meet-in-the-middle, 158, 166, 167
  on bended knee, 222–24
  Soviet Union, 25
  substitution type, 229
  types of, 229
  weakness, 236
Compromise
  ain't easy, 236
  Missouri, 81
  of 1790, 168, 176, 213
  patience, 207
  speed (not), 208
  The Great, 121, 166, 229, 230
  Three-Fifths, 79
  Trump, Donald, 199
Confederate States, 77
Congress
  apportionment, 79, 82, 83
  authority, 85
  committees, 169, 180, 212
  control of, 83, 162
  differentiation, 11, 142, 143, 148, 151, 158
  failure, 9, 10, 182, 185–87, 190–93

gridlock, 148
Gucci Gulch, 179–82, 212
House of Representatives, 81, 121, 123, 148, 162, 176, 180, 193
integration, 147–51, 148, 151, 158, 190–93
integrative complexity, 150
lobbyists, 179–82, 212
polarized, 10, 164
Senate, 79, 81, 82, 83, 104, 121, 148, 162, 166, 170, 180, 193
Southern influence, 104
subordination, 199
two minds, 158
war powers, 96, 199
conjunction compromise, 229
consensus, 4, 5, 14
Constitution, Confederate States, slavery, 78–79
Constitution, United States
  amending, 114
  amendment, 3, 100
  Article I, 203
  authority, 85, 91, 96
  Capitol, 167–68
  compromise, 187
  creation of, 44
  doctrine of incorporation, 100
  engrossing, 75
  factions, 109
  father of, 22
  First Amendment, 27, 99, 101, 245
  Fourteenth Amendment, 99, 100, 97–101, 101, 104
  framework, 119, 121, 178
  gridlock, 148
  nullification, 104
  parties, 109, 113, 133, 135, 139
  perpetual union, 141
  republic, 2, 139, 195, 209

sacred text, 74, 75
Shays's Rebellion, 44
slavery, 67, 78
Twentieth Amendment, 3
unit vote, 117
Constitutional Convention,
  22, 78, 97, 186, 195, 198
contact theory, 216
Cooper, Anderson, 113
coup d'état, 30, 35, 36, 37,
  40, 44, 49, 218
COVID-19, 149
Creed, American, 2, 62, 63,
  64, 66, 61–68, 71, 103,
  104, 158
Crisis, Cuban Missile, 77, 208
Cronkite, Walter, 47
Csikszentmihalyi, Mihaly,
  143

D

Daley, Richard, 47–49
Davis, Jefferson, 95
de Becker, Gavin, 4
Deal, the, 7, 9, 10, 20, 161,
  199, 200, 208, 207–11
Deal, the New, 128, 132, 134,
  169, 170, 211
dealmaking, 9
death, taxes, 178
decades, 28, 129, 130, 131,
  132, 133, 134, 135
  1950s, 29, 77, 100, 116,
    176
  1960s, 2, 46–49, 100, 128,
    171, 175, 177
  1970s, 165, 183–84, 187,
    191, 202, 205
  1980s, 163, 179–82
  1990s, 24–26, 74, 121,
    136, 184–85
Declaration of
  Independence, 75, 90
Decoy Effect, 155
decriminalize politics, 203,
  204, 205, 207

deliberation, 10, 147, 149,
  203
demagogue, 1, 2, 36, 47, 69,
  88, 189, 190
Democratic National
  Convention, 46, 173
Democratic–Republican
  Party, 152
Democrats
  Affordable Care Act, 176
  Civil Rights, 130, 175
  convention, 173
  cultural issues, 135
  differentiation, 10
  Electoral College, 114
  extremists, 137
  factions, 127
  foreign policy, 129
  healthcare, 176, 186
  immigration, 131
  longevity, 138
  Obamacare, 176, 186
  oldest party, 138
  party founded, 137, 173
  party realignment, 132,
    133–40
  populism, 134
  rage, 28
  Social Security, 170
  Southern, 169, 170
  states' rights, 134
  thugs, 47
  trade and tariffs, 133
Department of Government
  Efficiency, 210
Department of Justice, 40,
  202, 218
Depression, the Great, 2, 3,
  169
Dershowitz, Alan, 206
devils, nest of, 45
differentiation
  abortion, 146
  autocracy, 149
  bisociated compromise,
    167
  black-and-white thinking,
    145

Index

Congress, 142, 143, 147, 148, 158
  definition of, 143
  healthcare, 183, 185
  integrative complexity, 142, 146
  opposed ideas, 142
  political systems, 151
  political thought, 147
  prerequisite, 143
  timepiece examples, 143, 144
digital connectivity, 35, 39, 214
dinner at Jefferson's, 167–72, 193, 214
District of Columbia
  compromise, dinner, 167–68
  King, Martin Luther, Jr., 64
  Lincoln Memorial, 64, 70
disunion, 59, 79, 88, 89, 90, 98
diversity, American, 7, 11, 50, 57, 111
diversity, decision making, 112
Do Not Go Gentle, 29
doctrine of incorporation, 100
Douglass, Frederick, 67
Dream, American, 3, 63, 65
Dred Scott decision, 80, 84, 85
duck, lame, 3

E

E Pluribus Unum, 57, 62
  motto, 21
  translation, 21
East India Company, 31
Edison, Thomas, 70
Eisenhower, Dwight, 19, 67
Electoral College, 119
  abolish, 1, 123, 124, 127
  Adams–Jackson, 123
  amendments, 116
  arguments for, 115, 125, 126
  Biden–Trump, 30
  broad geography, 122, 125
  Civil War, 82, 220
  Clinton, Bill, 121
  Clinton, Hillary, 113
  compromise, 229, 230
  historical share, 116
  inversion, 115, 116, 120, 122
  Kennedy, John F., 117
  majority, 116, 120, 123
  one person, one vote, 118
  Perot, Ross, 124
  plurality, 116, 120, 122
  popular vote, 122, 125
  relic, 125
  Ross, Tara, 115
  Southern influence, 83, 104
  super plurality, 123
  system, 126
  three-body problem, 124, 127
  Trump, Donald, 30, 126
  Trump–Clinton, 114, 126
  unit vote, 117
  voters, faithless, 115
  voters, strategic, 123
Emancipation Proclamation, 103, 142
empire, 24, 25
engrossing, 75
ethics bureaucracy, 205–7
Europe
  armed conflict, 55, 58
  at-will union, 75–76
  Balkanization, 55, 58
  Brexit, 57, 74, 76
  coalition building, 12
  debt crisis, 76
  differentiation, 111
  ethnic diversity, 50, 51, 76
  factions, 128
  integrative complexity, 150, 151

lack of agreement, 111, 112
monarchs, 195, 235
multi-party, 11, 12, 18, 109
riots, 58
temporal parties, 131, 136, 138
Union, 74, 75
weak parties, 139
Everett, Edward, 70
Evil Empire, 24
experiment, American, 64
extremists, 32, 33, 38, 137, 197

F

factions, 53
  against faction, 56, 57, 62, 70, 139
  causes, 56
  compromise, 13, 168, 187, 192
  Congress, 174
  definition of, 53
  demagogue, 189
  Europe, 128
  extend the sphere, 22, 139
  extremists, 47, 197
  January 6, 47
  Madison, James, 22, 53–56, 108, 112, 190
  minority, 86, 97
  passion, 195
  riots, 197
  Ross, Tara, 125
  Soviet Union, 25
  system, 140
  Washington, George, 133
fascist, anti-, 32
fascist, neo-, 32
FBI, 38, 113, 165
fear, 67
  de Becker, Gavin, 4
  demagogue, 69
  Meacham, Jon, 67
  of Founders, 114, 133
  politics of, 66–68
  Roosevelt, Franklin D., 3–4, 169
  Shays's Rebellion, 43, 44
Fearon, James D., 50
federal
  courts, 99, 101
  customs, 86
  government, 98, 99, 183
  ports, 86
  tariffs, 86, 104, 133
Federal Negative, the, 98, 99, 100, 104
Federalist Papers, 139
  Number 10, 22, 53, 56, 139
  Number 37, 223
  Number 51, 63, 139, 209
  Number 62, 208
  Number 65, 206
  Number 70, 147, 148, 208
Feldman, Noah, 222
First Amendment, 232
First Amendment cases, 99, 101
Fitzgerald, F. Scott, 109–13, 111, 142, 158, 166, 216
Fort Pickens, 92
Fort Sumter, 91, 92, 93, 95, 96, 97
four-letter word, 18
Fourteenth Amendment, 98, 99, 100, 97–101, 101, 104
Fox, Gustavus, 93, 94, 96
Franklin, Benjamin, 5
  Boston Tea Party, 41
  death and taxes, 178
  on taxes, 178
  on the Constitution, 186, 195, 234
  printer, 75
  seal, 21
  sun rising or setting, 22, 91, 196, 207, 231
  wit, 195
freedom, 27, 30, 52, 85, 98, 103, 125, 141, 158, 207, 208, 234

Index

G

Genius of the And, 6, 16, 141, 159, 173
German healthcare, 191
Gettysburg Address
  anniversary, 77
  Bliss copy, 70
  full text, 70–72
  length, 72
  Lincoln's voice, 70
  other speaker, 70
  Stevenson, Adlai, 77
  the why, 68–73, 103, 235
Gilje, Paul, 27, 28, 54
Gingrich, Newt, 19
Goodwin, Doris Kearns, 172, 173, 188
Gorbachev, Mikhail
  compromise, 25
  resignation, 24
Gordon, John Steele, 76
Gramsci, Antonio, 210
Grant, Ulysses S., 66, 97, 202
gridlock, 148, 149, 167
Gucci Gulch, 179–82, 212

H

habeas corpus, 142
habits of a private citizen, 231–33
Haidt, Jonathan, 225, 226
Hamilton, Alexander
  assumption, 76
  dinner, 167–72, 193, 214
  Federalist Number 65, 206
  Federalist Number 70, 147, 148
  financial plan, 193, 214, 222
  integration, 147
  monarch, 152
  national bank, 152
  national blessing, 76
  national debt, 76, 152
  on decriminalizing politics, 206
  on deliberation, 148
  on human nature, 148
Hamilton, Ben
  eyewitness to January 6, 37, 198, 216–17
  mood change, 39, 217
  on stupidity, 37–41
  Shaman, 37
happiness, 10, 196, 208
healthcare
  Altman, Stuart, 184
  British system, 191
  Canada, 191
  Carter, Jimmy, 184
  Carter–Kennedy, 184
  Clinton, 184–85
  employer mandate, 183, 185, 191
  failure, 184
  German system, 191
  Medicare, 191
  Nixon–Kennedy, 183–85
  Obama, 186, 212
  Obamacare, 171, 175, 181, 186, 187, 189, 212
  out-of-pocket, 191
  third world, 191
  universal coverage, 183, 192
Heyer, Heather, 66, 67
Hilter, Adolf, 165
Hitler, Adolf, 57
Hoffman, Abbie, 46, 47, 48, 49, 198
Hoffman, Judge Julius, 46, 49
hope, 4, 22, 63, 66–68, 67, 103, 104, 169, 234
House of Representatives, 81, 162, 176, 193
human nature, 56, 62, 63, 64, 125, 152, 153, 156
Hurlbut, Stephen, 93

I

ideas, opposed, 109, 111, 140, 142

immigration, 26, 128, 131, 162, 189, 226, 227
impeachment, 201, 206
inaugural address, 3, 62, 76, 87, 89
inspiration in leadership, 69
institutional memory, 131
insurrection, 1, 2, 38, 39, 40
integration, 8
abortion, 146
bisociated compromise, 167
China, 12, 150, 151
Clintons, 185
coalitions, 13
Congress, 148, 158
definition of, 143
Europe, 12, 151
failure, 190–93
healthcare, 183, 191
integrative complexity, 142, 146
multi-party, 12, 109
political systems, 151
political thought, 147
prerequisite, 143, 145
single party, 12
Soviet Union, 12, 151
timepiece examples, 143, 144
two party, 147, 190
United States, 151
intersection compromise, 229

J

Jackson, Andrew
demagogue, 2
Electoral College, 115, 122, 123
nullification, 88
slavery, 2
states' rights, 88
Jackson, Mahalia, 65
January 6
Babbit, Ashli, 40
beginning, 36
costumes, 37
criminal actions, 218
curfew, 39
damage, 33
death, 40
demographics, 36–37
ending, 40
factions, 47
false claims, 30, 39, 40
four hours, 1, 36, 39, 40, 41, 217
insurrection, 1, 40
riot, 234
Sedition Hunters, 218
Shaman, 37, 41
shame, 216–19
shootings, 30, 40
Sparks, Michael, 36, 216
stupidity, 37–41
weapons, 40
window, broken, 36
zip cuffs, 39
Jefferson, Thomas
Adams, Abigail, 43
Democratic–Republican Party, 152
dinner, 167–72, 193, 214
on Boston Tea Party, 179
on Shays's Rebellion, 41–42
rebellion, 41, 42, 49
republicanism, 153
seal, 21
Jim Crow laws, 221
Jinping, Xi, 148, 149, 208, 235
Johnson Treatment, 177
Johnson, Ludwell, 87, 95
Johnson, Lyndon B.
bisociated compromise, 174, 176
Civil Rights, 175, 212
coalitions, 212
compromise, 175
dinner, 173
hell, 175
Kennedy, John F., 175
leadership, 67

Index

political ties, 177
the treatment, 177
Jones, Clarence, 64, 65

K

Kahneman, Daniel, 154, 155, 209
Kennedy, Edward
  blocked healthcare, 184, 185, 191, 193
  Carter, Jimmy, 184
  Clinton, Bill, 184
  healthcare, 183–85
  Jackson, Mahalia, 65
  Nixon, Richard, 182
  regret, 183
  single-payer, 184
Kennedy, John F.
  assassination, 38, 175
  Bentsen, Lloyd, 118
  Civil Rights, 175
  Crisis, Cuban Missile, 208
  Electoral College, 116, 117
  hero, Clintons', 116
  inaugural address, 76
  Qualye, Dan, 118
  statesman, 117, 126
  the solar system, 124
  unit vote, 117
King George, 31, 35, 112
King, Martin Luther, Jr., 67
  assassination, 38, 48, 52
  Jackson, Mahalia, 65
  Jones, Clarence, 65
  speech, Dream, 63, 64–66
Kirk, Charlie, xi, 40
knee, on bended, 222–24
Kremlin, 24

L

Lambert, William, 75
lame duck, 3
Lenin, Vladimir, 25
Leung, Tommy, 26
Lewin, Kurt, 149

liberty, 10, 52, 53, 58, 63, 158, 222, 225, 226, 234
life, 10, 178
Lijphart, Arend, 13
Lincoln Memorial, 64
Lincoln, Abraham
  Anderson, Robert, 92
  argument for perpetual union, 90, 91
  assassination, 97
  Chase, Samuel, 85
  Civil War, 61
  death, 97
  Emancipation Proclamation, 103
  first shot, 94
  Fort Sumter, 92, 93
  Gettysburg Address, 68–73
  habeas corpus, 142
  hope, 104
  inaugural address, 62, 89–92, 219
  integrative comlexity, 141–42
  leadership, 2
  militia proclamation, 96
  never declared war, 96
  Obama, Barack, 172
  provoked the Civil War, 95
  rejection by the South, 76
  Republican Party, 115
  rock and a hard place, 92
  Scott, Winfield, 92
  Stevenson, Adlai, 77
  Supreme Court, 84, 85
  swing of power, 85
  system, 115
  voice, 70, 71
  why they fought, 89–92
Lion King, 176
Lost Cause, 85

M

Madison, James
  ambition, 139

America's first political scientist, 53
Democratic–Republican Party, 152
error in public virtue, 54
extend the sphere, 22, 51, 53–56, 49–57, 63, 197–98
factions, 22, 53, 54, 55, 108, 112
father of the Constitution, 22
Federalist No. 10, 53, 139
human nature, 56, 63
Jefferson, Thomas, 41
on bended knee, 223
republicanism, 153
slavery, 79
willingness to change, 223
MAGA, 37, 38, 47
Many, the, 10, 16, 17, 18, 21–23, 46, 57, 63, 67, 97, 158, 161, 197–200
Marmion, 127
Marxist–Leninist, 25
Massachusetts, 41, 43, 45, 59
Matlack, Timothy, 75
Meacham, Jon, 62, 63, 67
Medicare, 164, 170, 177, 191
meme, 218
Microsoft Windows, 110
mind, human, 107, 108, 109, 110, 111, 154, 157, 216
minds, of two, 11, 17, 20, 107, 111, 112, 166
Missouri Compromise, 81
Montgomery, Alabama, 96
Monty Python, 37, 198
Moral Foundations Theory, 225, 226
moral relativism, 227
Moscow, 36
motto, national, 21, 57
Musk, Elon, 210

N

negotiation, 9, 138, 165, 187, 188, 223
news, cable, 30, 35, 162, 163
Nixon, Richard
Altman, Stuart, 184
employer mandate, 185
healthcare, 183–84
on environment, 192
political enigma, 192
productivity, 192
resignation, 184
villain, 19
Watergate, 201, 205
Nixon–Kennedy Healthcare Plan, 183–84, 193
nullification, 88, 90, 98, 100, 102, 104

O

O'Neill, Thomas (Tip), 162, 164, 162–64
Obama, Barack
arrogance, 173
blame, 176
Boehner, John, 164
citizenship, 201
cling to their guns, 145
confessions, 172
decriminalize politics, 201
Executive Orders, 189
go it alone, 175, 176, 185–87, 189, 191, 212
Goodwin, Doris Kearns, 173, 188
I won!, 173, 176, 187, 212
inexperience, 176, 177
Johnson, Lyndon B., 175
Obamacare, 171, 182, 212
Obamacare, naming, 181
on consequences, 173
pen, 189
regrets, 172–74
Obama, Michelle, 173
Obamacare, 171, 175, 181, 182, 186, 187, 189

Index

one person, one vote, 118
out-of-pocket healthcare, 191

P

Packwood, Bob, 180, 212
Palmito Ranch, 97
parchment, 74, 75, 139, 213
partisanship, 2, 139, 152, 153, 156, 171, 172
party system, multi-, 11, 12, 16, 18, 109, 111, 113, 130, 131, 136, 137, 151, 154
party system, single-, 12, 18, 25, 108, 109, 111
party system, two-, 8, 10, 13, 14, 18, 108, 109, 111, 115, 138, 153, 154, 155, 156, 157, 190
party, political
  Decoy Effect, 155
  emergence, 112
  integration, 147, 190
  Italy, 136
  longevity, 132, 136, 138, 139
  Prospect Theory, 154
  realignment, 133–40
  rival ambitions, 139
  role of, 133–40
  third party challenge, 155–56
party-line, 174, 175, 189
Paul, Alice, 67
Pelosi, Nancy, 164
Perkins, Nathan, 26
Perot, Ross, 121, 122, 123, 124
perpetual union, 76, 73–77, 87, 90, 141
phonograph, 70
physics, three-body problem, 127
pizza, 14, 15, 216
Plato, 62
poem
  Do Not Go Gentle, 28, 29

Marmion, 127
  Song of Myself, 31, 140
  The Winds of Fate, 101
polarization, 10, 154, 172, 227
police
  Capitol, 40, 48
  Chicago, 47–49
  January 6, 30, 39
  riot, 48
  shot, 30
popular vote, 114, 115, 116, 122, 123, 125, 126
population, 29, 50, 51, 52, 80, 81, 82, 104, 118, 119, 166
populism, 134
ports, customs, 86
printing press, 75
privacy, 232
private citizen, political office, 231
pro-choice, 227
pro-life, 227
Prospect Theory, 154
protests, 26
Proud Boys, 32, 38
Putin, Vladimir, 113
Putnam, Robert D., 214

Q

Qualye, Dan, 118

R

Ramaswamy, Vivek, 210
Reagan, Ronald
  Baker, James, 180
  bill naming, 181, 193
  compromise, 174, 212
  Consensus I, 181
  frenemies, 164
  Gucci Gulch, 179–82
  hardliner, 162
  Iran–Contra, 201
  O'Neill, Thomas (Tip), 162–64
  on compromise, 161–64

The Art of the Compromise

on Evil Empire, 24
on half a loaf, 161
on Pac-Man, 163
party stalwart, 19
Reagan I, 181, 193
tax reform, 161–64
Tax Reform Act, 188
tax team, 180
the impossible, 182
Reagan–O'Neill relationship, 162–64
realignment, electoral
  Civil Rights, 130
  Civil War, 128
  cultural issues, 135
  definition of, 128
  economic regulation, 132
  foreign policy, 129
  immigration, 131
  Nixon era, 192
  party longevity, 132
  populism, 134
  Reagan era, 129
  states' rights, 134
  system, 132, 133–40
  timeline limits, 128
  trade and tariffs, 133
Regan, Donald, 180, 181
republic, 2, 25, 120, 126
Republican Party, 115
  differentiation, 10
  party founded, 173
Republicans
  Affordable Care Act, 176
  Civil Rights, 130, 175
  cultural issues, 135
  economic regulation, 132
  Electoral College, 114
  extremists, 137
  factions, 127
  foreign policy, 129
  healthcare, 176, 186
  immigration, 131
  longevity, 138
  Obamacare, 176, 186
  party founded, 137
  party realignment, 132, 133–40

  populism, 134
  rage, 28
  Social Security, 170
  states' rights, 134
  trade and tariffs, 133
responsibility, 158
Reynolds, Glenn, 205
Richmond, Virginia, 96
riots, 42
  Gilje, Paul, 27, 40
  history, 27
  insurrection, 1
  overreact, 23, 44, 46, 58
  protests, 27
  yawp, 31
Roe v. Wade, 118
Rogers, Will, 215
Roosevelt, Franklin D., 3 4, 67, 171, 208, 211
Roosevelt, Theodore, 67, 232, 233
Ross, Tara, 115, 117, 120, 123, 125
Rostenkowski, Dan, 180, 212
Ruffin, Edmund, 91, 95

S

sailing, 102
Sanders, Bernie, 113, 137
Sartori, Giovanni, 13
Scalia, Antonin, 73
Scott, Winfield, 92
secession
  aggressor, 72, 86, 93, 95
  counterfactuals, 220
  dates, 89
  economics of, 78, 86
  first state, 87
  Jackson, Andrew, 89
  legality, 73, 74, 87, 88, 98, 103
  panic, 1
  reasons, 79–87
  slavery, 78–79
  spoiled child, 77, 91
  suppression, 96
  Texas v. White, 90

Index

Sedition Hunters, 218
Senate, 79, 81, 83, 104, 121, 148, 162, 166, 170, 180, 193
Shallus, Jacob, 75
Shaman, 37, 41
shame, 216, 217, 219
Shays, Daniel, 45
Shays's Rebellion, 218
  Adams, Abigail, 44
  history, 43–45
  insurrection, 2
  Jefferson, Thomas, 41–42
  possessive, 43
  unchecked, 198
Sinek, Simon, 69
slavery
  avoids term, 78
  Civil War, 77–79, 85, 86, 104
  Constitution of Confederate States, 78
  Constitution of United States, 78
  embraces term, 78
  Jackson, Andrew, 2
  Maidson, James, 79
  sin, 67, 103
  Stevenson, Adlai, 77
social media, 35, 38, 39, 126, 217
Social Security Act, 171, 172, 229, 230
Sojourner Truth, 67
son of a bitch, 1
Song of Myself, 31, 140
Sons of Liberty, 32, 33, 34, 35
soul
  of a nation, 62, 63
  of a person, 63
  poem, 102
  punish the act, not the, 59
  set of the, 101–3
Soul, American, 61, 62–68, 70, 74, 99, 100, 101–3, 208
South Carolina, 87, 88, 92, 93, 94, 95

Soviet Union
  authoritarian, 112
  backwater, 25
  collapse, 24–26
  Evil Empire, 24
  integrative complexity, 150, 151
  perpetual union, 74
  republic, 25
  single-party, 12, 25, 111
Sparks, Michael, 36–37, 36, 41, 45, 67, 216
special prosecutors, 202
sphere, extend the, 22, 49–57, 58, 63, 139, 152, 153, 197–98
spoiled child, 77, 91
Stalin, Joseph, 25, 200
Stanton, Elizabeth Cady, 67
Stasavage, David, 149
states' rights, 78, 85, 88, 134
Stein, Jill, 113, 126
Stevenson, Adlai, 77
stupidity, 37–41
substitution compromise, 229
superpower, 25
Supreme Court
  appointments, 84
  Baker v. Carr, 118
  Bill of Rights, 99
  Brandeis, Louis, 231
  Brown v. Board, 100, 118
  Chief Justice, 84
  court packing, 169
  Dred Scott decision, 80, 84, 85
  Lincoln, Abraham, 84, 85
  New Deal, the, 169, 170
  Republican efforts, 137
  Roe v. Wade, 118
  Roosevelt, Franklin D., 169
  Southern influence, 104
  Taney, Roger, 84
  Texas v. White, 90, 220
  Whitney v. California, 232

T

Taney, Roger, 84, 85
tariffs, trade and, 86, 133
tax code, length, 179
Tax Reform Act, 171, 172, 179, 182, 188, 212, 229, 230
taxes, death and, 178
Tea Party, the, 137
Tetlock, Philip, 141
Texas v. White, 90, 220
thinking
  binary, 209
  black-and-white, 145
  dichotomous, 145
third party challenge, 155–56
third-world healthcare, 191
Thomas, Dylan, 29
three-body problem, 127
Tocqueville, Alexis de, 214, 215, 240
total victory, 187
Truman, Harry S., 67
Trump, Donald
  2016 election, 126
  Art of the Deal, the, 9, 199
  as a business, 207–11
  Big Beautiful Bill, 189
  book, 9
  Charlottesville, 66
  Clinton, Hillary, 114
  coup, 30, 36
  decriminalizing politics, 201
  demagogue, 1, 36, 47, 137, 189
  Dershowitz, Alan, 206
  DOGE, 210
  Electoral College, 115, 126
  ethics, 206
  extremists, 137
  haters, 19
  Heyer, Heather, 67
  loyalists, 19, 38
  MAGA, 38
  on dealmaking, 9
  on the Bible, 9
  Pelosi, Nancy, 164
  popular vote, 114, 126
  protest tally, 26
  racist tones, 67
  social media, 40, 126
  son of a bitch, 1
Tversky, Amos, 154, 155
Two, the, 10, 16, 17, 18
two-party system, 7, 10, 13, 108, 111, 112, 113, 126, 127, 130, 132, 137, 138, 139, 140, 142, 147, 149, 154, 156, 157
tyranny, 63, 87, 205
Tyranny of the Deal, the, 7, 9, 10, 143, 146, 147, 158, 161, 162, 164, 171, 178, 187, 207
Tyranny of the Or, the, 9, 143, 200

U

union
  at-will, 75–76
Union Station, 39, 217
unit vote, 117, 127
United States
  armed conflict, 55
  integrative complexity, 150, 151
Uyghur Muslims, 58

V

Vietnam War, 47, 68
voters
  faithless, 115
  strategic, 123
  working-class, 145

W

war powers, 96, 199
Warsaw Pact, 25
Washington Monument, 89
Washington, Booker T., 67

Index

Washington, DC, 30, 64, 70
Washington, George
  chair at Convention, 196
  on Boston Tea Party, 31, 34, 41
  on political parties, 112, 133, 153
  public virtue, 53
  secret Convention, 195
Watergate, 183, 201, 203, 205
We, the People, 10, 23, 197, 206, 223, 231, 235
Weber, Max, 209
Weinberger, Caspar, 183, 192
Whitman, Walt, 31, 58, 140
Whitney v. California, 232
Wilcox, Ella Wheeler, 101, 102
Wilson, Woodrow, 67
wind, 101, 102, 105
Winds of Fate, The, 101
World War I, 2, 55, 58
World War II, 2, 57, 129, 165

Y

yawp, 31, 37, 39, 70, 231

Z

zingers, 118, 186

ABOUT THE AUTHOR

David Lon Page, Ph.D., is a Research Scientist specializing in computer vision and 3D imaging. He holds a doctorate in Electrical Engineering from the University of Tennessee and has published extensively in the field of computer vision. A lifelong political observer, he began volunteering on campaigns at the age of ten and has remained engaged in civic life ever since.

David lives in Knoxville, Tennessee, with his wife, Lisa, and their daughter, Grace. *The Art of the Compromise* is his first nonfiction book on American politics and governance. He is also the author of *Scruffy Little Essays* and the *Knox County 2012 Charter Review Committee*.

www.ingramcontent.com/pod-product-compliance
Lightning Source LLC
Chambersburg PA
CBHW070613030426
42337CB00020B/3774